D0350255

# WINSTON CHURCHILL, CEO

# WINSTON CHURCHILL, CEO

## 25 LESSONS
## FOR BOLD BUSINESS LEADERS

### ALAN AXELROD

STERLING

New York / London
www.sterlingpublishing.com

STERLING and the distinctive Sterling logo are registered trademarks of Sterling Publishing Co., Inc.

**Library of Congress Cataloging-in-Publication Data**
Axelrod, Alan, 1922-
Winston Churchill, CEO : 25 lessons for bold business leaders/Alan Axelrod.
p. cm.
Includes bibliographical references and index.
ISBN 978-1-4027-5805-8 (alk. paper)
1. Leadership. 2. Ability. 3. Decision making. 4. Churchill, Winston S. (Winston Spencer), 1940-I. Title.
HD57.7.A967 2009
658.4'092—dc22                                            2008044914


10 9 8 7 6 5 4 3 2 1


Published by Sterling Publishing Co., Inc.
387 Park Avenue South, New York, NY 10016
Copyright © 2009 Alan Axelrod
Distributed in Canada by Sterling Publishing
c/o Canadian Manda Group, 165 Dufferin Street
Toronto, Ontario, Canada M6K 3H6
Distributed in the United Kingdom by GMC Distribution Services
Castle Place, 166 High Street, Lewes, East Sussex, England BN7 1XU
Distributed in Australia by Capricorn Link (Australia) Pty. Ltd.
P.O. Box 704, Windsor, NSW 2756, Australia

*Book design and layout: Adam B. Bohannon*

*Manufactured in the United States*
*All rights reserved*

Sterling ISBN 978-1-4027-5805-8
               978-1-4027-7099-9 (export edition)


For information about custom editions, special sales, premium and corporate purchases, please contact Sterling Special Sales Department at 800-805-5489 or specialsales@sterlingpublishing.com.

**FRONTISPIECE:** Prime Minister Winston Churchill walking the deck of the HMS *Prince of Wales* during the Atlantic Conference, October 9, 1941. Courtesy the Library of Congress Prints & Photographs Division, LC-DIG-ppmsca-05407.

*For Anita, always*

"I also hope that I sometimes suggested to the lion the right place
to use his claws."

*~ Speech to both Houses of Parliament,*
*Westminster Hall,*
*on the occasion of his eightieth birthday,*
*November 30, 1954*

# CONTENTS

# WINSTON CHURCHILL, CEO

# Introduction
## *A Leader's Life*

From the beginning, his greatest urge—his greatest need—was to be at the center of the action. This fact is not in itself sufficient to explain Winston Churchill, but Winston Churchill cannot be explained without understanding this fact. He was born on November 30, 1874, in a bedroom of Blenheim Palace, the family's magnificent seat in Woodstock, Oxfordshire. That he entered the world two months premature was a fitting prelude to a life lived in perpetual impatience to make upon that world one indelible mark after another. When, as a twenty-three-year-old cavalry subaltern (second lieutenant) in 1898, he prevailed on the senior-most officer in the British army, Lord Horatio Kitchener, to accept him for service in his Nile River Campaign, Churchill's fellow junior officers denounced him as "super-precocious" and "insufferably bumptious." He was, in fact, much more than that. Not content with a mere army career, he also wrote newspaper dispatches from the front lines of Britain's colonial wars, and his firsthand account of an expedition against a rebellious Pashtun tribe in Malakand (now part of Pakistan), *The Story of the Malakand Field Force* (1898), published just before he left India to join Kitchener's campaign in North Africa, was a sensational bestseller. Literary critics also called it "precocious," but they meant this in the best sense of the word, because the book exhibited the narrative skill and historical authority of a much more mature author. In no small part, this effect was the result of the author's writing about the conduct of the senior officers of the field force as if *he* had been their commander, and *that* did little to endear Churchill to the many officers he portrayed.

Not that their opinions much mattered to him. A premature baby, Winston grew into a premature historian and a premature general. It was, as it were, only natural.

On the face of it, he started life with a leg up in society and politics. His father, the prominent Tory politician Lord Randolph Churchill, was descended from John Churchill, the first duke of Marlborough and hero of the War of the Spanish Succession (1701–14). Named for the Battle of Blenheim (August 13, 1704), Britain's greatest victory in the war, Blenheim Palace was Parliament's gift to Marlborough, commander at Blenheim. The descendents of the first duke—the second through the sixth dukes of Marlborough—sharply deviated from the heroic prototype and were universally described as profligates and wastrels, who manifested signs of deep mental instability, to boot. The seventh duke, Winston Churchill's grandfather, managed to restore the family's name to greatness, redeeming a large measure of proper Victorian respect, but he proved unable to replenish the family's material fortune. It was, in fact, a mighty struggle for him to maintain Blenheim, which he did only by selling off other properties, the Marlborough family jewels, and—most galling to Winston—the magnificent Blenheim library. Winston's uncle, the eighth duke of Marlborough, continued the fire sale in 1886, unloading a staggering collection of Old Master paintings in a single lot for £350,000 (a sum that has been calculated as the equivalent of well over fifty million modern dollars). But he also resumed the Churchill tradition of profligacy, so that, despite this influx of funds—as well as a marriage to an American heiress (which followed a scandalous divorce from his first wife)—the family fortune continued to dwindle, leaving the ninth duke, known as "Sunny," with Blenheim Palace but very little else. He, too, married a very wealthy American (one of the Vanderbilt girls) but was later divorced from his bride as well as her cash. Sunny died on the verge of bankruptcy.

Lord Randolph Churchill, Winston's father, married yet another American heiress, the extraordinarily beautiful Jennie Jerome, daughter of a New York financier and stockbroker who was at one point part owner of the *New York Times* and a string of racehorses. In Lord Randolph, the two major strains of the Churchill family merged. On the one hand, he was larger than life—a Tory politician who nevertheless appealed to the working classes, and an orator of dazzling brilliance. A member of Parliament, he attained the post of secretary of state for India, followed by chancellor of the exchequer, analogous to the U.S. secretary of the treasury, but also a stepping-stone to even higher office. As his son would also prove to be, Lord Randolph was driven by an irrepressible impatience. Not content with working his way conventionally to the top spot in Conservative Party leadership, he attempted to force the marquis of Salisbury to cede to him the position of first lord of the treasury, which would have put him in position to become prime minister in the next Conservative government. Salisbury stood firm, however, and became prime minister himself in the general election of 1886, whereupon Lord Randolph summarily resigned as chancellor of the exchequer in the vain belief that this would be sufficient to topple Salisbury. He was relying on his great popularity in Parliament to bring this about, and popular Lord Randolph was, but not sufficiently so to incite an outright rebellion among the Tories. Salisbury held on to his office, and Lord Randolph Churchill, having resigned his, found himself suddenly on the outside looking in.

He had, quite simply, thrown away his political career, but the worst was yet to come. Running parallel with his life as a respectable Tory politician was something many regarded as the Churchill bad seed, which increasingly manifested itself in dementia and other neurological symptoms widely interpreted as the telltale signs of tertiary syphilis. Victorians were quick to ascribe mental debility to venereal disease, and some modern medical authorities believe it far more likely that Lord Randolph suffered from a brain tumor. Nevertheless, the man's colleagues, the public, and his own family—Winston included—believed he had syphilis, which served to render more poignant and painful the rapid decline of what had been a fine mind. The great orator became a great stammerer, adding slobbering incoherence to his rambling non sequiturs, which were punctuated by fits of public weeping, as if he were perpetually in his cups. Jennie, unfaithful through much of the couple's marriage, stood by him faithfully during the worst of his decline. In 1894, she took him on a sea voyage (Victorians saw travel as a sovereign cure), but his descent into neurological collapse continued, and he died on January 24, 1895, shortly after the couple returned to London.

> *"All my dreams of comradeship with him, or entering Parliament at his side and in his support, were ended. There remained for me only to pursue his aims and vindicate his memory."*
>
> ~ *My Early Life*, 1930

Young Winston Churchill was enrolled as a cadet at Sandhurst, Britain's Royal Military College, during his father's final months and at the time of his death. He idolized his father, but—and this is characteristic—he did not idealize him. He saw him through his own romantic sensibility, not as the failed leader that he was, but as the great leader that he might have been. There was substantial imagination in this vision of his father but not a trace of delusion. Winston knew what his father was, and when he came home from Sandhurst for the funeral, he demanded the full details of his last illness. Learning that he had died of what was believed at the time to be advanced syphilis, Winston Churchill betrayed not the slightest shame. He spoke later of the sense he had at his father's funeral that it now fell to him to "lift again the tattered flag I found lying on a stricken field," and he decided on the spot that he would win a seat in Parliament for the purpose of pursuing his father's unrealized goals and to "vindicate his memory."

■

Winston Churchill adored his beautiful mother, and he admired her for the devotion she showed his father during his dying months. If he was aware, as a child and young man, of the serial infidelities that had preceded this final spasm of connubial fidelity, he did not allow the knowledge to diminish his adoration. Even more remarkably, he never seemed to feel any resentment about his mother's indifference toward himself. She was neither a demonstrative nor a loving parent, but, on the contrary, distant and cool. For that matter, Lord Randolph Churchill had also done little to earn his son's admiration, let alone quasi-worship. He was not merely cold to Winston, but unremittingly harsh in his criticism of the young man, perhaps seeing in him the seeds of his own life of error.

> *"My mother made the same brilliant impression upon my childhood's eye. She shone for me like the Evening Star. I loved her dearly—but at a distance."*
> ~ *My Early Life,* 1930

Winston Churchill was by no means blind to the failings of his mother and father. He had been, for all practical purposes, raised by a nanny. Mrs. Anne Everest (he called her "Woom") lavished upon her charge all the warmth and love Lord and Lady Churchill could not give. Winston was devoted to Woom, and when, after she had served the family for some nineteen years, the Churchills cut her loose with only the most threadbare of pensions, Winston saved what he could of his own meager allowance to contribute toward her support. He understood his mother and father had treated her abominably, and he meant to make it right. When she was stricken with peritonitis just four months after his father died, he rushed to her bedside, hired a doctor and a private nurse, and was with her in her final hours. He then paid for her funeral, her burial, her head-stone, and even the perpetual upkeep of her grave. They were all things, he believed, his mother should have seen to, but he never criticized her for her neglect. Instead, what he could do and what needed to be done for Woom, he himself did.

> *"My nurse [Mrs. Everest] was my confidante . . . my dearest and most inti-mate friend."*
>
> *~ My Early Life, 1930*

As for his father's harshness toward him, young Winston seems never to have resented it, rather excusing it because he recognized that there had been much about him to merit harsh reproof. He had been a sickly and unruly child, bright but frustratingly incompetent in anything resembling disciplined study. A half-dozen generations of Churchills had prepped in the storied halls of Eton, but Lord and Lady Churchill believed their son would founder there. They set-tled on Harrow as a lesser though still eminently acceptable alterna-tive, but, as Winston wrote years later in *My Early Life* (1930), he was humiliated by the entrance exam: "I wrote my name at the top of the page. I wrote down the number of the question, '1.' After much reflection I put a bracket around it thus, '(1).' But thereafter I could not think of anything connected with it that was either relevant or true." The thirteen-year-old Winston noted the arrival "from nowhere in particular" of a blot and several smudges on the other-wise blank page. "I gazed for two whole hours at this sad spectacle; and then merciful ushers collected up my piece of foolscap and car-ried it up to the Headmaster's table." Winston Churchill was admitted to Harrow nevertheless. He must have understood that this could hardly have been based on his own demonstrated merit.

One of the enduring myths about Churchill is that he was a total failure as a student. It is true that his grades in French, the classical languages, and mathematics were inconsistent, sometimes rather good, but sometimes failing. History always appealed to him, and he consistently excelled in it, but it was considered a "minor" subject. Nevertheless, his teachers were concerned less about his academic performance than his often wild conduct. For at least three school activities, he actually showed a positive flair: fencing (he took a prize at a public schools championship), recitation (he won another prize for declaiming, from memory, several hundred lines of Thomas Babington Macaulay's *Lays of Ancient Rome*), and English composition. Still, he was remanded to what he himself later described as a kind of remedial class run by one Robert Somervell. Whereas the boys in the regular and advanced classes learned Greek and Latin, Somervell devoted most of his time to teaching the English language, with an emphasis on composition. In Winston Churchill, the lessons took, getting into his very "bones" (he later wrote) "the essential structure of the ordinary British sentence—which is a noble thing."

By his early teens, Winston had acquired both a love of and facility with the English language, particularly as it was incarnated in the "ordinary British sentence." This had gotten into his bones, and, with it, the sense of the nobility not of language, but of *his* language, the language of the British people. It has often been observed that nationalism—the perception that one's personal identity is inseparable from that of the nation—is rooted in language. When the minions of a rapacious empire invade a nation, the conquest is not complete until the native language has been stamped out. In train behind the conquering armies come laws of the severest kind, imposing the invader's tongue on the conquered people and banning the use of the native language, at least in public. At an early age, then, Winston Churchill drew on his identity as a Briton with the very words he read, wrote, or spoke. At a level deeper than intellectual understanding, deeper even than mere emotion, he perceived this national identification as inherently noble. Being British was thus second nature for Winston Churchill. It defined him, and it satisfied him infinitely.

> *"[My classmates at Harrow] went on to learn Latin and Greek and splendid things like that. But I was taught English. We were considered such dunces that we could learn only English."*
>
> ~ *My Early Life,* 1930

Yet a talent for English composition and a love of country were hardly sufficient qualifications for a career. In late Victorian England, entry into a life in government came about by one of three routes: the foreign service, the civil service, or the military. All three required proof of academic achievement as measured by rigorous entrance examinations, for which even a grand family name would not be accepted as a substitute. Both the foreign service and the civil service called for high marks in precisely the academic disciplines Winston had proved either unwilling to master or incapable of mastering—the classics, foreign languages, and mathematics. That left the army.

For Winston Churchill, about to graduate from Harrow, the army loomed as an attractive choice. Among his favorite childhood pastimes was playing with toy soldiers. Although he had been frail and often sickly, he also loved horses and the out-of-doors. Prowess with the saber came to him easily. Getting onto the track that would lead to a commission in the officer corps of the Royal Army was far more feasible than entering either the civil or foreign services, but there was still an examination to pass. Winston assumed he would have little trouble with it, but he nearly failed, barely scoring high enough to gain admission to the cavalry, which had lower academic requirements than the infantry, artillery, and engineers.

There was a good reason for this. The low standards of the British cavalry were the stuff of legend, and Lord Randolph put his foot down, insisting that Winston take the examinations again in the hope of getting a more respectable infantry commission. Dutifully, he took them again, and this time he failed—even to qualify for admission into the cavalry. As rarely as Lord Randolph intervened on his son's behalf, he did so now, perhaps out of guilt or the shame a father feels for the failure of a son. He secured for Winston a military tutor, who managed to cram enough knowledge into the boy's head to enable him to scrape by the entrance examination to Sandhurst in June 1893. Yet again, he qualified for nothing more than the cavalry, but Lord Randolph, now terminally ill, capitulated, though not without letting his son know that he was a deep disappointment to him.

■

Young Churchill entered Sandhurst ranked ninety-fifth out of an incoming class of 104 cadets. By the time he completed his training there, he had ascended to twentieth out of his graduating class of 130. He excelled in drill, gymnastics, riding, and tactics, and while his great improvement could have gotten him a berth with an infantry regiment, the 60th Rifles, which would have mollified his father, Winston chose instead to join the 4th Hussars, an elite and quite fashionable cavalry regiment.

> *"For years I thought my father with his experience and flair had discerned in me the qualities of military genius. But I was told later that he had only come to the conclusion that I was not clever enough to go to the Bar."*
> ~ *My Early Life,* 1930

Taking up his new assignment in February 1895, he passed his time in drill and the fierce pursuit of such hazardous sports as polo and the steeplechase while awaiting departure with his regiment for service in India—a routine requirement of any British professional soldier. But Winston Churchill had no patience for routine. Officers about to leave for India were given a long period of leave before embarking—the term of service abroad, after all, was nine long years—and Subaltern Churchill decided to spend his in Cuba, where a revolution was under way against the island's Spanish rulers. His idea was to cover the war for a newspaper, getting himself as close to the action—and in as much danger—as possible.

Getting into the action was always important for Churchill. Risk—physical danger—was a bonus. Yet there was nothing merely impulsive about his decision to go to Cuba. Not only did he see it as an opportunity to fast-track his military reputation, but he also saw it as a means of earning quick and much-needed cash through combat journalism and of getting into the public eye in preparation for an eventual Parliamentary campaign. Moreover, he did not simply pack up and go. Instead, he did what he would always do when he wanted something: he identified the person or persons who had the power and authority to give him what he wanted, and he made his appeal directly to them. Before leaving, Churchill prevailed on his mother to call on her friend, the British ambassador to Spain, who gave him letters of introduction to all the top Spanish civil and military officials. His next visit was to the British commander in chief, from whom he formally secured permission to join the war in Cuba, and then he called on the British director of military intelligence, obtaining from him official instructions to gather intelligence on the island. By the end of November 1895, Winston Churchill was attached to a Spanish unit fighting the Cuban insurgency.

Some men—very few—like to be shot at. In 1754, George Washington discovered that he was such a man. Writing to his half-brother, John Augustine Washington, from his camp at Great Meadows, Pennsylvania, on May 31, 1754, following his first firefight, the young colonel declared, "I can with truth assure you, I heard Bulletts whistle and believe me there was something charming in the sound."

In 1896, Winston Churchill wrote similarly. While taking a swim in a river his unit forded, Churchill came under small arms fire. His press dispatch lingered over the sound of the bullets—"sometimes like a sigh, sometimes like a whistle, and at others like the buzz of an offended hornet"—and he wrote to his mother that he "heard enough bullets whistle and hum to satisfy me for some time."

> *"A single glass of champagne imparts a feeling of exhilaration. The nerves are braced; the imagination is agreeably stirred; the wits become more nimble. A bottle produces a contrary effect. Excess causes a comatose insensibility. So it is with war; and the quality of both is best discovered by sipping."*
> ~ The Story of the Malakand Field Force, 1898

The thrill—really, the savor—of high danger was one great lesson he took away from his experience in Cuba. The other was more profound: it was the revelation of the power possessed by an absolutely determined people. Churchill was officially attached to the forces of Spain—one empire aiding another—but he quickly learned to admire the Cuban insurgents. Not only were they supremely skilled in unconventional warfare and guerrilla tactics—the use of which Churchill would champion during World War II in such units as the Special Operations Executive (SOE) in Europe and the Chindits in Burma—they also thrived on adversity, drawing their strength, it seemed, in direct proportion to Spanish efforts to crush them. It was a lesson in the compelling force of skillful defiance.

After making a name for himself as a war correspondent in Cuba, Churchill rejoined his regiment. At home on leave in the spring of 1897, he got news of fighting on India's North-West Frontier and fired off a telegram to General Sir Bindon Blood, assigned to command a punitive expedition against insurgents in Malakand (a region of modern Pakistan), requesting a combat assignment. As if that weren't an impetuous enough action for a junior officer, Churchill didn't even wait for Blood's reply. He boarded the first available ship for Bombay (Mumbai), and only after disembarking in that city did he pick up Blood's answer. "No vacancies," it began, but then continued, "Come as correspondent. Will try to fit you in. B. B."

In this way, Churchill came to join the Malakand Field Force. Every day on the march, he dispatched 300 words to the Allahabad *Pioneer* in India and—thanks to his mother's influence—also wrote a series of highly paid columns for the *Daily Telegraph* in London. Nor did he just write. On September 16, 1897, his brigade fell under attack by Pashtun tribal forces, suffering heavy casualties and narrowly avoiding total annihilation in the mountainous passes of the northwest borderland. In typical Churchill fashion, the subaltern had moved far in advance of the main column during this engagement and, with four other officers and eighty Sikhs, he was cut off near a hostile village. As an officer, Churchill carried only a sidearm. On this occasion, however, he grabbed a Lee-Enfield rifle from a wounded Sikh and fired a steady barrage against the attacking Pashtuns, determined to drive them off, despite being hopelessly outnumbered. The Sikhs, however, had other ideas, commencing a retreat that soon turned into a rout. With his "army" melting around him, Churchill had no choice but to follow on his gray charger, although he noted that he "remained till the last."

As previously mentioned, the book Churchill wrote of his experiences with the punitive expedition, *The Story of the Malakand Field Force*, made a sensation. It also made him that much more eager to get to the next hot spot, which was the Egyptian-Sudanese border region. Senior army officers, taken aback by what they regarded as the many impertinences of Churchill's book, ignored his pleas for a posting with Kitchener in North Africa. Prime Minister Salisbury, however, was enthralled by *The Story of the Malakand Field Force*. He summoned Churchill to 10 Downing Street, expressed his admiration, and asked if there was anything he could do for him. When Churchill blithely replied that he wanted an assignment in Egypt, Salisbury wrote to the British agent in Cairo. As luck would have it, the 21st Lancers had a vacancy. Largely indifferent to the comings and goings of the likes of Winston Churchill, Kitchener raised no objection, so the young officer took ship for Cairo, embarking so precipitously that he neglected to inform his own commanding officer of his transfer out of the 4th Hussars.

The highlight of Churchill's assignment with Kitchener's Nile army came on September 2, 1898, about three miles outside of Khartoum, Sudan, in the Battle of Omdurman. On that date, 40,000 hostile dervishes descended upon him and an Anglo-Egyptian army of 26,000. Vastly outnumbered though they were, Kitchener's men wielded modern magazine-fed rifles, machine guns, and artillery. Holding fast, they mowed the charging dervishes, and the battle was won by nine in the morning—conveniently before the heat of day became overly oppressive. Lord Kitchener, a prudent commander, was determined to ensure that the defeated enemy did not regroup. As the battle came to a close, therefore, he ordered the 21st Lancers to mop up, sweeping the field clear of any lingering enemy. The 21st consisted of just over 300 riders. Following Kitchener's command, they threw themselves headlong into more than 3,000 dervishes still at large. A more traditional cavalry officer would have wielded his saber against the enemy. Churchill instead drew his Mauser pistol, with which he subsequently claimed to have killed six dervishes—more precisely, three "certain" kills, two "doubtful," and one "very doubtful."

As in his action against the Pashtuns, he fought from the forefront, at one point nearly finding himself cut off. Of the 300-plus Lancer force, twenty-one were killed and forty-nine were wounded. Half the regiment's horses fell in battle. That was the price of a mission accomplished. The enemy had been killed or scattered, vanquished utterly.

*"The great struggles of history have been won by superior will-power wresting victory in the teeth of odds or upon the narrowest of margins."*
~Speech in the House of Commons, June 25, 1941

Vanquished also, at least for the time being, was Winston Churchill's passion for army life. As soon as Kitchener's Nile Campaign had been officially concluded early in 1899, he resigned his commission, returned to England, and wrote his second book, *The River War*, an account of the expedition. Once again, he found himself a celebrity, and, seizing the moment, the Conservatives ran him for Parliament from working-class Oldham, Lancashire. He lost—though not by a wide margin—and promptly took off for South Africa, determined to earn a handsome living as a correspondent covering the Second ("Great") Boer War for the *Morning Post*.

As usual, he was far more than a reporter. With the British stronghold of Ladysmith under siege by the Boers, Churchill boarded an armored train carrying 150 troops from Estcourt, outside of Ladysmith, toward the town of Colenso for the purposes of reconnoitering. In an era before the invention of the tank and other armored vehicles, the armored railway train was the height of mobile military technology. Yet it was also a conventional product of conventional warfare, and on November 15, 1899, Boer commandos exploited its greatest vulnerability: they sabotaged the tracks and derailed the train.

Churchill efficiently directed efforts to uncouple the derailed cars from those still on the tracks and to get the locomotive back into action, but he and his companions were quickly surrounded by more than 500 Boers and had no option but surrender. Churchill was confined in a schoolhouse-turned-POW camp in Pretoria, the capital of the Transvaal province. It was not surrendering that he resented so much as confinement, and he soon joined two fellow prisoners in an escape scheme. When the time came to make their move, his comrades remained behind while Churchill leapt the prison wall and ran into the night.

The next day, he hopped a freight train and managed to reach the house of an English mine manager, who hid him for three days at the bottom of a mineshaft until the arrival of a freight train, which had a car loaded with wool bound for Mozambique, at the time a Portuguese colony. The railway worker secreted Churchill among the woolen bales, and he managed to evade detection by one Boer inspector after another throughout the long ride to the port town of Lourenço Marques (Maputo), from which he boarded a ship to Durban, British South Africa, which he reached on December 23.

The capture, prison break, and successful escape, coming as they all did during what was the nadir of British fortunes in the Great Boer War, made Winston Churchill a national hero. He parlayed his fame into an appointment as assistant adjutant of the South African Light Horse, with which he fought in and around Ladysmith—actions culminating in the relief of the siege on February 28, 1900—and then participated in the victorious British advance through the Transvaal. He had the poetic pleasure of participating in the liberation of the Pretoria POW camp that had briefly held him, and then he survived a near-death experience at Dewetsdorp, when his horse, spooked by intense gunfire, galloped off without him, and he had to be rescued by a trooper who pulled him up onto his own mount. That horse, shot with an explosive bullet, rapidly bled out under the strain of carrying two riders at full gallop, but survived long enough to convey the pair to safety. A second close encounter with death came when he left Pretoria for Cape Town aboard another armored train. Like the first, it fell under ambush, including heavy artillery bombardment. Churchill took charge of the train's troops and, this time, was able to drive off the attackers.

On his return to England, a new book quickly flowed from his pen, *London to Ladysmith via Pretoria*, earning him a modest fortune. He stood again for election to Parliament in 1900, and this time won a seat, which he took in February 1901. Rapidly gaining a reputation as a brilliant orator, Churchill also drew attention for his sudden defection in 1904 from the Tories to the Liberals, primarily over the issue of free trade—Churchill was for it, while the Conservative Party was opposed. The Liberal Party embraced their celebrated convert. Churchill quickly rose to the ministerial post of undersecretary of state for the Colonies, and, in 1908, to the presidency of the Board of Trade, which included a seat on the Cabinet. In this same year, he married Clementine Hozier, a Mayfair peeress and woman of striking beauty and indomitable will. She would prove to be her husband's lifelong support and inspiration.

*"There is a good saying to the effect that when a new book appears one should read an old one. As an author I would not recommend too strictly an adherence to this saying."*
~Quoted in J. A. Sutcliffe's *The Sayings of Winston Churchill,* 1992

As president of the Board of Trade, Churchill guided national labor policy away from laissez-faire, dog-eat-dog capitalism and toward social reform, introducing an eight-hour day for miners, attacking so-called sweated labor (sweatshop) practices, and inaugurating a set of minimum wages as well as measures to reduce unemployment. His reforms brought charges that he had turned traitor to his Tory class, but the more opposition he faced, the more enthusiastically he went about the business of reform. He played a key role in securing passage of the Parliament Act of 1911, which greatly curtailed the powers of the hereditary House of Lords, earned Churchill popular approval, and catapulted him to the office of home secretary. In this post, however, his liberal zeal came up against hard reality. Faced with widespread strikes and labor violence, Churchill responded by deploying the police, a policy that undermined his hard-won liberal credentials.

It was just as well that, at this juncture, in October 1911, he left the Home Office to become first lord of the Admiralty. In the midst of a growing military crisis—an arms race with Kaiser Wilhelm II's Germany—Churchill championed and directed the rapid modernization of the Royal Navy and ensured that it remained superior in number to the expanding German fleet. He successfully campaigned to secure the largest naval expenditure in British history, so that the Royal Navy, far more than the army, was adequately prepared when World War I broke out in August 1914.

At the commencement of the Great War, Churchill's confidence in the navy he had been instrumental in creating knew no bounds. It led him, early in 1915, to plan a daring amphibious assault on the strait dividing the Balkans from Asia Minor, the Dardanelles, which was held by German-allied Turkey. Gain control of the Dardanelles, Churchill reasoned, and a supply line would be opened wide to Britain's key ally on the Eastern Front, Russia. This was Winston Churchill's first essay in grand strategy, and it was characteristically bold, yet its architect lacked the patience to pursue the tactical and logistical details necessary to execute it. The failure of the naval assault resulted in Churchill's removal as first lord of the Admiralty. As the architect of the offensive, he was also held responsible for the Gallipoli Campaign, the land component of the assault, which also failed, more catastrophically, with Allied losses amounting to 252,000, including 46,000 battle deaths, over eight agonizing months. Churchill severed all connection with the government in November 1915.

Winston Churchill had good reason to believe, as he did, that Gallipoli meant an end to his political career. To console himself, he took up painting, which became both a solace and a passion for the rest of his life. But not everyone had counted him out. J. L. Gavin, the astute editor of the London *Observer*, wrote, "He is young. He has lion-hearted courage. No number of enemies can fight down his ability and force. His hour of triumph will come." And, indeed, Churchill found that he could not long remain out of the war. He accepted an offer to serve as lieutenant colonel of the 6th Royal Scots Fusiliers, leading them in combat on the Western Front until May 1916, when he returned to England. In July of the following year, his friend, political ally, and new prime minister, David Lloyd George, named him to the post of minister of munitions.

Although the new office was not the equivalent of First Lord of the Admiralty—it did not carry a cabinet seat—Churchill dedicated himself to the work with great energy and imagination, increasing munitions production so dramatically that an actual shell surplus was achieved before the war ended. He also championed the development and manufacture of what was called at the time the *land cruiser*, but soon became known as the *tank*. Despite formidable technological problems encountered in its development, Churchill believed that this heavily armored, heavily armed, all-terrain vehicle was precisely the weapon needed to break the horrible stalemate of the Western Front. If it could be made fully and reliably operational in time, the tank had the capability of traversing trenches and shell holes, breaking through barbed wire and other obstacles, and even withstanding the withering fire of machine guns. Although the tank remained unperfected in World War I, it did have an impact on that conflict, and it would become a major weapon in the following war—forever transforming the way ground wars were fought.

Immediately after the armistice in 1918, Churchill advanced from the Munitions Ministry to secretary of state for war and air, stunning everyone by zealously slashing military expenditures, even as he called for British intervention in Russia's ongoing Bolshevik Revolution. He moved to the Colonial Office in 1921, where he wrestled with British mandates in the Middle East, listening closely to the legendary if mercurial guerilla leader T. E. Lawrence ("Lawrence of Arabia") and affirming Britain's support for Palestine as a Jewish homeland while also recognizing Arab rights. In 1922, when insurgent Turks threatened the Dardanelles "neutral zone" created after World War I, Churchill urged a firm stand, but the shell-shocked British public, fearing the outbreak of a new war, turned against him. An acute attack of appendicitis prevented his defending himself or campaigning in the elections, and, as Churchill himself put it, he suddenly found himself "without an office, without a seat, without a party, and even without an appendix."

His involuntary hiatus from politics gave him time to write, and his personal history of the Great War, *The World Crisis*, earned him enough money to finance the purchase of a fine country estate, Chartwell, in Kent. It was not as grand as Blenheim Palace, to be sure, but it was a magnificent piece of old England Churchill would love dearly for the rest of his life.

In 1923, Churchill lost his seat in Parliament and, the following year, accepted nomination for a Conservative seat from the London suburb of Epping. At the time, he was still a member of the Liberal Party, but during the campaign, he described himself as an "independent constitutionalist anti-socialist," yet threw his support behind the Conservatives, thereby effectively crossing the aisle to the Tory side. He remained a Conservative for the rest of his life.

> *"Some men change their Party for the sake of their principles; others change their principles for the sake of their Party."*
>
> ~ Speech during 1906 general election

Seeking to form a coalition government, the new Conservative prime minister, Stanley Baldwin, appointed Churchill chancellor of the exchequer. If anyone deserved the well-worn label *Renaissance man*, it was—to be sure—Winston Spencer Churchill. Yet part of his ancestral heritage was an incurable incompetence when it came to money matters, and the one talent he assuredly lacked was a gift for financial administration. No sooner was he seated in the cabinet

than he restored the gold standard, which instantly triggered deflation, followed by widespread unemployment and a miners' strike
that exploded into the nationwide general strike of 1926. For this
cluster of crises, Churchill could suggest no more useful solution
than painful belt tightening. Worse, he took profound offense at the
general strike, choosing to interpret it as a kind of revolution and
therefore refusing to negotiate an end to it. Instead, he fanned the
flames of discord by appointing himself editor of the *British Gazette*,
a vehemently anti-strike official newspaper published by the government. Churchill's unwillingness to bend brought what he now most
deplored, the ascendancy of the hyper-liberal Labour Party, and in
1930, Churchill withdrew from the Baldwin government and took
up a strident campaign against a bill designed to give India the
status of a self-governing dominion.

> *"He occasionally stumbled over the truth, but hastily picked himself up and
> hurried on as if nothing had happened."*
> ~ Attributed to Churchill, on Prime Minister Stanley Baldwin

Throughout the 1930s, Churchill languished outside of the inner
circle of British government. He remained in the public eye as a
vehement critic of Baldwin's pro-independence policy for India and
was equally adamant during this period about the dangers of the situation developing in Nazi Germany, continually sounding a
warning—both in the press and in Parliament—that "Hitlerism" was
bound to bring the world to war yet again. To counter this threat, he
advocated putting Britain on a full war footing. In particular, he
urged a program to match Germany's growing air power, reasoning
that Hitler would first attack Britain from the air in an attempt to
bring the nation to its knees and soften it up for invasion. Churchill
became the leading opponent of the policy Baldwin's successor,
Neville Chamberlain, introduced: "appeasement," the attempt to

buy off rather than resist Adolf Hitler's aggressive expansionism. In an effort to avoid a war for which he felt Britain was woefully unprepared, Chamberlain connived in Germany's annexation of the Sudetenland, the German-speaking region of Czechoslovakia. Churchill argued that no dictator could be appeased and that, moreover, sacrificing Czech sovereignty was not only immoral and cowardly—it was also strategic folly. Czechoslovakia's central position made it the keystone of middle Europe, and its coal fields were of great value to any power. When Chamberlain returned from the Munich Conference (September 29–30, 1938), having yielded to Hitler the Sudetenland and claiming to have achieved thereby "peace for our time," Churchill bluntly labeled the act a "total and unmitigated defeat."

Events, of course, proved Winston Churchill right, and after Hitler invaded Poland in September 1939, bringing general war to Europe, Chamberlain offered Churchill his former post of First Lord of the Admiralty. With his characteristic aggressiveness, Churchill proposed an immediate assault on Norway to dislodge the Germans there. Like the Gallipoli campaign of World War I, the invasion proved a fiasco and had to be aborted. This time, however, it was Chamberlain—not Churchill—who took the fall. He resigned in May 1940, and Churchill replaced him as prime minister during the very darkest period of World War II.

Such was Churchill's character in a crisis that he did not for a moment brood on the Norway disaster, but instead went about the business of saving his nation—and did so in the knowledge that, by defending England, he was defending the entire free world.

Churchill took upon himself all the responsibilities of a war leader. With Europe rapidly falling to the Germans, he turned to the United States, a neutral nation reluctant to involve itself in yet another "European" war. Churchill established an intensely personal relationship with President Franklin D. Roosevelt, whom he readily persuaded to drift away from neutrality. The first step was the development of the lend-lease policy, which provided England (and, soon, other Allies, most notably the Soviet Union) with arms, matériel, aircraft, and ships, not on the former cash-and-carry basis, but in a moneyless exchange for strategic cooperation with the United States.

Lend-lease was a great step forward in Britain's war effort, but in 1940, the German juggernaut seemed unstoppable. In late May/early June, the British army was beaten back—and very nearly annihilated—at Dunkirk on the North Sea coast of France. Only a nearly miraculous trans-Channel evacuation saved the mass of the army. Later in the summer, the Battle of Britain commenced as the German Luftwaffe (air force) unleashed what Churchill had predicted years earlier: a massive bombing campaign of London and other English cities. Britons prepared to be invaded—or, more accurately, Churchill prepared his people to resist invasion with everything they had. On June 4, 1940, he delivered one of his most celebrated speeches to Parliament, declaring that Britain would "defend our Island, whatever the cost may be, fight on the beaches . . . fight in the fields and in the streets . . . we shall never surrender."

Churchill possessed the personal character and rhetorical skill to maintain his courage and to fire the courage and determination of his people. To the stunned surprise of Nazi Germany and, for that matter, the rest of the world, it was the British who emerged victorious in the Battle of Britain, the Royal Air Force (RAF) defeating the Luftwaffe and foiling invasion.

Nor was Churchill merely a cheerleader. He engaged fully in every aspect of the conduct of the war. In contrast to Hitler and Mussolini, who dominated their military commanders—always to the detriment of effective strategy—Churchill formed a true working partnership with the military. What he did insist on, however, was that British forces never permit themselves to be tied down in a defensive posture. Churchill believed that the best defense was a vigorous offense, and he boldly diverted an entire armored division—one of only two in Britain—to take the offensive against the armies of Hitler and Mussolini in the Middle East. At the same time, he forged an alliance with the Soviet Union, pledging to aid it after it had been invaded by Germany, even though Churchill was an outspoken and implacable foe of communism.

With the entry of the United States into the war following the Japanese attack on Pearl Harbor on December 7, 1941, the prime minister stepped in to hammer out a three-way alliance among the United States, Soviet Union, and Great Britain. His war strategy for the Allies was controversial, and its wisdom is still debated by historians. He proposed postponing any invasion of the European mainland until what he called the "soft underbelly of Europe" had been penetrated by clearing North Africa and the Mediterranean of the enemy. He did not want to face another Dunkirk, but he did want to institute vigorous offensive operations where he believed they stood a good chance of success. Over the objections of top U.S. generals George C. Marshall and Dwight Eisenhower, President Franklin D. Roosevelt ultimately acceded to Churchill's plan, and it was not until the summer of 1943 that the Allies invaded Sicily and Italy, having fought the first part of the "European" war in North Africa. A year later, Churchill was instrumental in supporting the principal invasion of Europe, via Normandy, on "D-Day": June 6, 1944.

> *"I cannot help reflecting that if my father had been an American and my mother British, instead of the other way round, I might have got here on my own."*
>
> ~Address to the U.S. Congress, December 26, 1941

Although Churchill's "soft-underbelly" strategy governed much of the war in Europe, his influence diminished once the Normandy campaign was under way. With victory in sight, Churchill now saw the Soviets as a postwar threat. It was not only that he hated communism, but that the hard lessons of two world wars had taught him to oppose *all* totalitarian regimes. He therefore advocated a drive by the Western Allies directly into Berlin, specifically to preempt the city's occupation by Soviets. Exercising great prescience, Churchill foresaw the dangerous shape of a postwar "Cold War" world. With the concurrence of President Roosevelt and his successor, Harry S. Truman, Churchill's proposal was overruled by Supreme Allied Commander Dwight D. "Ike" Eisenhower, who believed it necessary first to crush any remaining German resistance in southern Germany and Austria. While British and American forces turned away from the German capital, the Russians fought a tremendously costly battle to take eastern Germany, including Berlin.

For immediate tactical purposes, Ike's plan was the soundest and least costly, but Churchill typically looked beyond the tactical range to see the overall strategic consequences of an action. In this case, he looked beyond World War II itself. Later, in a speech delivered at a small Presbyterian men's college in Missouri, he would popularize the phrase *iron curtain* to describe the hard pall of Soviet influence and tyranny that had descended across Eastern Europe, thanks to the inroads made as a result of the Allies' war strategy.

In some ways, Churchill was disappointed by the final conditions of the Allied victory in Europe. On top of this came a blow any other man would have felt as crushing. In July 1945, a general election failed to return him to office following the unconditional surrender of Germany and shortly before the capitulation of Japan. Churchill was flabbergasted, but he refused to be crushed. He received the first dismal election returns while taking a bath: "There may well be a landslide and they have a perfect right to kick us out," he calmly observed. "That is democracy. That is what we have been fighting for. Hand me my towel."

Ousted in 1945, Churchill was returned to office as prime minister in 1951, and was subsequently knighted in recognition of his service to the nation and the world. In July 1953, he suffered a stroke that left him weakened and ailing. Nevertheless, he fought back to partial recovery and continued in office until April 1955, when he was succeeded by his handpicked candidate, Anthony Eden.

Churchill spent his final decade pursuing his favorite recreation, painting, and seeing to the publication of the last of his great literary works, the four-volume *History of the English-Speaking Peoples*. Published in 1956–58, it followed his even more epical six-volume *The Second World War* (1948–53), which earned him the Nobel Prize for literature. A man of prodigious achievement, Winston Spencer Churchill would be remembered as a great journalist and historian even if he had not been a war leader and a leader of the free world. In 1963, two years before Churchill's death on January 24, 1965, President John F. Kennedy and the U.S. Congress conferred upon him honorary American citizenship. Churchill was the first of only five people to receive this distinction.

# Always Savor
# the Thrill

"Nothing in life is so exhilarating
as to be shot at without result."
~ *The Story of the Malakand Field Force*, 1898

*Malakand.* No one knows for certain the origin of the name of this forbidding province, in what is now Pakistan's North-West Frontier, abutting Afghanistan. Some guess that it derives from the Pashto words for flower garland and water (*aamail* and *ubo*) and was applied to the region because, from the perspective of a traveler on the treacherous route along the high and rugged Malakand Pass, the River Swat below has the appearance of a string or garland of delicate flowers. Others have speculated that the name is a combination of the words *mullah* and *kandao*. A *mullah* is a "holy man" or "saint," and *kandao* signifies "a high place." Yet others point out that *mlakandao* is an adjective meaning "curved like a human backbone." To anyone who ever had to walk the Malakand Pass, this was the etymology that rung true. It is a backbreaking journey, prompting many travelers to beg for *kund* (Pashto for a "soothing tonic," a "curative," or an "unguent") after making the trek. Add to that the word *mala*, which signifies "for me," and to pronounce *mala kund* is to request "a pain reliever for me."

Whatever the origin of its name, Malakand was and remains hard and unforgiving country.

In the late summer and fall of 1897, it was also lethal country—and that is precisely what made it irresistible to Winston Churchill, a cavalry subaltern freshly minted from the Royal Military Academy at Sandhurst.

At the time, the Russians were pushing their own frontier uncomfortably close to India, prompting the British government to enforce what was called the *Forward Policy*, which held that the key passes into India through the Hindu Kush would be held by the Anglo-Indian government through its vassal tribes and at the military direction of Anglo-Indian garrison forces. When an uprising in Chitral menaced the British garrison in that region, a force was sent to its relief. This force was based in Malakand, and, by subsidizing local warlords and other rulers, it maintained the peace and held the mountain passes. After a time, however, Pashtun tribes rose up yet again and attacked the Anglo-Indian Malakand camp. Although the troops beat off the assault, the Colonial Office decided to muster a punitive expedition for the purpose of suppressing the tribes once and for all.

Practically all the "fierce and warlike tribes of Afghan stock are in revolt," Churchill wrote excitedly to his brother, Jack, on August 31, and he wangled a place in the punitive expedition dubbed the Malakand Field Force, sent to put down the uprising. He would serve as both a soldier and a war correspondent.

> *"I have faith in my star, that I am intended for something in this world. If I am mistaken—what does it matter? My life has been a pleasant one and though I should regret to leave it, it would be a regret that perhaps I should never know."*
>
> ~Quoted in John Keegan's *Winston Churchill*, 2002

But he could hardly wait. On the twelfth, he joined a cavalry detachment riding through the Mohmand Valley, bound for

Nawagai, where he was to be formally attached to the Field Force. In high anxiety that he might miss any of the action, he spurred his gray pony far in advance of the detachment. Suddenly, some fifty tribesmen materialized out of the craggy landscape. Alone now, Churchill responded by galloping at full tilt straight through them, pistol drawn. As it turned out—and as Churchill was later told—these men were friendly to the British, and they gaped in astonishment at the subaltern's behavior. "But," he wrote to his mother, "how could I tell? I was so close on them that there was nothing for it but a dash."

> **"Suddenly, some fifty tribesmen materialized out of the craggy landscape. Alone now, Churchill responded by galloping at full tilt straight through them, pistol drawn."**

"How could I tell?" The question, posed rhetorically, reveals much about young Churchill's embrace of a situation about which he understood only one thing for certain. It was deadly dangerous. *How could he tell?* He could not tell, of course, because he had chosen to ride alone into territory he knew nothing about. Foolhardy? For Winston Churchill, it was the very essence of adventure, and he craved it as other men craved food or sex or money.

By the time he reached Nawagai, Churchill got a vivid lesson in the rules of engagement that were to prevail in this fight. He looked on as a group of Sikhs—Indian troops in the imperial British service—heaved a wounded Pashtun tribesman unceremoniously into an incinerator, where he was burned alive. He wrote later, "There is no doubt we are a very cruel people. . . . I feel rather a vulture. The only excuse is that I might myself become the carrion." For he well knew that it was "a point of honour on the Indian frontier not to leave wounded men behind. Death by inches and hideous mutilation are the invariable measure meted out to all who fall in battle into the hands of the Pathan [Pashtun] tribesmen." Kill or be killed. He accepted this as the morality of the conflict and as the price of the adventure he craved.

The shooting, which started on September 16, elicited from Churchill these four sentences, which convey the essence of what was the young man's maiden battle, his baptism of fire:

There was a ragged volley from the rocks; shouts, exclamations, and a scream. One man was shot through the breast and pouring with blood; another lay on his back kicking and twisting. The British officer was spinning round just behind me, his face a mass of blood, his right eye cut out. Yes, it was certainly an adventure.

During World War II, Britain and its allies would live and die by Churchill's eloquence, and in later years, his genius with language would earn him the Nobel Prize for literature. It is not surprising, therefore, that the writing here is spectacular—coruscating, rhythmical, precise, devoid of false sentiment, telling nothing while showing all. Yet it is not the screams, the blood, the agonized writhing, or the mutilation that most shocks the reader. It is the final summary sentence: "Yes, it was certainly an adventure." The violence, the pain, the mayhem exist, in this account, to satisfy the writer's appetite for dangerous sensations.

He had plenty of them.

Officially attached to the Malakand Field Force on September 15, Churchill accompanied one of the unit's three brigades the next day in a ride to a position just outside of the hostile frontier village of Markhanai. In the best tradition of the British cavalry, he rode to the sound of the guns, putting himself in the vanguard of the Anglo-Indian force by trotting along with the 35th Regiment, a unit of Sikhs. When the firing became so intense that it posed a danger to his mount, he tied the horse under cover and proceeded on foot. Always, he pushed ahead. He pushed himself into the very heart of the enemy, daring them to surround him, to cut him off as he fired in all directions.

When the order came to pull back, Churchill resisted. "I remained till the last." Two British officers near him were cut down by Pashtun rifle fire. An enemy soldier approached the body of one of the officers and set about mutilating it with his knife. Churchill fired on him. "He dropped but came on again," whereupon Churchill took aim and finished him off.

To his mother, he wrote that "had there been any gallery" to observe his performance, he might "have received some notice." It is a revealing remark, evidence of how Churchill's motives evolved in the course of his first battle. The prime mover, the primal motive, was the adrenalin rush of danger. That, however, was followed closely by the expression of a new motive: the need to distinguish himself, to be recognized as a hero. Moreover, these motives continued to evolve, and did so very quickly. Under heavy fire, Churchill and another subaltern had pulled a wounded Sikh toward the main column of the retreating 35th Regiment. ("My pants are still stained with the man's blood," he wrote to his mother after the battle.) The greatest danger to any military force comes when it is in retreat, and the art of the retreat is both strenuous and delicate. It lay in staging the movement tactically. It is fatal simply to turn and run. Instead, at intervals, the retreating troops must turn around and make a stand, returning fire against those who pursue. Churchill and his companion did just this. As they dug in to fire back, the enemy closed to within no more than 40 yards (about 37 meters), hurling a storm of stones before opening fire.

**"Always, he pushed ahead. He pushed himself into the very heart of the enemy, daring them to surround him, to cut him off as he fired in all directions."**

> *"In war, which is an intense form of life, chance casts aside all veils and disguises and presents herself nakedly from moment to moment as the direct arbiter over all persons and events."*
>
> ~ *Thoughts and Adventures*, 1932

Now Winston Churchill felt entirely new sensations. "It was a horrible business," he said, "for there was no help for the man that went down." Compassion stole upon what had been an entirely amoral hunger for adventure. "I felt no excitement and very little fear. All the excitement went out when things became really deadly." With enemy swarming around them, Churchill found his officer-issue Mauser pistol inadequate and took up the rifle of another wounded soldier. He fired forty rounds without pause. "I cannot be certain, but I think I hit four men. At any rate, they fell." (Later, he claimed three "certain" kills in addition to two that were "doubtful" and one he called "very doubtful.")

After an hour under fire—a continuous hail of bullets as well as hurled stones—it ended, imperceptibly at first, petering out from heated battle to fitful skirmish. That evening in camp, when he sat down to describe the events of September 16 to his mother, Churchill returned to a somewhat earlier state of moral evolution. He wanted glory: "I rode on my grey pony all along the skirmish line when everyone else was lying down in cover. Foolish perhaps," he admitted, "but I play for high stakes and given an audience there is no act too daring or too noble."

Compressed into the space of a few violent hours was Winston Churchill's personal journey from mere sensation, to heroism, to compassion, and then back to heroism, risking all for the sake of garnering admiration. This was just the beginning, however. On September 30, less than two weeks after the battle near Markhanai, Churchill went into action again, this time with the 31st Punjabi Regiment at Agrah. He endured five hours under continuous fire, an experience that affected him less than the crushing news that a gallant British regiment, the Royal West Kents, had broken and run, committing the cardinal infamy of leaving one of their wounded officers on the ground.

Back in camp, Churchill broke down and cried when, first, he

## Absorb All the Lessons

Churchill's experience in Malakand had profound physical and spiritual aspects. It also had an intellectual dimension. He saw firsthand the devastating effectiveness of the new generation of breech-loading weapons, especially the modern repeating rifle. The Pashtun tribesmen, who were armed with old-fashioned single-shot rifles, did not stand a chance. Fierce as they were, and although they enjoyed an overwhelming superiority of numbers, the tribal warriors were unable to overrun the British camps because the effectiveness of the camps' relatively small number of defenders was multiplied by the speed with which they were able to fire, especially from the cover of carefully prepared trenches.

The evidence was unmistakable. Pashtun corpses were piled man-high outside of many advance encampments. At Malakand, Churchill came to understand that the repeating rifle—and, the machine gun—gave defenders an extraordinary advantage over attackers. When the Great War—World War I—came in 1914, the trench warfare stalemate that rapidly developed on the Western Front stunned many military thinkers. Winston Churchill, however, had already learned that the state of weapons technology allowed for almost unlimited defense of a dug-in position, making it extraordinarily difficult for an attack to progress decisively. He absorbed the lesson of the Malakand defense, which was the necessity of avoiding costly and fruitless assault against men wielding modern defensive weapons. This insight would drive his future thinking about strategy, motivating the ill-fated assault on the Dardanelles in 1915, and tactical technology, moving him to champion the development of the tank and the airplane as weapons.

saw the officer's body, recovered from the battlefield, "literally cut in pieces on a stretcher" and, second, as he gazed on the Royal West Kents, broken men who had been "really unsteady under . . . fire and tired of the game." Contemplating these twin spectacles, he wrote to his mother that he hoped, in his next battle, to be commanding a company—a hundred men—which would give him "some other motive for taking chances than merely love of adventure."

**"In the crucible of Malakand, a leader had been forged."**

In the crucible of Malakand, a leader had been forged. To the raw steel of a young man's craving after adventure for adventure's sake, a thirst for heroism was annealed. Succeeding upon this was a powerful flow of compassion, and, last of all, the sense of a need to do more than merely feel, merely perform, or even merely care. There came the need to lead. It was a need compounded of every other motive, including adventure, heroism, and compassion, but it was catalyzed—made active—by a compelling desire to prevent another British force from losing heart and from abandoning one of their own to the enemy's cruel mercy. Subaltern Winston Churchill had plunged into battle selfishly. He now emerged from it selflessly, ready not just to command others, but to lead them.

**Many books have been written on leadership,** most suggesting that it is a skill and, as such, can be learned. Doubtless, many aspects of leadership can be learned. But the case of Winston Churchill suggests that, underlying whatever skills a leader may acquire is a kernel—irreducible, almost certainly inborn—from which the original motive to venture, to excel, and ultimately to lead develops. As a leader, Churchill was heroic, compassionate, self-sacrificing, and inspirational. Driving all of these varied qualities was his primal hunger for adventure, risk, and danger—an irresistible urge to savor the thrill. By itself, this was certainly not sufficient to greatness in leadership, but without question, it was indispensable to it.

# Engage
# the Realities

"I pass with relief from the tossing sea of Cause and Theory
to the firm ground of Result and Fact."
~ *The Story of the Malakand Field Force,* 1898

Churchill's first task in writing *The Story of the Malakand Field Force,* as
with any writer, was to determine just what his story would be. On
the one hand, his experience with the field force offered the opportunity for a simple, exciting narrative of an intensely violent clash
between Pashtuns, who followed a militant religious leader
Churchill referred to as the "Mad Mullah," and the officers and
men of the Anglo-Indian Malakand Field Force. Yet Churchill was
also well aware that there was a back story, which was anything but
simple. It involved the web of motivation—purposes and cross-
purposes—from which both sides operated. The Pashtun militants
might be guided by a Mad Mullah, but, Churchill knew, they were
also moved by issues of trade and kinship among tribes, as well as
by what they regarded as their solemn religious duty to kill the
infidel: the Christian interlopers and invaders in their midst. For
their part, the British were driven by motives of empire, of international power politics, of trade, and of concepts of racial and religious
superiority.

*"Writing a book was an adventure. To begin with it was a toy, an amusement; then it became a mistress, and then a master, and then a tyrant."*
~Speech, London, November 2, 1949

A big part of writing—or, at least, of writing intelligibly—is making choices. Churchill began by explaining the choice he made:

The book does not pretend to deal with the complications of the frontier question, nor to present a complete summary of its phases and features. In the opening chapter I have tried to describe the general character of the numerous and powerful tribes of the Indian Frontier. In the last chapter I have attempted to apply the intelligence of a plain man to the vast mass of expert evidence, which on this subject is so great that it baffles memory and exhausts patience. The rest is narrative, and in it I have only desired to show the reader what it looked like.

Essentially, Churchill's choice was *to get to the story*, by which he meant to narrate the action of combat. He explained this more fully a bit farther along in the book:

The historian . . . is always oppressed by the difficulty of tracing the silent, subtle influences, which in all communities precede and prepare the way for violent outbursts and uprisings. He may discover many causes and record them duly, but he will always be sensible that others have escaped him. The changing tides of public opinion, the undercurrents of interest, partisanship and caprice, the whirlpools of illogical sentiment or ignorant prejudice, exert forces so complex and numerous, that to observe and appreciate them all, and to estimate the effect of each in raising the storm, is a task beyond the intellect and industry of man. . . .

In an attempt to state the causes of the great tribal upheaval of 1897, these difficulties are increased by the fact that no European can gauge the motives or assume the points of view of Asiatics.

Though he champed at the bit to get to the action and despaired of even trying to account for the multifarious causes behind that action, young Churchill couldn't quite bring himself to suppress the prelude entirely. "It is," he almost grudgingly wrote, "impossible to pass the question by, and ignoring the detail, I shall endeavour to indicate some at least of the most important and apparent forces, which have led to the formidable combination with which the British power in India has been confronted." In the course of a single chapter, he filled in some of the background, laying both the blame and the emphasis on the religious—"superstitious," as he put it—motives of the Pashtuns. The chapter is not a long one, and at the end the reader cannot fail to recognize the author's evident joy at having finally disposed of the burdensome preliminaries: "I pass with relief from the tossing sea of Cause and Theory to the firm ground of Result and Fact." With this sentence, Winston Churchill begins his narrative in earnest and tells a very exciting tale of a modern army's clash with fierce medieval warriors.

The sentence "I pass with relief from the tossing sea of Cause and Theory to the firm ground of Result and Fact" is found in every collection—and there are a great many—of Churchill quotations, sayings, and maxims. In the context of *The Malakand Field Force*, it may be interpreted

**"Essentially, Churchill's choice was *to get to the story*, by which he meant to narrate the action of combat."**

as nothing more or less than an author extending a courtesy to his reader by marking a thematic transition. Yet the sentence is not so easily disposed of. It seems to cry out for a life of its own beyond merely serving as a rhetorical bookmark. It seems, in fact, to be a kind of manifesto in miniature—the expression of a life's philosophy. "Cause and Theory," after all, are presented as a "tossing sea," from which it is a "relief" to pass "to the firm ground of Result and Fact." True, this may be no more than a writer—and a young writer, at that—expressing his preference for action over thought, but that isn't how the sentence reads. What it really seems to say is that result and fact are somehow inherently superior to cause and theory.

### All Leadership Is Practical

Take the phrases "practical leader" and "practical leadership" and discard them. They are redundant. All true leadership is practical leadership, because there can be no such thing as "theoretical leadership." By definition, a leader engages people and things on a practical level. Those who remain on the level of theory have no contact with people or things, and a "leader" without such contact cannot possibly be a real leader. You may freely imagine a machine loaded with gears, but until the teeth of one gear actually mesh with those of another, no real work is produced.

Certainly, this describes Churchill's approach to leadership. A champion of democracy and an enemy of communism, fascism, Nazism, and all other forms of totalitarianism, he conceived of democracy as a system of government that sought to promote and protect individual liberty and initiative, and he thought of all forms of totalitarianism as systems that sought to suppress and destroy individual liberty and initiative. That was the extent of his ideological orientation, the limit of his interest in the "Cause and Theory" of government. Of far greater concern to him, when it came to governing a nation, was how to feed, shelter, and defend the people—or, rather, how to inspire and guide them to feed, shelter, and defend themselves. This required very little theoretical understanding, but a great deal of practical application. For Churchill, leadership was a hands-on affair. It is no accident that he came to it, not through an education designed to groom civil servants or foreign service diplomats—an education based almost exclusively on Cause and Theory—but through the army, through the business of leading a body of men in desperate battle—while also seeing to their physical and spiritual well-being, their feeding and sheltering, and their good order and discipline. He came to civil leadership through the nitty-gritty of military leadership—leadership as measured strictly by "Result and Fact."

Winston Churchill was not anti-intellectual. A voracious reader and prodigious historian, he also possessed a consuming amateur's interest in science. But his approach to the intellect was largely through the universe of his own senses—what he could see, touch, and manipulate. Though his taste in poetry ran to Shakespeare, Tennyson, and Kipling, he would have readily understood and heartily subscribed to the maxim of the twentieth-century American modernist William Carlos Williams. "No ideas but in things," Williams wrote, by which he cast aside abstract, abstruse, and vague expression and replaced it with language based on the firmest of firm ground: that which could be heard, seen, tasted, smelled, and felt. From the very beginning of his career, Churchill, too, was a man of things, but also of ideas *in* things. To him, the saga of empire was not an abstract dissertation on imperial policy and administration, but rather *The Story of the Malakand Field Force*, a story of combat at the frontier of what was then generally understood as "civilization." Through a career in Parliament and in the higher leadership of government, democracy was never for him a philosophy of

**"Of far greater concern to him, when it came to governing a nation, was how to feed, shelter, and defend the people—or, rather, how to inspire and guide them to feed, shelter, and defend themselves. This required very little theoretical understanding, but a great deal of practical application."**

human rights, but rather a vivid narrative of danger, defeat, recovery, survival, and victory in politics as well as in two desperate wars—a narrative nevertheless founded on the leading themes of liberty, justice, and human rights.

> *"Perfect solutions of our difficulties are not to be looked for in an imperfect world."*
>
> ~Speech, Sheffield, April 17, 1951

As a leader, Churchill could not sever ideas from things or principles from people. There was no division between theory and reality. In the leadership and management of government, theory had to be made manifest in result and fact. Apart from these, it had no meaningful existence whatsoever.

Do you want to create a new theory of government? Find new facts and create new results. Winston Churchill neither denigrated nor denied ideas, but he always worked with them hands-on, through what they produced. Firm ground was infinitely preferable to a tossing sea. On the one, it was quite possible to build wonderfully and to virtually any height. On the other, you were fortunate to get away with your life, let alone leave behind anything of utility or value.

**Effective, genuine leadership** is never a matter of imposing ideas and ideals on a set of people, but rather of connecting ideas, ideals, values, and goals to the members of the enterprise and to the realities of the environment in which the enterprise exists and operates. Allow this connection to break, and you relinquish leadership in any meaningful sense of the word.

# Define
# Your Destiny

"It is better to be making the news than taking it;
to be an actor rather than a critic."
~ *The Story of the Malakand Field Force,* 1898

Growing up, we all face the problem of making our way in the world. For some of us, it is more or less easy. The world offers a path—doctor, lawyer, teacher, accountant, engineer, whatever—and, for better or worse, we follow it. For others, it is more challenging.

Winston Churchill came of age in the middle of the Victorian era, in a place and of a social class that were rife with certain expectations. The paths potentially open to him were in the civil government or in the military. Because he could not achieve sufficiently lofty marks in school to prepare him for a career in either the civil or foreign service, young Churchill was shunted into a less intellectually demanding military career—something, fortunately, that interested him and for which he possessed an aptitude.

But Churchill quickly found that this well-worn path would not likely lead to a rewarding career. Such a realization comes to many people, yet most remain on their original path, resigning themselves to a life lived more or less in dissatisfaction. Not Churchill. First, he leveraged his commission as a junior cavalry officer into as much hazardous adventure as he could get. Second, he combined his

profession as a soldier with that of a journalist, becoming that
hybrid of modern combat, the war correspondent. It was an unconventional approach to military service, and young Churchill freely
moved back and forth across the indistinct line that separated combatant from reporter.

## If You Fail to Define Yourself, Others Will Define You

In business, whether within your own enterprise or in the wider
world of colleagues, competitors, clients, and investors, it is
crucial to fashion an effective identity and to maintain control
over it. Present yourself as a blank slate, and others will rush to
fill it in. Instead, build yourself into a brand, an identity that
marks you as both unique and valuable.

It was not that he couldn't make up his mind. Quite the contrary,
he was always intensely single-minded. Soldier, reporter—it didn't
much matter. All that mattered was that he be at the center of the
action—not just watching it or even experiencing it, but influencing,
managing, and controlling it. So after marching with the Malakand
Field Force in 1898, he secured reassignment to a new fight on a different continent, voyaging to South Africa to report on the Second
("Great") Boer War.

In November 1899, the town of Ladysmith was under heavy
siege by the Boers, the settlers of Dutch ancestry who wanted independence from the British Empire. Churchill and the British troops
were in nearby Estcourt when Captain Aylmer Haldane was
ordered to reconnoiter into enemy-held territory in the direction of
the town of Colenso. The expedition of slightly more than 20 miles
would be made aboard an armored train—considered the safest way
of traveling in country held by insurgent forces at the time—and
Haldane asked Churchill, with whom he had served in India, if he
would like to go along. Churchill hesitated briefly, but realizing that

such an expedition might well be productive of some exciting news dispatches, he agreed, and at ten minutes after five on the morning of November 15, the train pulled out of Estcourt.

On reaching Chieveley station, more than halfway to Colenso, Haldane received word of the presence of Boers and ordered the train to back up about four miles to the town of Frere, where he intended to wait and watch the situation. As the train chugged around a hill, Boer artillery, emplaced on the hill, began to rain down shells, one of which hit the lead car. The engineer poured on the steam, intending to push past the Boer ambush. Boers had placed a large rock on the tracks, however, which derailed three cars. Because the train had been traveling in reverse, the three derailed cars, which were being pushed rather than pulled, now blocked the locomotive. Without hesitation, Churchill offered Haldane his services. While Haldane and some of his men kept up a covering fire against the Boers, Churchill supervised a work gang to manhandle the derailed cars clear of the tracks. As they did this, he told the engineer to move forward and backward in an effort to push the wreckage clear.

### Pitch In

Problems are invitations to action. Take ownership of a problem, and you suddenly own a stake in the enterprise.

All the while, the Boers maintained fire with small arms as well as artillery, and when a shell fragment struck the engineer in the head, he turned to Churchill.

"I'm finished," he declared in disgust.

Churchill calmly replied: "Buck up a bit. I will stick to you."

Expressed in just nine words, it was the very message Churchill would deliver more grandly throughout the darkest hours of World War II. It was a call to courage and endurance, supported by a pledge of solidarity, personal and absolute.

*"Broadly speaking, the short words are the best, and the old words best of all."*

~Speech, London, November 2, 1949

To this, Churchill added something more pragmatic, promising the engineer that if he kept at the throttle, he would be cited for distinguished gallantry in action and earn a medal. Whether inspired by the prospect of honorable celebrity, the Churchillian promise of sharing his fate, or both, the engineer stayed at his post. Captain Haldane later wrote that the efforts to clear the tracks continued for more than an hour, under intense fire and at first without success.

**"Churchill . . . , 'with indomitable perseverance, continued the difficult task,' all the while 'exposed to the full fire of the enemy.'"**

Churchill, Haldane observed, "with indomitable perseverance, continued the difficult task," all the while "exposed to the full fire of the enemy." There was nothing frantic about his direction of the work. In a letter, one of the privates on board the train described how Churchill "walked about . . . as coolly as if nothing was going on," his "presence and way of going on . . . as much good as fifty men would have been."

After little more than an hour, Churchill achieved a breakthrough, and the engine eased past the wreckage. He ordered the engineer to steam into position to couple with the cars that remained on the rails, so that as many men as possible could be brought safely back to Frere. The coupling, however, had been hit by artillery and was useless. Churchill then helped the engineer hoist about twenty wounded men onto the coal tender. At least, running the locomotive without cars, the engineer would be able to evacuate them. With Churchill still on board, the locomotive set off for the Frere station, picking up more wounded on the way. As soon as he was satisfied that the engine had cleared the field of fire, Churchill hopped off and walked back into the ambush to help Haldane.

Haldane's plan was to take refuge, along with the fifty men who remained with him, in a farmhouse just off the right-of-way and fight from its cover. But as he was about to rally the troops for this, two of Haldane's men took it upon themselves to wave their white handkerchiefs. Haldane had no choice now but to order a general surrender.

In the meantime, Churchill was still walking along the track, back to Haldane's position. Intercepted by a pair of Boers, who leveled their rifles at him, he did not surrender, but turned on his heel and ran back along the tracks. The Boer bullets, "sucking to right and left, seemed to miss only by inches."

He sought cover in the shallow cut through which the tracks ran, but, feeling the "soft kisses" of another two bullets draw the air beside him, climbed up the embankment, crawled through a wire fence at the top, and then found a small hollow into which he pressed his body. Seeing a river gorge about 200 yards away, he decided to run for it, knowing that it afforded plenty of cover and concealment. No sooner had he made this decision, however, than a young Boer cavalry officer pounded up to him, shouting something Churchill could not understand.

*"Although prepared for martyrdom, I preferred that it be postponed."*
~ *The Story of the Malakand Field Force,* 1898

Churchill rose to his feet and reached for his pistol, only to discover an empty holster. He had left the weapon in the locomotive. With the cavalry officer's rifle in his face, Winston Churchill put up his hands and surrendered.

The "greatest indignity of my life," he later called it. He was herded with the other prisoners, "like cattle," onto a train bound for Pretoria, where they were confined to the States Model School, which had been converted into a makeshift POW camp. He lodged formal protests, pointing out that he was not a soldier but a war correspondent, and should therefore be released immediately. Unknown to Churchill, it was precisely his reporting that the Boer leaders most feared. They considered his accounts highly damaging to their cause. And thus, each of his letters of protest was filed away by the Boer authorities, unanswered.

On December 10, the twenty-fifth day of his captivity, learning that Haldane and a Sergeant-Major Brockie were planning an escape, Churchill invited himself to join them. The school was surrounded by a high wall; however, in the corner where the latrine was located, the wall butted up against a kind of ledge, making it possible to vault quietly over the wall and into the garden of a private house next door to the school. Traveling by night and hiding by day, the trio planned to make their way—on foot—the hundred miles to the neutral Portuguese colony of Mozambique. Agreed on the plan, the men set the very next night, December 11, as the night of their escape.

The trio passed a restless day, anxious for the sun to set. After dark, they watched the wall by the latrine, waiting apprehensively for a lapse in the attention of the sentries. It did not come.

As Churchill later recalled it, Haldane counseled patience while he, Churchill, was all "for making a desperate venture and risking the chance of detection." December 12 was passed in a state of high tension as the three men argued over the necessity of action. Haldane recorded in his diary that Churchill insisted, "We must go tonight," to which he responded, "There are three of us to go, and we will certainly do so if the chance is favourable." Writing a dozen years after the events, Churchill admitted that he "was insistent that at whatever risk, we should force the thing through that night."

That night, before moonrise, Churchill and Haldane ventured to the latrine, only to dither in spluttering indecision. The sentry hardly ever looked away, it seemed, and both men were intimidated. When they returned to the verandah, Brockie mocked them. They responded by inviting Brockie to go to the latrine and survey the situation for himself. He did so, and when he did not return, Churchill announced to Haldane that he was going across, advising Haldane to follow him after a few minutes.

> *"Whatever risk, we should force the thing through that night."*
>
> ~Quoted in Martin Gilbert's *Churchill: A Life,* 1991

On his way, Churchill encountered Brockie returning to the verandah. The sergeant-major muttered something Churchill could not make out. A sentry was within earshot, and Brockie dared not raise his voice. As for Churchill, he kept walking toward the latrine. As he approached the wall, he later recalled, he had "come to the conclusion that we should waste the whole night in hesitations unless the matter were clinched once and for all." Seeing the sentry turn away to light his pipe, Churchill jumped up the ledge of the wall and, after a few seconds, had dropped down on the other side.

> *"It is a mistake to try to look too far ahead. The chain of destiny can only be grasped one link at a time."*
>
> ~Speech to the House of Commons, February 27, 1945

Would Haldane and Brockie follow? He waited, crouched in the dark garden of the neighboring house. A quarter of an hour passed . . . a half hour . . . an hour. His only cover was a few small, scrubby, leafless bushes. The house was lit, and through its windows, he could see people passing to and fro. Twice, a man walked out and into the garden, approaching no more than a few yards from Churchill.

At last, Churchill walked back to the wall. He tapped gently on it until he had attracted the attention of a prisoner. He whispered to him to tell Haldane that he had gotten over and that he should do his best to join him. Then he waited some more.

After receiving the message, Haldane approached the wall, but each time he got ready to make his move, the presence of the sentry thoroughly discouraged him. After an hour of agonizing indecision, Haldane approached the wall and tapped on it. Churchill, just outside, tapped back. Haldane whispered that neither he nor Brockie would make it over that night. Churchill now chewed over his options. He considered climbing back over the wall, back into prison, since he did not think he had much of a chance getting to Mozambique on his own. But because there was no ledge on the garden side, it would be much harder to climb back in than it had been to climb out. At the very least, noise would be unavoidable. He and Haldane therefore agreed that his only option was to go it alone.

It was a desperate prospect, but Churchill had a genius for negotiating desperate prospects without desperation. He thought the matter through and rapidly concluded that the original plan, which had been simply to walk through some hundred miles of enemy-controlled territory to the border with Portuguese Mozambique, would be very much an act of desperation and therefore he rejected it. He knew, however, that a rail line ran from Pretoria to the Portuguese port of Lourenço Marques, a port from which he could take ship to solidly British Durban. His best chance, he decided, was to find a freight train and hide in it.

**"It was a desperate prospect, but Churchill had a genius for negotiating desperate prospects without desperation."**

Nobody enjoyed military pomp, pageantry, and elaborate uniforms more than Winston Churchill, but, functioning in South

Africa as a journalist, he had made a point of wearing plain civilian clothes, and, attired as he now was, in an unassuming brown suit, he decided (after passing the rest of the night concealing himself as best he could in the garden) that the best way for him to hide in Pretoria was out in plain sight. He even made a point of walking the streets humming a tune while waiting for nightfall. In the dark, he watched for the headlamp of a slow-moving freight train. Running alongside it, he jumped up on the coupling between cars, and then climbed into a car that was filled with empty coal bags. Just before daybreak, fearful that he would be discovered in the light of day, he jumped off near the mining town of Witbank, about 60 miles east of Pretoria. He hid near the tracks until night returned, and then walked toward a cluster of lights visible on the horizon. Hungry and thirsty, he approached a house adjacent to a coal mine. The man who answered the door brandished a pistol. Churchill pretended to take no notice.

"Are you an Englishman?" he asked with perfect calm.

By way of answer, the man simply kept his pistol trained on him.

"I am Dr. Bentinck," Churchill continued. "I have fallen off the train and lost my way."

With his pistol, the man silently motioned Churchill inside. Then he demanded that he tell him the truth.

"I am Winston Churchill."

The answer was much like leaping over the wall. It was just something you did—and hoped for the best.

"Thank God you have come here!" the man exclaimed. He went on to explain that the Boers had issued a bulletin with his full description and that this house was the only house for some 20 miles round where he would not have been turned in—or shot on the spot.

**"The answer was much like leaping over the wall. It was just something you did—and hoped for the best."**

John Howard was a British mine manager. He hid the fugitive at the bottom of a mineshaft and supplied Churchill with a candle, which the albino rats infesting the mine soon made off with, leaving him in total darkness.

Churchill spent three days in the hole before Howard fetched him back to the surface, ushered him into a storeroom, and locked him in. Here, he awaited the arrival of the next freight train bound for Lourenço Marques. At last, on the nineteenth, bearing with him the gift of two roasted chickens, a few slices of cold meat, a bread loaf, a melon, three bottles of cold tea, and a Mauser, he climbed into a freight car and hid himself among bales of wool. The train clattered along the tracks and made many stops, each one a close call as inspectors searched the cars. It was four in the afternoon on the twenty-first when the freight eased into the rail yard of the Portuguese coastal town. The floor of his rail car had been thick with coal dust, so Churchill emerged black from head to toe and, in this condition, called on the British consul, who sent a polite telegram: "Please inform relations that Winston Churchill arrived today."

Soon all of England and the empire knew that Winston Churchill had escaped from a Boer prisoner-of-war camp. When he reached Durban in British South Africa on December 23, he was greeted by a tumultuous crowd. The tumult was echoed throughout the empire. Magnificent as it really was, Churchill's feat was magnified many fold by the historical moment in which it had occurred. The war was going badly for Britain, and the escape was greeted as a triumph just short of sudden and total victory. The first great fame of Winston Churchill was born, and his destiny—now defined—awaited only fulfillment.

**"Look before you leap,"** the old saying goes, but sometimes it is better just to leap. Insofar as thought creates hypothetical situations, it also produces imaginary problems and therefore does not always make decisions better, let alone easier. Action, in contrast to thought, has a way of clarifying the present and defining the future, paring your choices to a crucial few and prompting quick, clean decisions, which provide the opportunity to appear as a person of bold decisiveness and self-confident vision. Despite the risks, taking timely action may well allow you to define yourself, not only dramatically but before others do it for you. Never allow yourself to be confined in the prison of somebody else's ideas.

# 4

# Fail and Learn

"You will make all kinds of mistakes;
but as long as you are generous and true, and also fierce,
you cannot hurt the world."

~ *My Early Life,* 1930

Hard though it is to believe, "think outside the box" was once a fresh and stimulating admonition to solve problems creatively. It has been repeated so often since it made its first appearance sometime in the 1970s that the phrase has become a cliché of threadbare thought—a prisoner, as it were, of the very box from which it sought to liberate decision makers and their decisions. Try nevertheless to imagine it as a brand-new piece of advice, and you will appreciate the problem Winston Churchill, First Lord of the Admiralty, faced at the very end of 1914, some five months into World War I, the so-called Great War.

Together with all the other combatants on the Western Front, his army was stuck in a hemorrhaging gash of trench running more than 600 miles from the English Channel coast in the north to the border of neutral Switzerland. In the summer of 1914, it looked as if the war would be over in its first month, as the German armies wheeled through Belgium and northern France, descending precipitously upon Paris. But then execution of the celebrated Schlieffen Plan, which had guided this sweeping advance, faltered, sputtered, and broke down completely. On September 5, 1914, the invading German armies halted, digging in along the Marne within 30 or so miles of the French capital. From this, the French and the British drew hope of salvation, but from this, too, the horror of the bloody stalemate grew.

The Western Front was a box, and no one was more aware of the nature of this box than Winston Churchill himself. After the war, in his magisterial five-volume history of the conflict, *The World Crisis, 1911–1918* (1923–31), he would write that battles were "won by slaughter and maneuver." The superior general relied on maneuver rather than slaughter. In fact, this was a kind of index to the quality of the commander: The more he exploited maneuver and the less he depended upon slaughter, the better he was. Maneuver was the economical and efficient approach to war; slaughter, the wasteful and costly. The problem of the ossified Western Front was that it did not permit maneuver. On a field of battle, opposing forces strive to flank one another—that is, to get around one another so that they can attack from the side (flank) or, better yet, swing around to attack from the rear. Head-to-head combat is slaughter. Flanking combat is maneuver. Yet, on the Western Front, each time one side would try to get around the other, extending its trench to the north or south, the other side would do the same. Soon, there was no more room for such sidestepping. All that was left was slaughter along a front that bisected Western Europe.

Like any truly enterprising leader, whether of a military force, a nation, or a corporation, Churchill endeavored to think outside of the box. His insight was startlingly simple. The Western Front was a box; therefore, get outside of it. If maneuver was impossible on the Western Front, move to a front where it was still a possibility.

> *"All the greatest things are simple, and many can be expressed in single words: Freedom; Justice; Honour; Duty; Mercy; Hope."*
> ~Speech at Albert Hall, London, May 14, 1947

Churchill understood that the "Great War" was a *world* war, so he looked beyond Europe. He looked at the world. What he saw was that Turkey, which had sided with Germany, represented a threat to Russia, the eastern ally of Britain and France. Turkey menaced the southern border of Russia, tying up troops that could otherwise be used directly against Germany and Austria. The more troops Russia could hurl against Germany and Austria on the Eastern Front, the fewer those nations would have to use against Britain and France on the Western Front. Turkey also controlled the Dardanelles, the long, narrow strait separating the Balkans from Asia Minor. If the Allies could seize the Dardanelles, they could open a direct passage to Russia, allowing for the free flow of supplies and troops from the West to the East. Moreover, Turkey would find itself menaced. It might even be possible to knock that country out of the war altogether. In either case, Turkish troops would have to be withdrawn from the Russian border, thereby freeing up many Russian troops for service against Germany and Austria. Finally, a successful move against the Dardanelles would probably bring Italy into the war on the side of the Allies, as well as some of the other uncommitted Balkan countries, particularly Greece.

Taking the Dardanelles was much easier said than done. The narrow strait was lavishly fortified, presenting an extreme hazard to warships. Earlier in the century, Churchill himself had declared his opinion that the fixed fortifications and heavy guns of the Dardanelles made it virtually impossible to "force" the strait, and it would therefore be foolhardy to "expose a modern fleet" to it. But Churchill had also recently presided over a massive modernization of the Royal Navy, including the production of ships with advanced armor plating, much larger guns, and far more accurate fire-direction systems. In January 1915, he sent a query to Admiral Sackville Carden, commanding the eastern Mediterranean fleet. Given the advances in technology, he asked, would it be possible to reduce and breach the Dardanelles by naval action alone? Carden replied that, given a sufficient number of ships, it was possible. Because the object was to create truly massive firepower, this meant supplementing the modern battleships with older, even obsolescent battleships. Equipped with less formidable armor plating, those ships would be more vulnerable to fire from the Turkish shore batteries, but, Churchill reasoned, their age made them more or less expendable. Besides, the sacrifice of some older ships—together with their crews—would be more than compensated for by the lives that would be saved from fruitless carnage on the Western Front.

## Consider Value, Not Cost

Most of us have been raised to evaluate decisions in terms of cost. This is a mistake. The more important dimension is always value, which is the sum of benefit minus cost. The loss of warships and their crews is a high cost; however, the benefit purchased by this cost may well represent a great value—the saving of more lives, the breaking of a destructive stalemate.

That the assault on the Dardanelles failed is beyond question. Nearly a century after this disastrous operation, however, what remains very much in dispute is the wisdom of the strategic concept. Some military historians have blamed—and some continue to blame—Churchill for rushing headlong into a tragically foolish gamble. Others, however, believe that the operation exhibited not only sound strategy, but brilliant strategy. The failure, they point out, was in the execution rather than the concept.

It is a principle of war fighting, as it is of any complex, high-stakes enterprise, that whereas good tactics efficiently applied can often rescue flawed strategy, even the most brilliant strategy will fail if it is not served by good tactics properly executed. That is, strategy—no matter how brilliant—cannot compensate for inadequate tactics. The wisdom of the Dardanelles strategy can be debated, but the tragic inadequacy of the tactics supporting it is beyond debate.

The failure of those tactics began before a single ship got under way. As First Lord of the Admiralty, Churchill had great authority, but even more responsibility. He was a member of a War Council that included Prime Minister Asquith and Lord Herbert Kitchener, who headed the army. It also included other naval and army officers. Neither Churchill nor anyone else, acting alone, could override the council. For all practical purposes, the war was conducted by committee, and the committee was indecisive, wracked with self-doubt, second-guessing, and inconsistency. From the end of 1914, when the prospect of attacking at the Dardanelles was first broached, to March 1915, when the attack was launched, the War Council chewed over the operation no fewer than fifteen times, according to

**"Whereas good tactics efficiently applied can often rescue flawed strategy, even the most brilliant strategy will fail if it is not served by good tactics properly executed. . . . strategy—no matter how brilliant—cannot compensate for inadequate tactics."**

Churchill's official biographer, Martin Gilbert. Beyond the question of whether or not it was feasible to take the Dardanelles, the other decision that repeatedly vexed the council was whether to attack only with ships or to make this an amphibious operation, combining naval and land forces. Originally, both Churchill and his first sea lord, Admiral Lord Fisher, favored the amphibious approach. They were opposed, however, by Asquith and Kitchener, the latter protesting that he had no troops available and could not afford to deplete the Western Front for the operation. This is when Churchill asked Admiral Sackville Carden if a navy-only attack would work, and when he received a hopeful answer, the War Council focused on this option.

The war planners discussed the naval attack during the second and third meetings of the War Council. At the fourth meeting, however, Kitchener suddenly reversed himself, suggesting that a land component was also necessary. Less than a week after this, he returned to his original position, insisting that he had no troops to spare. Two weeks later, at the sixth War Council meeting, he offered the possibility of contributing a division, but he wanted it to be used on the Turkish mainland, in an independent assault on Salonica, a port city in northeastern Greece, rather than in an operation coordinated with the naval assault on the Dardanelles.

Amid the growing confusion, the first sea lord floundered. After telling Churchill that a navy-only attack was feasible, Admiral Fisher suddenly voiced opposition to the idea—only to reverse himself yet again, insisting that the ships acting alone could do it. This was followed, however, by a new round of waffling, and War Council meetings seven, eight, and nine were devoted to discussion of a combined sea-land operation, with the navy pounding the straits and the 29th Division making a coordinated attack on shore, at Gallipoli. With this apparently settled at last, a date for the operation was set. At meeting ten, three days later, Kitchener told Churchill that the 29th Division would not be available after all. Meetings eleven and twelve were devoted to argument, rancorous and fruitless. Acting on his own authority—and without even informing Churchill, who bore the responsibility for overseeing the entire Dardanelles operation—Kitchener cancelled preparations to transport the 29th Division. Having done this, however, he came to the meeting number thirteen again willing to offer the 29th Division.

*"A fanatic is one who can't change his mind and won't change the subject."*
~Quoted in *Bartlett's Familiar Quotations,* 1992

By this time, the clock had all but run out. The naval component of the operation had been proceeding, with ships already steaming into position. At the time of the War Council's thirteenth meeting, the navy was set to attack in just one week. Now that Kitchener had canceled troop transport, there was not even a plan, let alone the means, of landing the division. This meant that the fleet commanders had to go into desperate battle without even knowing when—or even whether—a land army would follow up on their attack. Nothing is more fatal to success than operating from slippery footing on an uncertain foundation. Churchill and his War Council sent the men of the Royal Navy into combat without resolute and decisive backing.

The real surprise was that the naval assault, which commenced on February 19, 1915, initially showed promise. Early in the morning, a pair of destroyers cautiously probed the straits. They were followed by the battleships *Cornwallis* and *Vengeance*. This opening attack was somewhat disappointing, but

**"Nothing is more fatal to success than operating from slippery footing on an uncertain foundation."**

seven days later, on February 25, the naval bombardment was repeated. This forced the Turks to evacuate the outer defenses of the straits and allowed the British fleet to enter and begin firing on the intermediate fortifications. At first thrilled by this progress, the British commanders found themselves thwarted by the Turkish minefields, against which the fleet's minesweepers—merely converted fishing trawlers operated mostly by civilian crews—were largely ineffective. The resulting delay gave the Turks both time and incentive to reestablish a vigorous defense. It was not until March 15 that Admiral Carden received approval from the Admiralty to make an all-out attack in an effort to break the defenses once and for all. His idea was to use the heavy guns of the battleships to cover the minesweepers, giving them free rein to do their work and thereby clearing the way for the fleet to push through the remainder of the straits.

It was a good idea. Unfortunately, on the fifteenth, Carden fell seriously ill and had to be replaced by Rear Admiral John de Robeck, who lacked his confidence in the ability of the fleet to silence the guns of the Dardanelles fortifications. A leader who undertakes a high-risk enterprise without much hope for its success is clearly doomed to failure.

The British planned to make their move on March 18, aiming to knock out the fortifications covering the first five lines of mines. Once this was accomplished during the day, the minesweepers could do their work the following night. With the mines cleared, the fleet would then be free to move up the Narrows and fire upon the remaining shore defenses. That done, the minesweepers could then clear the remaining five minefields. After that, the Dardanelles strait would be clear, troops could be freely transported and supplied for a vigorous invasion, and a line of communication and supply would be opened directly to Russia.

### The Curse of the Committee

The proper purpose of a committee is to pool brainpower in preparation for decision making. Decisions themselves should never be made by the committee, but by a person assigned the responsibility for making decisions and invested with the authority to execute them. Committees dilute responsibility and dissolve authority.

Firing began about eleven in the morning. The combined British and French fleets took a pounding, but did manage to suppress— though not destroy—the intermediate Turkish defenses. Instead of pressing forward, however, Admiral de Robeck pulled back, maneuvering for a fresh assault. In the process, a French battleship struck a mine and was lost, and, hours later, the British battle cruiser *Inflexible* also struck a mine and had to be beached on the Turkish island of Bozcaada. *Irresistible*, another battleship, also hit a mine, was cast adrift, and had to be abandoned. HMS *Ocean* was dispatched to tow the ship, but also struck a mine, which rendered her unable to steer and therefore helpless.

With one French battleship sunk and three British vessels beached or drifting abandoned, de Robeck, disheartened, broke off the attack and withdrew.

*"Never give in, never give in, never, never, never, never. . . ."*
~Speech, Harrow School, London, October 29, 1941

It was an ignominious defeat. Churchill called for the attack to
be renewed and informed de Robeck that he was sending four
replacement ships. He refused to be discouraged by the loss of
the ships. Of those sacrificed, only *Inflexible* was a modern
combat vessel. The rest were obsolescent and expendable.
Churchill believed—quite accurately, as it turned out—that the
Turks had nearly depleted their ammunition, so a renewed naval
attack would have met with far less opposition. Moreover,
whereas the minesweepers had initially been manned by civilian
crews, the loss of the battleships had freed up a great number of
Royal Navy sailors willing to take over sweeping operations, even
under fire. They were determined to get rid of the mines. Based
on reports from Henry Morgenthau, at the time U.S. ambassador
to Turkey, Constantinople anticipated imminent attack, and no
one expected the Turkish capital to hold out. If the city fell, the
Turkish government itself would collapse, and Turkey would be
out of the war.

But Admiral de Robeck, who never had heart for the operation,
lost his stomach for the fight. He was appalled by the loss of one
ship after another. On March 23, he sent a message to the
Admiralty, calling for the support of land forces before he dared to
renew the sea assault. The result was a lost opportunity of vast pro-
portions as the naval assault gave way to an army invasion, which
did not commence until April. The Turks used the long interval
between the naval attack and the troop landings to reinforce their
positions, rendering them virtually impregnable and creating on the
Gallipoli peninsula the very conditions that prevailed in the
Western Front: a battlefield of trenches—static, doomed, deprived of
the option of maneuver, leaving only slaughter. From April 25, 1915,
to January 6, 1916, Australian and New Zealand troops would fight

and die on the peninsula; there were 252,000 casualties, including 46,000 battle deaths, and all without productive results.

At the time, Churchill absorbed almost all of the blame. On May 15, 1915, Admiral Fisher resigned, an action that prompted Prime Minister Asquith to struggle for political damage control by forming a new coalition government—one in which Winston Churchill would no longer be First Lord of the Admiralty. "Let me stand or fall by the Dardanelles," Churchill appealed to Asquith on May 21, "but do not take it from my hands." The plea was in vain.

> *"Success is the ability to go from one failure to another with no loss of enthusiasm."*
>
> ~ Frequently quoted saying attributed to Churchill

The catastrophe of the Dardanelles would have crushed a lesser man. Churchill was, indeed, both heartbroken and enraged, but he was also determined to recover. On a personal level, he achieved recovery by temporarily retreating to canvas and paints—which would become a lifelong avocation, more a spiritual restorative than a mere hobby—and then flung himself back into the center of the action. He assumed command in the front lines of France of the 6th Royal Scots Fusiliers, serving in the trenches from November 1915 to May 1916. In July 1917, David Lloyd George, who had replaced Asquith as prime minister, offered Churchill a new position, of decidedly lesser status than First Lord of the Admiralty, yet one Churchill embraced with neither complaint nor regret, eager to reclaim a place in the government, in the administration of the war, and in the political destiny of Great Britain.

**Churchill did much more than survive the catastrophe** of Dardanelles and Gallipoli; he learned from the failure. He learned that strategy without adequate tactics is like an idea without adequate expression: stillborn. He learned that the counsel of experts, authorities, and advisers was valuable, but that no committee could ever make effective decisions. One leader, one thinker, one decision maker had to reign above all. But that was not enough. The person who held the responsibility for making decisions must also possess the authority to execute those decisions. He cannot be second-guessed, countermanded, or sabotaged.

The principle of possession of full authority was perhaps the most important lesson of the Dardanelles disaster. In later years, Churchill added four additional principles that, he believed, must govern any major decision, whether in a military or other context:

1. Any proposed operation should have a reasonable prospect of success. This did not mean that it had to be a sure thing—far from it. Churchill was willing to take great risks and make substantial sacrifices, but he drew the line at foolish desperation.
2. No operation or campaign should be undertaken if it is likely to compromise greater interests. When the United States was propelled into World War II, for example, the public hungered for instantaneous revenge on Japan for its attack on Pearl Harbor. Churchill and Roosevelt, however, agreed that the united efforts of America and Britain had to be directed first against Hitler. The powerful motive of vengeance had to be subordinated to addressing the greater and more immediate threat of the European war.
3. Preparation is key. Whatever else went wrong at the Dardanelles, valuable time was wasted in debate and indecision rather than actual preparation.
4. Finally, Churchill came to understand that the successful execution of a plan requires absolute determination and the full vigor of an unswerving commitment. Both of these qualities were tragically lacking at the Dardanelles.

# 5

# The Job: Do It

"The maxim of the British people is 'Business as usual.'"
~ Speech, Guildhall, London, November 9, 1914

Historians still debate whether—or to what degree—the disastrous naval assault on the Dardanelles and the even more catastrophic land campaign on Gallipoli during World War I were the fault of First Lord of the Admiralty Winston Churchill. At least one thing is beyond debate: As the British war bureaucracy was structured at the time, Churchill had to accept virtually total responsibility for these operations, but was not given anything approaching total authority over them. For any leader, responsibility without authority is a fatal combination, and, for Churchill, the immediate result was, indeed, fatal. He absorbed all of the blame, and—call his fate richly deserved or call it scapegoating—he was sacked.

Initially after this blow, Churchill again withdrew into his favorite private passion, painting, but he soon decided that he had to return to an active role in the war. He accepted an invitation to take command of the 6th Royal Scots Fusiliers as regimental lieutenant colonel in the late fall of 1915. Perhaps no one has ever called combat on the Western Front a therapeutic experience, but for Churchill, it was just that. The reason for this is not difficult to fathom. Leading a thousand men in combat, assigned to carry out a specific mission, and, as lieutenant colonel, enjoying unquestioned responsibility as well as authority over both the men and the mission was far more satisfying—at least in the short term—than becoming ensnared in a lumbering bureaucracy, where responsibility and authority were apportioned unequally but blame was served up in heaps. Churchill's experience on the front, successfully facing intense physical danger as he had done as a young officer in the North-West Frontier of India and in South Africa, restored his general morale and his confidence in himself as a leader.

**"For any leader, responsibility without authority is a fatal combination, and, for Churchill, the immediate result was, indeed, fatal."**

> *"To do justice to a great man, discriminating criticism is necessary. Gush, however quenching, is always insipid."*
> ~ Quoted in Sir James Marchant, ed., *Winston Spencer Churchill: Servant of Crown and Commonwealth,* 1954

Still, the disincentive to return to high-level government service was strong. He had been disgraced, he had been fired, and he felt he had been blamed unjustly. Nevertheless, his need to serve his country and to distinguish himself proved stronger than any self-righteous sense of unjust treatment. When H. H. Asquith's successor as prime minister, David Lloyd George—a friend and supporter of Churchill—invited him on July 16, 1917, to rejoin the government, he accepted. Asked what available post he wanted, he chose minister of munitions.

It was decidedly a step down from First Lord of the Admiralty, because it did not carry with it membership in the War Cabinet, the inner circle of government in which the major strategic and policy decisions relating to the war were made. Churchill acknowledged this, but he seems to have seen it as something of a tactical retreat. In congratulating him on his appointment, his Aunt Cornelia cautioned: "My advice is to stick to Munitions, and don't try to run the

Government." At this point, she was clearly preaching to the choir. Winston Churchill's intention was not to tell the prime minister how to run the government, but to run the Ministry of Munitions better than anyone had ever run it before. It was the job he had accepted, and it was the job he intended to do. If, cast out of the War Cabinet, his ego still pained him, he never let on, and he never let it interfere with his performance.

He faced a good deal of hostility, both from the staff of the Munitions Ministry and from a large segment of the press. Convening his staff for a first meeting, Churchill spoke with his customary candor, stating his awareness that he "started at scratch in the popularity stakes." Having said this, he did not proceed to the next logical step or, rather, the next conventional step—the offer of an apology. Instead, he threw down the gauntlet, leaving the issue of personal popularity and instead announcing that it would be his policy to produce munitions faster and in greater quantity than ever before. The result was an instantaneous about-face among staff members. Churchill had issued a challenge, and they eagerly took it up. He had refused to keep the focus on himself or his unpopularity and had instead begun his tenure by focusing on the mission, offering his staff an opportunity to excel. They were thrilled.

**"Winston Churchill's intention was not to tell the prime minister how to run the government, but to run the Ministry of Munitions better than anyone had ever run it before. It was the job he had accepted, and it was the job he intended to do."**

The press was another matter. The *Morning Post* greeted Churchill's appointment by calling him that "dangerous and uncertain quantity . . . a floating kidney in the body politic." He knew that the only way to win over the press—and the people—would be through performance.

*"Ideas acquire a momentum of their own. The stimulus of a vast concentration
of public support is almost irresistible in its potency."*

~ *Thoughts and Adventures,* 1932

His first major test came within days of his appointment. For a
year and a half, workers in several munitions plants along the Clyde
River in Glasgow, Scotland, had been locked in a dispute with management. This culminated in a general strike—potentially disastrous
in time of war. Churchill's predecessor had ordered the firing of the
strike leaders, who were also forced into exile, forbidden to live in
Glasgow, where they might continue to make trouble. Month after
month, the exclusion order stood, and the plants remained idle.

*"[The Ministry of Munitions] is a very heavy department, almost as inter-
esting as the Admiralty, with the enormous advantage that one has neither got
to fight Admirals nor Huns!"*

~ Quoted in Martin Gilbert's *Churchill: A Life,* 1991

When Churchill invited David Kirkwood, the leader of the
"Clyde deportees," to a meeting, Kirkwood anticipated being
greeted by "arrogance, military precision, abruptness." Instead,
Churchill "came in, his fresh face all smiles, and greeted me simply,
without a trace of side or trappings." In an instant, Kirkwood felt he
"had found a friend." A smile can go a long way, Churchill knew,
but he intensified his charm offensive by ringing a bell and saying to
Kirkwood as their talk began, "Let's have a cup of tea and a bit of
cake together." The effect of this simple gesture was electric. "Here
was the man supposed never to think of trifles," Kirkwood later
recalled, "suggesting tea and cakes." But, even as he wrote this,
Kirkwood realized that what Churchill offered was actually no mere
"trifle." The tea and cakes were "a sort of bread and salt of friendship." This minister of munitions was a master of the symbolic ges-

ture, and the symbolism was not lost on Kirkwood: "It was magnificent. We debated over the teacups."

Despite being under tremendous pressure—to redeem himself after the Dardanelles-Gallipoli disaster, to make good on his pledge to increase production, and to prove himself to the public—Churchill entertained his "enemy" as a friend, person to person, and proceeded with calm courtesy. When Kirkwood promised to end the strike if the "Clyde deportees" were reinstated, Churchill agreed, and he saw to it that Kirkwood himself was given the job of manager at London's Mile End shell factory. The *Morning Post* derided the settlement as an act "extending the hand of fellowship to . . . a gang of as dangerous and desperate agitators as ever fomented trouble in the labour world." Despite the derision, not only did the strike immediately end, but Kirkwood devised a worker bonus scheme that boosted production at the shell plant to the highest level in all Britain. Churchill got results. He did not posture. He did not call names. He did not preach of patriotism. He simply did the job.

*"You don't want to knock a man down except to pick him up in a better frame of mind."*

~Speech, New York, March 25, 1949

Churchill was more than willing to compromise in order to do the job. The Munitions of War bill he introduced in the House of Commons on August 15 was intended to increase output while preserving "industrial peace." He included in the bill wage incentive awards for workers with specialized skills and a guarantee that no worker would be penalized for belonging to a union or punished for taking part in a labor dispute. In presenting the bill, Churchill explained that the war would be won only with the support of "the great masses of the labouring classes." That support could not be coerced, but had to be given "with a loyal and spontaneous determination," in the absence of which "we must expect disastrous results."

As minister of munitions, Churchill introduced the great principle that would guide him as prime minister in the next war: self-restraint. Acquire as much power and authority as possible, but exercise the utmost restraint in using it. It was far better to elicit voluntary and wholehearted participation in programs for the common good than merely to coerce compliance. Volunteerism—spontaneous loyalty and commitment—not coercion and compulsion, were to be "business as usual."

## Win Your Authority Every Day

Too many managers believe that their authority comes from their official title or job description when, actually, it is bestowed by those the manager is assigned to manage. Leaders require followers. The most effective leaders ensure that those who follow them do so voluntarily. To the degree that authority is coerced, loyalty and commitment are hollow. Earn authority by persuasion. Make followership a matter of choice. Win your authority every day.

Churchill sought to increase the rate of war production not only by looking to workers and war plants, but also by turning inward to the Ministry of Munitions itself. He streamlined the bureaucracy of his ministry, replacing some fifty semi-autonomous departments with a single, eleven-member Munitions Council, each member of which exercised authority and responsibility over a specific area. The Munitions Council included a council secretariat, which coordinated the purchase of raw materials and oversaw production methods. This ensured economical and efficient consistency throughout all munitions production operations. Churchill kept close tabs on the Munitions Council, which met weekly and produced reports that he read closely and approved or questioned, as the need might be. The council established committees on an ad hoc basis in order to bring on board industrialists and businessmen, who could make things happen in the private sector far more quickly and efficiently than any number of civil servants or government executive authorities. Churchill was not an empire builder. He felt no need to exercise control for the sole sake of control. His object always was to achieve results. As he put it in a letter to Prime Minister Lloyd George, "I am delighted with all these clever businesspeople who are helping me to their utmost. It is very pleasant to work with competent people."

## Aim for Results

Churchill needed to increase munitions production. One essential step toward this goal was to end labor strife in war plants. Accordingly, he focused all of his effort on obtaining this result. He did not yield to the temptation to brandish his power by punishing labor leaders or coercing compliance. He understood what all effective managers understand: it is far easier to fix problems than to try to fix people. This led him to make compromises with labor leaders and to emphasize positive incentives for workers rather than punitive measures. The Conservative press criticized him for "giving in" to "dangerous elements." Maybe he did, but he achieved the result that he wanted and that the nation desperately needed. His policies greatly increased war production.

Even if we set aside all issues of assigning blame, we still must conclude that Winston Churchill failed as first lord of the Admiralty. He failed, that is, by the only objective and meaningful measure: results. But, having failed, he was willing to accept "demotion" to minister of munitions, a job with less authority and no standing in the War Cabinet. Not only did he embark on his new job without even the smallest of chips on his shoulder, he also embraced the work wholeheartedly and enthusiastically, he established cordial and highly productive relations with labor, he streamlined and revitalized the Ministry of Munitions itself, and he presided over a war production machine that, incredibly, produced a surplus of shells by the day of the armistice, November 11, 1918. Was this a step down, a lesser job? All that mattered to Winston Churchill was victory, and as minister of munitions, he was instrumental in achieving it.

**The first thing a manager must successfully manage** is his own ego. Having failed as First Lord of the Admiralty, Churchill refused to feel or behave as one who had been humiliated or wronged. Instead, he took up a "lesser" job and turned it into a triumph—a triumph not measured in terms of ego, but in terms of results and the further advance toward victory. Most leaders have a natural inclination to dominate and mold others. This trait, although common, drives the misdirection of energy and effort. The real goal of leadership is to create the best results possible: higher profits, more efficient production, better products, more advanced service—however the success of a particular enterprise may be defined. Set aside ego, and do the job at hand. Fix problems, not people. Rule over the results that are produced, not over the people who produce them.

# 6

# See for Yourself

"Change is the master key. A man can wear out
a particular part of his mind by continually using it and tiring it,
just in the same way as he can wear out the elbows of his coat."
~ *Thoughts and Adventures*, 1932

If you were to sit down and draw up a quick list of leadership traits, the chances are slim that you would include "curiosity" among them, and even slimmer that you would put it at the head of your list. Nevertheless, you don't have to look far for examples of what happens to leadership in the absence of curiosity. Britain's King George III showed no curiosity about the nature of the discontent in "his" American colonies, and therefore did nothing constructive to avert revolution. The result: he lost "his" colonies. More recently, another George—this one, the forty-third president of the United States—was repeatedly criticized for his lack of "intellectual curiosity" as he led the nation into an unnecessary war and presided over its mismanagement, mismanagement due in large part to his failure to ask probing questions of his policy and intelligence advisers.

So much for incurious leaders. Turn now to Winston Churchill. Whatever you might jot down on your short list of leadership traits, it is a good bet that Winston Churchill possessed them in abundance. But it is that one leadership trait you probably didn't include—curiosity—that he possessed in the greatest abundance of all.

*"Personally I am always ready to learn, although I do not always like being taught."*

~Speech, House of Commons, May 21, 1952

Practically everything interested Churchill: geography, politics, science, technology, literature, history, and biography. His personal store of curiosity is reflected in the multiple nature of his career, as soldier, journalist, Nobel laureate author and historian, omnivorous reader, politician, painter, bricklayer, and connoisseur of whiskey and cigars. Curiosity was no idle trait in Churchill. It made him want to see up close anything of any importance for himself. To the extent possible, he refused to rely on secondhand assessments of whatever truly mattered. His final government post during World War I was minister of munitions, the official in charge of weapons development, production, and supply. Most members of the government would have regarded it as a desk job. Churchill, however, could not sit still—he ventured to the Western Front at every opportunity. He believed that it was not sufficient to review reports on such issues as weapons performance and the consumption of ammunition without seeing all of these things, in action, for himself.

## Get Your Hands Dirty

Many CEOs would rather be accused of embezzlement than micromanagement, which they consider the cardinal sin of running a company. It is true that you cannot be everywhere at once, nor should you feel you have to be. Nevertheless, it is better to risk some degree of micromanagement than to insert multiple layers between you and your operations. At the very least, any *major* leadership decision should be based on firsthand knowledge of the area or areas the decision will affect. Gather the impressions, perceptions, and analyses of others, but do not rely on them exclusively. Get down in the trenches. Get your hands dirty. In addition to giving you a dose of the unvarnished truth, showing yourself in the front lines lifts the morale of everyone by demonstrating that you are in touch with your enterprise.

As the war approached its end in the fall of 1918, Churchill followed up each British advance with a personal visit to the front—often at significant hazard to himself—in order to assess the effectiveness of artillery, mustard gas, and the weapon he believed had the potential of being a war-winner, the still-evolving tank.

He strained to make his firsthand assessment as objective as possible. He took personal inventories of ammunition consumed and on hand, warning Prime Minister Lloyd George that the expenditure of artillery shells was so heavy that there was a very real danger of shortages beginning in 1919. Churchill by no means advised conservation of ammunition—quite the contrary, he believed that its prodigal use would hasten the end of the war—but he did call for increased production on the worst-case assumption that the war, which had already lasted four years, would continue well into 1919.

*"I have always loved butterflies. . . . The butterfly is the Fact—gleaming, fluttering, settling for an instant with wings fully spread to the sun, then vanishing in the shades of the forest."*

*~ My Early Life, 1930*

Churchill did not merely count shells and crater holes. A champion of the tank—a weapons system few generals welcomed at the time—he wrote dramatically to Lloyd George on September 10 to describe what happens when there are not enough tanks available to support an infantry attack. Wherever advancing infantry got too far ahead of the tanks, they rendered themselves horrifically vulnerable to enemy machine gunfire. Churchill observed that in one portion of the battlefield just 380 yards wide, 400 Canadians were buried as opposed to fewer than a hundred Germans. "You would be shocked," he wrote the prime minister, "to see the tragic spectacle of the ground where our attack for the time being withered away. It was just like a line of seaweed and jetsam which is left by a great wave as it recoils." With this vivid picture, a picture possible only for an eyewitness, Churchill made his case for increased production of tanks and stepped-up training of tank crews. Moreover, he called for faster tanks, which could keep pace with any infantry advance, so that the foot soldiers would not have to outrun their vital support and protection.

Churchill's visit to the front also gave him additional insights. He wrote to his wife, Clementine, on September 9 that the "ruin of the countryside was complete" and described the "pain & litter & squalor & the abomination of desolation" that were everywhere in evidence. Such scenes not only persuaded him that war was in itself an "abomination"—in contrast to most British politicians, Churchill avidly supported the creation of the League of Nations after the armistice, believing it was the best chance the world had to make future wars "impossible"—they also moved him to do whatever was necessary to push this war to as quick an end as possible. Accordingly, on September 12, he wrote to Clementine of his eagerness "to give the Germans a first good dose of the mustard gas"—at the time, a new addition to the British arsenal, although the Germans had introduced it to the battlefield back in July of 1917. It was, in fact, not a gas at all, but rather a fine aerosol that caused severe, painful, and debilitating burns on contact. If a high concentration was breathed in, it turned the lungs to liquid, causing men to drown in their own secretions. Mustard gas mist condensed, falling from the air like a fine rain, collecting in trenches and shell holes, where it remained long after the end of a battle. The unlucky soldier who settled into a contaminated trench or shell hole—or leaped into one, seeking cover—found himself bathed in liquid fire. At the direction of the Ministry of Munitions, British chemical warfare specialists had produced an especially potent form of mustard gas, "and we shall I think have enough to produce a decided effect." The "whining" of the Germans "in defeat is very gratifying to hear." It was Churchill's hope that the new mustard gas would push the exhausted and demoralized German soldiers over the brink. He wrote to Clementine on September 15 that the gas was on its way to the front. "This hellish poison will I trust be discharged on the Huns to the extent of nearly 1,000 tons by the end of this month." It was awful to contemplate, of course, but far more awful to see—month after month—row upon row of British dead. He took satisfaction in having his own two eyes on the war and his own two hands in the war. He explained in his letter to his wife that he no longer had reason to complain about not being "able to direct general policy" as part of the War Cabinet. He saw that his work was having a positive, definite impact on the war, and he confessed himself "content to be associated with the splendid machines of the British Army, and to feel how many ways there are open to me to serve them."

**An effective leader is incurably curious.** She wants to see everything for herself. She wants to learn the details of every operation in which her company engages. She craves a direct and unfiltered vision of the enterprise she leads and is willing to risk accusations of micromanagement to follow wherever her curiosity beckons.

# Be Just

"One ought to be just before one is generous."
~Speech, Manchester, December 6, 1947

Immediately after the armistice that concluded World War I, Prime Minister David Lloyd George asked Churchill to leave the Ministry of Munitions and assume the combined offices of secretary of state for war and air on January 9, 1919. This put Churchill in charge of the War Office and made him responsible for directing the demobilization of a British army of some 3.5 million men. The sheer numbers alone made the job a daunting one, but it was even more complex than it appeared. Running the War Office required more than dismantling the army. Although the war had ended, the need for a substantial military remained. Germany required occupation and the anti-Bolsheviks in Russia needed assistance. The Middle East was also a flashpoint for armed conflict. But even if Britain were in a position simply to disband the army, sending everyone home, to what kind of home would the veterans be sent? With the sudden end of war production and the mass cancellation of industrial contracts, England had far more men than livelihoods to give them.

Army mutinies and riots broke out two days before Churchill officially took office. Thousands gathered at Whitehall, London's government district, shouting that the war was over, they had done their bit, and they wanted to go home. Some simply refused orders to return to the Continent for deployment to German occupation duty. Some mutinied when they received marching orders to far-off Russia, wracked by civil war.

> *"[Vladimir I. Lenin] alone could have led Russia into the enchanted quagmire: he alone could have found the way back to the causeway. He saw; he turned; he perished. . . . The Russian people were left floundering in the bog. Their worst misfortune was his birth, their next worst—his death."*
>
> ~ *The World Crisis*, 1923–31

Churchill took charge of the situation one day before he was officially installed as secretary. As always, he insisted on seeing the situation for himself. He asked the general in charge of the London District how many troops were available to deal with the mutineers. Receiving an answer, he then asked, "Are they loyal?" The general replied that he hoped they were. "Can we arrest the mutineers?" Churchill asked next, to which the general replied, "We are not certain." Without comment, Churchill asked him if he had any other suggestions, and when the general replied that he had none, Churchill issued a terse command: "Then arrest the mutineers."

## Vintage Churchill

Handling the "Whitehall mutineers" was vintage Churchill, and any manager can learn from it: Inspect the situation, consult with the man in charge, solicit his suggestions, and then, if nothing better is forthcoming, act on your own. When something has to be done, choose the best available thing. Then do it, just as Churchill did.

He did not expect the arrests to go easily, but to his surprise, the mutineers did not resist being surrounded, and they voluntarily surrendered. Churchill saw in their yielding an opportunity to defuse an explosive situation. He did not want to crack down, not on those who were now complying. Instead of taking a punitive approach, he decided to reward compliance by introducing a settlement that would be not only fair in fact, but also in appearance. He wanted to resolve the current crisis *and* set an example for the millions more who were awaiting demobilization.

> "Instead of taking a punitive approach, he decided to reward compliance by introducing a settlement that would be not only fair in fact, but also in appearance."

Under the existing War Office policy, any soldier who had served at least four months could go home, but only if he could prove that he had an industrial job waiting for him. Even a soldier who had served for the duration of the war—four long and arduous years—would not be demobilized if he could not show that he had a civilian job waiting for him. Just four days after the Whitehall mutineers dispersed, Churchill announced a major revision of policy. Those who had served in the war, at the front, would be released first—the order of demobilization based on length of service. This was true whether or not a civilian job was in the offing. Additionally, all men who had enlisted prior to 1916 would be automatically and instantly demobilized. Those who had served two years or fewer would have to await the demobilization of those who had served longer—again, regardless of their civilian job situation. Moreover, among those who had served two years or less, special demobilization priority would be given to wounded men.

## The Greatest Power Is the Power of Self-Restraint

Under Churchill, demobilization proceeded smoothly, except at Calais, where 5,000 troops mutinied because they were not demobilized. Field Marshal Sir Douglas Haig led a force to suppress the mutiny. He arrested three soldiers identified as ringleaders and informed Churchill that they were to be shot to create a deterrent example. Churchill intervened immediately, telegraphing Haig that, unless the men had been guilty of bloodshed, "I do not consider that the infliction of the death penalty is justified." Executing the men was not only unjust, Churchill believed, but would alienate public opinion. He directed Haig to find a punishment that was more proportionate to the crime. As Churchill saw it, the greatest power a leader possessed was self-restraint.

The nation warmly greeted the justice of Churchill's scheme, and he himself was very proud of it, remarking to a friend that "It was one of the best things I did." However, there remained the problem of maintaining a sufficient army to occupy the Rhine. Churchill believed he needed to retain the military draft to the extent of continuing to field a million-man army. It took an effort to persuade Prime Minister David Lloyd George that this was indeed necessary, but in the end, Churchill was allowed to conscript his million.

*"At his best he could almost talk a bird out of a tree."*
~ On David Lloyd George, in *Thoughts and Adventures,* 1932

It was Britain's first peacetime draft. Churchill believed that the Rhineland occupation force was absolutely necessary to enforce the provisions of the armistice and was, in effect, an extension of wartime duty. He had, therefore, no compunction about committing draftees to the assignment. He did not believe it right or proper, however, to send conscripts to distant Russia to stiffen the anti-Bolshevik forces; moreover, he did not think that the British public would stand for it. Indeed, he believed there would also be widespread objection to sending regular army personnel to Russia. Service in Russia against the Bolsheviks, he believed, should be the exclusive province of those who explicitly volunteered for the assignment. As head of the War Office, Churchill had the authority to order any soldier to serve anywhere, but he believed that finding a manifestly fair and just solution trumped any authority he might possess.

**The exercise of power without justice** is tyranny. Winston Churchill was no tyrant, and he believed that the British people would never tolerate one. At various times and in various circumstances, a leader may or may not be able to provide all the food, shelter, clothing, or even protection that his constituents need, but by practicing thoughtful restraint in the exercise of his power, a leader can always act fairly and provide justice. On that commodity—justice—no leader need ever stint.

# 8

# Draw a Line

"We would rather see London laid in ruins and ashes
than that it should be tamely and abjectly enslaved."
~Broadcast, London, July 14, 1940

Inflexible companies, like inflexible people, are unresponsive to change and therefore doomed. Depending on the nature of the organization, the market, the competitive environment, and the industry, this doom may mean instant death or perhaps a slow, lingering demise. A third possibility is the creation of a ceiling above which neither you nor your enterprise can rise. As Ralph Waldo Emerson said, "A foolish consistency is the hobgoblin of little minds." Yet it is also the case that overly flexible companies, like overly pliable people, are properly called spineless. They lack identity and principles, and this absence creates a vacuum. As nature abhors a vacuum, so do your colleagues, subordinates, bosses, competitors, clients, and customers. If you and your organization have a vacuum where an identity should be, others will rush in to fill it. Your identity, including your values and principles, will be defined for you by others—quite possibly in ways neither to your advantage nor liking.

The ability to improvise, to respond creatively to change and to create change, is vital to success in any endeavor. Yet there comes a point at which a line must be drawn—a core identity defined, a set of principles laid down. At every level of his career, Churchill had a strong and sure sense of where to draw this line, and he knew how to draw it unambiguously. As secretary of war and air in 1920, for example, he approved using aircraft to "disperse" Sinn Fein (militant Irish nationalists) with "machine-gun fire" or "bombs," but he drew the line at what had recently taken place in another part of the empire, at Amritsar, India. There, on April 13, 1919, General Reginald Dyer earned the epithet "Butcher of Amritsar" for the infamous order he gave to open fire on unarmed civilians, including women and children, who were gathered at the Jallianwala Bagh for the annual Baisakhi celebrations, a Punjabi cultural and religious festival. The Jallianwala Bagh was a space of some six or seven acres surrounded by a wall, which had only five entrances. Four of the entrances were very narrow, and the fifth was blocked by Dyer's troops and two armored cars, each mounting machine guns.

**"If you and your organization have a vacuum where an identity should be, others will rush in to fill it. Your identity, including your values and principles, will be defined for you by others—quite possibly in ways neither to your advantage nor liking."**

> *"Responsibility is a wonderful agent when thrust upon competent heads."*
> ~Comment on the nonviolent police action
> that dispersed Irish Republican protestors
> in Dublin, September 1922, quoted
> in Martin Gilbert's *Churchill: A Life,* 1991

Intent on teaching the Indians a lesson after an anti-British mob assaulted a female English schoolteacher, Dyer ordered his soldiers to fire directly into the crowded festival grounds. In a ten-minute fusillade, some 1,650 rounds of ammunition were exhausted. Dyer personally led the assault, directing fire precisely where the crowd was densest, and then concentrating on the narrow exits, so that people who sought escape were cut down in great number. Officially, it was reported that more than 379 civilians were killed and 1,200 wounded. Unofficial reports—including those from British civil servants—counted more than 1,000 killed. Churchill never liked using ground troops against civilians, and after seeing to it that Dyer would never hold command again, he condemned the Amritsar massacre as a "monstrous event." He went on to promulgate what he described as "one general prohibition" for commanders to observe when handling riots and other civil strife: "I mean a prohibition against what is called 'frightfulness.' " This was the line he drew, and he defined it carefully:

> What I mean by frightfulness is the inflicting of great slaughter or massacre upon a particular crowd of people, with the intention of terrorizing not merely the rest of the crowd, but the whole district or the whole country. We cannot admit this doctrine in any form. Frightfulness is not a remedy known to the British pharmacopoeia.

He took care to draw this line, not only as a personal moral statement, but as the product of national values. "Frightfulness" was wrong for many reasons, the foremost of which was its essential un-Britishness.

Churchill was outraged by Amritsar, but he subordinated his personal outrage to a formulation of collective outrage—the line he drew on behalf of the British people. He expressed this in the form of an eloquent and unambiguous statement of principle. Churchill never turned his cheek when wronged. He endorsed vigorous action to suppress civil disorder and other attacks, but always with the purpose of protecting lives and never at the cost of compromising a basic code of morality, decency, and humanity. Six years later, when Churchill was serving as chancellor of the exchequer in the cabinet of Prime Minister Stanley Baldwin, he enthusiastically

## Measuring the Line

As the leader of an enterprise, you are expected to embody and act upon the identity and values of the enterprise. The ethical decisions you make have to be more than personal. You both guide and represent your organization. Yet this does not mean that you should abandon your personal values. They should inform—not necessarily determine—the ethical and policy lines you draw. Measure company policy against your personal ethics, and measure your personal ethics against the policies of your organization. Your leadership task is to reconcile them.

endorsed the cabinet's decision to send reinforcement troops to China, in response to attacks by Chinese warlords on Britishers in two Chinese ports. He wrote to the prime minister:

> Short of being actually conquered, there is not evil worse than submitting to wrong and violence for fear of war. Once you take the poison of not being able in any circumstances to defend your rights against the aggression of some particular set of people, there is no end to the demands that will be made or to the humiliations that must be accepted.

Here was Churchill's earliest stand against appeasement—the policy of submitting to wrong in order to avoid war—which preceded by a dozen years his famous stance against Prime Minister Neville Chamberlain's attempt to "appease" Adolf Hitler by acquiescing in his annexation of Czechoslovakia's Sudetenland. Clearly, an anti-appeasement policy was an unwavering principle for Churchill, essentially unchanged between 1926 and 1938. Winston Churchill's willingness to boldly draw a line and his great skill in articulating both the nature of the line and the rationale behind its having been drawn would serve him and the people of Britain splendidly during World War II, even—indeed, especially—when it seemed as if the British people were in no position to enforce such a line. For example, on July 10, 1940, Adolf Hitler ordered the first of the many massive bombardments of Britain that would become known as "the Blitz." His intention was to prepare the way for "Operation Sealion," the full-scale invasion of the British Isles. On the fourteenth, four days after the Blitz began, Prime Minister Churchill made a radio broadcast from the BBC studios in London. The significance of the date—Bastille Day—was not lost on Churchill, who told his audience how, a "year ago in Paris I watched the stately parade down the Champs Élysées of the French Army and the French empire. Who can foresee what the course of other years will bring?" It was an acknowledgment of uncertainty in a time of terrifying uncertainty. From terror and anxiety, however, Churchill quickly passed to faith, "Faith is given to us to help and comfort us when we stand in awe before the unfurling scroll of human destiny. And I proclaim my faith that some of us will live to see a fourteenth of July when a liberated France will once again rejoice in her greatness and in her glory, and once again stand forward as the champion of the freedom and the rights of man. When the day dawns, as dawn it will, the soul of France will turn with comprehension and with kindness to those Frenchmen and Frenchwomen, wherever they may be, who in the darkest hour did not despair of the Republic."

"Winston Churchill's willingness to draw a line and his great skill in articulating both the nature of the line and the rationale behind its having been drawn would serve him and the people of Britain splendidly during World War II."

As he had done in prior speeches and would do in many yet to come, Churchill used words to create in language what could not—at least, not at the moment—be wrought in physical reality. In a handful of sentences, he took his listeners from frightful uncertainty, to faith, to absolute confidence—"*When* the day dawns, as *dawn it will*"—and imagined how, on that certain day of certain deliverance, those citizens of France who did not despair would be rewarded. The message to the people of Britain was clear: *Emulate these French men and women. Be confident. Do not despair, no matter how dark the present hour.*

**"For Churchill, no principle was more absolute than duty. Its precise nature would change, depending on the situation, but the principle was invariable."**

The prime minister went on to pledge assistance to France, Britain's "friend . . . smitten down by a stunning blow," vowing on behalf of the British people "to conduct ourselves that every true French heart will beat and glow at the way we carry on the struggle; and that not only France, but all the oppressed countries in Europe may feel that each British victory is a step towards the liberation of the Continent from the foulest thralldom into which it has ever been cast." This salvation, not only of France and Britain, but of all Europe, was the "duty" of the nation. For Churchill, no principle was more absolute than duty. Its precise nature would change, depending on the situation, but the principle was invariable.

Doing one's duty would not be easy. "All goes to show that the war will be long and hard," Churchill admitted. And the war would also be heavily freighted with uncertainty—"No one can tell where it will spread"—yet, "One thing is certain: the peoples of Europe will not be ruled for long by the Nazi Gestapo, nor will the world yield itself to Hitler's gospel of hatred, appetite and domination." Thus, from a call to grim duty, a summons to fight in a long, hard uncertainty, Churchill led his listeners directly to the triumphant certainty of their common destiny: the defeat of Adolf Hitler. The first step toward the realization of that destiny was now "to stand alone in the breach, and face the worst that the tyrant's might and enmity can do."

Bearing ourselves humbly before God, but conscious that we serve an unfolding purpose, we are ready to defend our native land against the invasion by which it is threatened. We are fighting by ourselves alone; but we are not fighting for ourselves alone. Here in this strong City of Refuge which enshrines the title-deeds of human progress and is of deep consequence to Christian civilization; here, girt about by the seas and oceans where the Navy reigns; shielded from above by the prowess and devotion of our airmen—we await undismayed the impending assault. Perhaps it will come tonight. Perhaps it will come next week. Perhaps it will never come. We must show ourselves equally capable of meeting a sudden violent shock or—what is perhaps a harder test—a prolonged vigil. But be the ordeal sharp or long, or both, we shall seek no terms, we shall tolerate no parley; we may show mercy—we shall ask for none.

Here, finally, is where he drew the line. No matter how hard the coming battle, there would be no surrender, no negotiation, no abject plea for mercy.

Churchill was keenly aware that it was one thing for him to draw the line, but quite another to enforce it with London under bombardment and Hitler's armies having already rolled over most of Europe.

I can easily understand how sympathetic onlookers across the Atlantic, or anxious friends in the yet-unravished countries of Europe, who cannot measure our resources or our resolve, may have feared for our survival when they saw so many States and kingdoms torn to pieces in a few weeks or even days by the monstrous force of the Nazi war machine. But Hitler has not yet been withstood by a great nation with a will power the equal of his own. Many of these countries have been poisoned by intrigue before they were struck down by violence. They have been rotted from within before they were smitten from without. How else can you explain what has happened to France?—to the French Army, to the French people, to the leaders of the French people?

But here, in our Island, we are in good health and in good heart. We have seen how Hitler prepared in scientific detail the plans for destroying the neighbor countries of Germany. . . . We have seen how the French were undermined and overthrown. We may therefore be sure that there is a plan—perhaps built up over years—for destroying Great Britain, which after all has the honor to be his main and foremost enemy. All I can say is that any plan for invading Britain which Hitler made two months ago must have had to be entirely recast in order to meet our new position. Two months ago—nay, one month ago—our first and main effort was to keep our best Army in France. All our regular troops, all our output of munitions, and a very large part of our Air Force, had to be sent to France and maintained in action there. But now we have it all at home. Never before in the last war—or in this—have we had in this Island an Army comparable in quality, equipment or numbers to that which stands here on guard tonight. We have a million and a half men in the British Army under arms tonight, and every week of June and July has seen their organization, their defences, and their striking power advance by leaps and bounds. . . .

Having drawn the line, Churchill was at pains to show that it was real, and that it could be held. And should the Royal Navy and Royal Air Force fail to stop the invasion, "there will be no placid lying down of the people in submission before him, as we have seen, alas, in other countries."

We shall defend every village, every town, and every city. The vast mass of London itself, fought street by street, could easily devour an entire hostile army; and we would rather see London laid in ruins and ashes than that it should be tamely and abjectly enslaved. I am bound to state these facts, because it is necessary to inform our people of our intentions, and thus to reassure them.

After presenting the worst-case scenario—a street fight in London—Churchill went on to detail what he called "a great week for the Royal Air Force, and for the Fighter Command. They have shot down more than five to one of the German aircraft which have tried to molest our convoys in the Channel, or have ventured to cross the British coast line." He also touted the "the power of the Royal Navy. With over a thousand armed ships under the White Ensign, patrolling the seas, the Navy, which is capable of transferring its force very readily to the protection of any part of the British Empire which may be threatened, is capable also of keeping open communication with the New World, from whom, as the struggle deepens, increasing aid will come." Would Hitler starve Britain out? "Is it not remarkable that after ten months of unlimited U-boat and air attack upon our commerce, our food reserves are higher than they have ever been, and we have a substantially larger tonnage under our own flag, apart from great numbers of foreign ships in our control, than we had at the beginning of the war?"

"Why do I dwell on all this?" Churchill asked, rhetorically. "Not, surely, to induce any slackening of effort or vigilance. On the contrary. These must be redoubled. . . . I dwell on these elements in our strength, on these resources which we have mobilized and control—I dwell on them because it is right to show that the good cause can command the means of survival; and that while we toil through the dark valley we can see the sunlight on the uplands beyond."

Churchill acknowledged that the British Empire was vast and varied, "but there is one bond which unites us all and sustains us in the public regard—namely (as is increasingly becoming known), that we are prepared to proceed to all extremities, to endure them and to enforce them. . . ." As usual, Churchill followed the grand, broad strokes with specifics: "all depends now upon the whole life-strength of the British race in every part of the world and of all our associated peoples and of all our well-wishers in every land, doing their utmost night and day, giving all, daring all, enduring all—to the utmost—to the end."

It was he who drew the line, but he did so on behalf of the people. As he explained, this was "no war of chieftains or of princes, of dynasties or national ambition," and, certainly, it was no war of Prime Minister Winston Churchill. Instead, "it is a war of peoples and of causes. There are vast numbers, not only in this Island but in every land, who will render faithful service in this war, but whose names will never be known, whose deeds will never be recorded. This is a War of the Unknown Warriors; but let all strive without failing in faith or in duty, and the dark curse of Hitler will be lifted from our age."

**In Emerson's quote,** "A foolish consistency is the hobgoblin of little minds," the key word is the first adjective: *foolish.* Flexibility and responsiveness are important in any organization or leader, but underlying whatever endeavor you undertake must be a base of consistency. Call that foundation what you like—policy, principles, values, or identity—it is an indelible and absolute line that neither you nor your enterprise can cross under any circumstances. Draw it, define it, broadcast it, and explain it.

# 9

# Never Wear
# Another Man's Hat

"Never give in, never give in, never, never, never, never—in nothing, great
or small, large or petty—never give in except to convictions
of honour and good sense."
~Speech, Harrow School, London, October 29, 1941

In 1924, at the age of forty-nine, Winston Churchill left what appeared to him to be the moribund Liberal Party to join the Conservatives. He won a seat in the House of Commons as a Conservative, but, because his "crossing to the other side" had been sudden, he did not expect to be "invited to join the Government"— that is, offered a cabinet post. As it turned out, he was wrong. His defection to the Conservative cause was seen as a plum, and Prime Minister Stanley Baldwin, after considering many offices that might be appropriate for Churchill—including presidency of the Board of Trade, secretary of state for war, a posting in the Colonial Office, a return to the Admiralty, and others—asked him if he would consider becoming chancellor of the exchequer.

Churchill found the offer impossible to resist. "This fulfils my ambition," he replied. "I still have my father's robe as Chancellor. I shall be proud to serve you in this splendid Office."

Had Stanley Baldwin been a savvier judge of personnel, these remarks would have given him pause. Churchill might have responded to Baldwin's invitation in many ways. He might have spoken about his great interest in economics; that would have been appropriate for the person tapped as the approximate equivalent of the U.S. secretary of the treasury. But, in fact, he had little interest in economics, except for a notion that taxes on unearned wealth (mainly inherited wealth) should be high, whereas taxes on earned wealth (produced by productive labor) should be low. Churchill's belief—and in this, he shared something with the radical American economist Henry George—was that reducing taxes on earned wealth would stimulate production, whereas increasing taxes on unearned wealth would (at least) not reward idleness. The thought here, however, was not so much that of a man thinking like an economist, but rather a man thinking like a moralist.

In any case, Churchill did not respond to the offer by talking of economic policy. Instead, he cited personal ambition, which included redeeming the pledge he had made when his father died more or less in disgrace—namely, to vindicate Lord Randolph's tarnished memory. The position of chancellor of the exchequer was a stepping stone to prime minister, which was another good reason to take on the job. But Churchill seemed eager mainly to take up his father's mantle—both figuratively and literally. He was, however, not well suited to the job.

Winston Churchill was a modern Renaissance man, no doubt, with a staggering range of interests and accomplishments. But finance was never among them. Although he made a great deal of money as a journalist and bestselling author, he did not manage his funds prudently, lived lavishly, and almost always spent well above his head. In every other field he took up, from the military to social welfare, Churchill either possessed or acquired extensive, practical, hands-on knowledge, which served him well as the foundation of a genuine strategic vision. As chancellor of the exchequer, however, his vision was largely without foundation. Churchill's great strength was original thought. He almost always worked through an idea before he attempted to put it into practical motion. He revolved every proposal thoroughly in his mind and in his imagination. Yet at the exchequer, he made the fatal mistake of embracing a second-hand idea—someone else's idea—and one that he not only understood poorly but failed to think through to all of its consequences.

## Wing It?

In 1968, Dr. Laurence J. Peter and Raymond Hull published the bestselling *The Peter Principle*, a tongue-in-cheek study of hierarchical organizations centered on the Peter Principle: "In a hierarchy, every employee tends to rise to his level of incompetence." That is, hierarchies reward performance with promotion, ultimately promoting each employee to a position at least one step beyond his or her ability. Thus, in a hierarchy, one rises to a level of incompetence.

The question to ask is whether or not the Peter Principle is inevitable. In any hierarchy, it is difficult for an employee to refuse promotion—to say, "I am not qualified for that job." Indeed, we are often told to stretch. As the poet Browning wrote, "A man's reach should exceed his grasp, or what's a heaven for?" And it is true that many people rise to the responsibility given them. When President Franklin D. Roosevelt died suddenly on April 12, 1945, in the midst of World War II, many feared his vice president, Harry S. Truman, was grossly inadequate to take his place. No one feared this more than Truman himself. But, seeing his duty, he quickly rose to the occasion. Yet, in some cases, it may be the greatest test of leadership character to decline a promotion for which you are convinced you are unsuited or unprepared. Make no mistake, doing so puts your career on the line, but failing in office or, even worse, presiding over a significant institutional failure is of far greater consequence. *Do or die* is a fine maxim, unless you believe the second alternative is substantially the more likely.

Before Churchill assumed office, the treasury had already decided to return to the gold standard. When World War I began in 1914, the British government suspended the gold standard—that is, ended the policy of backing Bank of England notes with gold—in order to create more money to finance the war. This was a common practice for governments during war. After the armistice, Britain remained off the gold standard, which brought on inflation but also created a "loose money" climate favorable to industry and generally to those whose incomes depended on productivity—in other words, those whose wealth was earned as opposed to inherited. The former class was the one Churchill wished to encourage and support. He was accordingly reluctant to follow through on the treasury policy and approve the return to the gold standard. He argued that doing so "favoured the special interests of finance at the expense of the interests of production," and he went on to declare that he "would rather see Finance less proud and Industry more content." He was, in fact, so reluctant to return to the gold standard that, on March 17, 1925, he hosted a dinner for economist and gold-standard opponent J. M. Keynes and the treasury officials with the hope that Keynes's authoritative eloquence would prevail. At this point, Prime Minister Baldwin, who had himself held the post of chancellor of the exchequer, weighed in, advising Churchill (in the words of biographer Martin Gilbert) "not to rock a boat which was already virtually launched, and to which the Bank of England was committed."

Churchill found himself in a painfully similar position to the one he had been in when he made the decision to assault the Dardanelles in World War I. He was being denied full authority to make a decision for which he would nevertheless have to accept full responsibility.

The situations were similar, but not identical. In 1915, First Lord of the Admiralty Churchill had been saddled with a bureaucracy that made it impossible for him to wield full authority for his decisions. From 1924 to 1925, however, he was in charge, and he could have stood firm, no matter how inconvenient that would have been for the treasury and the Bank of England, and even if the prime minister did not want him to. Churchill had the authority, painful though it would have been for him to wield it.

Why, then, did he yield? The most likely answer is that he did not feel confident enough in his knowledge of economics to stand against so many authorities. This was a perfectly good reason for him to give way, but, of course, it was an even better reason for him to have declined the appointment to the exchequer in the first place. However, having for better or worse taken the job, Churchill should have stood firm on his instinct that returning to the gold standard was a bad idea.

To give Churchill his due, returning to the gold standard did have some theoretical validity. Money cut loose from gold certainly interfered with a free market by artificially managing prices, but the war and its aftermath interfered with the free market even more, creating pressures that badly distorted it. If every nation could repay its war debts in a timely fashion, there would have been a sound practical—as well as theoretical—reason to restore the gold standard immediately, but many nations were not willing or even able to repay their debts. In response to this, the British government sought to recoup some of the war debt by heavily taxing imports in order to protect and stimulate domestic industry. The debtor nations retaliated by taxing British exports. The result was a trade deadlock, which the treasury and its advisers sought to break by returning to the gold standard, a move that would effectively set the price of goods on the international market by providing a single standard of value. In theory, this was also quite sound, but it failed in practice

**"Churchill found himself in a painfully similar position to the one he had been in when he made the decision to assault the Dardanelles in World War I. He was being denied full authority to make a decision for which he would nevertheless have to accept full responsibility."**

because the other European nations did not follow England's lead; unlike Great Britain, they delayed their return to the gold standard. This meant that the price of British exports rose beyond what importing nations were willing or able to pay. Thus stricken, British manufacturers sought to lower wages, and this wage-reduction movement quickly rippled throughout the British manufacturing sector, triggering, in May 1926, a nationwide general strike.

> *"The inherent vice of Capitalism is the unequal sharing of the blessings; the inherent virtue of Socialism is the equal sharing of miseries."*
> ~Speech, House of Commons, October 22, 1945

Drastic reductions in miners' wages had triggered the general strike, and Churchill responded by condemning the mine owners, but he also took charge of a government newspaper, the *British Gazette*, and printed frustrated, intemperate screeds against the strikers, thereby incurring the lasting enmity of British labor. It was exactly the opposite of the way he responded to strike leaders when he was minister of munitions, and it is difficult to account for the change in his approach. After all, his original inclination to remain off the gold standard was a product of his identification with those who worked for a living. It seems most likely that his intemperate reaction against labor's position was the result of his own frustration at having to defend a policy in which he did not truly believe.

Although the strike itself was resolved in a week, depressed wages persisted as high export prices put a ceiling on production, which, in some parts of England, resulted not only in low wages but also a sharp spike in unemployment. These depression-generating forces were only exacerbated by what Churchill did next. Higher gold prices and inflation followed the wartime suspension of the gold standard. Tradition dictated that, after war, gold conversion payments be restored at the prewar—rather than current—gold price. Without exercising much independent thought, Churchill yielded to tradition, so that the reintroduction of the gold standard at a prewar exchange level brought a sudden deflation throughout the British Empire. Then, when other European countries finally began reintroducing the gold standard as well, the demand for gold rose sharply relative to the demand for goods. This further depressed the price of goods, deepening a depression for which Winston Churchill and the Conservative Party were widely blamed. In 1929, the Labour Party trounced the Conservatives in the general election, and Winston Churchill found himself out of the government. Although he remained in Parliament, he would not return to a cabinet post until after the outbreak of World War II.

*"Whatever one may think of democratic government, it is just as well to have practical experience of its rough and slatternly foundations."*
~ *Great Contemporaries,* 1937

Although Churchill himself later confessed that buckling to pressure to reintroduce the gold standard was the greatest mistake of his life, he defended the decision on many occasions throughout the rest of his long career, pointing out that he was following the advice of everyone in the government finance community and that it was, after all, ultimately important to connect money policy to the "reality" of gold rather than allow currency to continue to inflate and lose value. But while he may have publicly defended the decision, the most enduring lesson he took away from it was deeply personal. He passed it on in a wartime speech to the students at his public school alma mater, Harrow, on October 29, 1941:

You cannot tell from appearances how things will go. Sometimes imagination makes things out far worse than they are; yet without imagination not much can be done. Those people who are imaginative see many more dangers than perhaps exist; certainly many more than will happen; but then they must also pray to be given that extra courage to carry this far-reaching imagination. But for everyone, surely, what we have gone through in this period—I am addressing myself to the School—surely from this period of ten months this is the lesson: never give in, never give in, never, never, never, never—in nothing, great or small, large or petty— never give in except to convictions of honour and good sense. Never yield to force; never yield to the apparently overwhelming might of the enemy. We stood all alone a year ago, and to many countries it seemed that our account was closed, we were finished. All this tradition of ours, our songs, our School history, this part of the history of this country, were gone and finished and liquidated.

Very different is the mood today. Britain, other nations thought, had drawn a sponge across her slate. But instead our country stood in the gap. There was no flinching and no thought of giving in; and by what seemed almost a miracle to those outside these Islands, though we ourselves never doubted it, we now find ourselves in a position where I say that we can be sure that we have only to persevere to conquer.

Mistakes, provided we survive them, are highly valuable. Stumble we do, but as long as we stumble forward, we make progress. What Churchill learned from his uncharacteristic lapse of will in 1924–25 was never, never, never to let it happen again. It was a lesson that guided him, his nation, and the free world during the darkest period of modern history.

**Knowing when to stand firm**—even against a powerfully swelling tide—and when (as well as how much) to yield is one of the most vexing problems of leadership. There are times when stubbornness is nothing more than stubbornness— unproductive and even destructive. However, yielding to pressure and abandoning your own instinct and better judgment is rarely a good idea. Any policy adopted half-heartedly is doubly doomed. If it is a bad policy, it should never have been adopted in the first place, and if it is a perfectly good policy, giving it inadequate support may well ensure its failure. When you hesitate to embrace a particular decision, idea, or policy, don't let anyone push you forward. Carefully examine the reasons behind your hesitation. Review the proposal carefully. If you continue to find it difficult to buy in to, don't. This is not the time to bend over and be saddled with the consequences of a decision you never really wanted to begin with.

# 10

# Speak Truth
# to Power

"The flying peril is not a peril from which one can fly.
We cannot possibly retreat. We cannot move London."
~Speech, House of Commons, November 28, 1934

Winston Churchill was congenitally truthful. In December 1931, Churchill was in New York City during a lecture tour of the United States—he was determined to earn back the fortune he lost in the American stock market crash of 1929. On the thirteenth, he was about to cross Fifth Avenue (at the time a two-way street) in search of the house of financier and presidential adviser Bernard Baruch, who had invited him to a high-level gathering. He looked to his left and, seeing nothing, began to cross the street. That is when a car struck him from the right.

Fifty-seven-year-old Churchill had been painfully injured, sustaining trauma to his forehead and thighs. A police officer who rushed to his aid asked him what had happened. In agony, Churchill nevertheless calmly explained that he was an Englishman and, forgetting that Americans drive on the right, had looked the wrong way before crossing. The accident, he insisted, was entirely his fault. That was the truth and, because it was the truth, he had no choice but to tell it.

*"There is an end to everything, and happily nothing fades as quickly as the memory of physical pain."*

~ *My Early Life*, 1930

He had to tell the truth as well when it came to the evil that was gathering and growing in Germany. It was a truth he would tell throughout the decade of the 1930s, as Adolf Hitler gathered more power, tightened his grip around the throat of his own nation, raised an army, built an air force, and began to look with hungry eyes to the rest of the world. It was a truth hard to tell, because almost no one in the government wanted to hear it, and when they were compelled to hear it, they denied it insistently and shrilly.

In 1932, the government of Stanley Baldwin was fully committed to disarmament, intent on setting, through arms reduction in Britain, an example for the rest of the world. The government enthusiastically participated in the World Disarmament Conference ongoing in Geneva, Switzerland. In Germany, while the Swiss conference was under way, Adolf Hitler came in second to Field Marshal Paul von Hindenburg in the contest for the presidency of the German republic. This forced Hindenburg to bring Hitler on board the government as chancellor, making him the second most powerful man in the nation. Hitler fiercely bucked the tide of European disarmament, demanding revision of the Treaty of Versailles to permit the rearming of Germany. To his complacent countrymen, Churchill pointed out that the new chancellor of the German republic was rising rapidly to power and, before long, would displace the moderate but superannuated Hindenburg. Hitler would not rest, Churchill pointed out, until Germany was remilitarizing and rearming at full tilt.

The response to Churchill's warning came from Foreign Secretary Sir John Simon, who insisted that the rise of Hitler was yet one more reason to press ahead with a speedy and comprehensive disarmament. He argued that, if Britain and France did not reduce their military might, Germany, under threat, would have no alternative but to rearm. Reduce British and French arms, he argued, and Hitler would surely follow suit.

> *"The story of the human race is War. Except for brief and precarious interludes, there has never been peace in the world."*
>
> ~ *The World Crisis,* 1923–31

Winston Churchill considered Simon's view the product of willful self-delusion and wishful thinking. The truth was that Hitler's response to talk of British and French disarmament was not to reduce but to *increase* his military strength. Churchill replied to Simon's call for disarming in order to create "parity" of strength between Germany and France with a question: "I would say to those who would like to see Germany and France on an equal footing in armaments: 'Do you wish for war?'"

The ugly truth Churchill saw and was not afraid to acknowledge was the fact of German rearmament. The great truth that he regarded as a corollary to this was the certainty that a nation could not prevent or avoid war by rendering itself weak. Far from averting war, disarmament would hasten its coming.

He understood, as he wrote in an article for the *London Daily Mail* on May 26, 1932, that the Great War had produced "such a horror of war . . . that any declaration or public speech against armaments, although it consisted only of platitudes and unrealities, has always been applauded; and any speech or assertion which set forth the blunt truths had been incontinently relegated to the category of 'warmongering.' "

He understood this, he wrote, but his sympathy for the feelings of his countrymen would not stop him from telling the truth: that, as the Disarmament Conference continued, each state did nothing more or less than urge the other states to reduce their arsenals while retaining its own arsenal at present strength—or even adding to it. It was unrealistic, Churchill pointed out, to expect France—population 40 million—to reduce its air and naval fleets when Germany—population 60 million—could always field the larger army. Moreover, the newly independent nations that had come into being with the Treaty of Versailles and associated agreements were always in danger of being swallowed up by Soviet Russia. Could *they* be expected to cut back on advanced weaponry?

"Mush, slush, and gush" was how Churchill characterized the means by which the British government hoped to attain European disarmament. This, he said, would never work. Disarmament "will be advanced steadily by the harassing expense of fleets and armies, and by the growth of confidence in a long peace." Disarmament and peace cannot be achieved by weakness and idealistic talk. The burdensome reality of fleets and armies was the sovereign deterrent to war. Only a nation prepared to fight, to resist aggression, was in a position to invite the world to become peaceful.

## Don't Be Seduced by Mush and Gush

Never underestimate the powerful appeal of telling people what they want to hear. Sugared words are an addictive drug, producing an effect both soothing and deadly. The truth can be a lot harder to swallow, but the survival of your enterprise depends on it.

In the meantime, the German government continued to hammer away at "equality of status" for German armaments, demanding that Germany be allowed to rearm to parity with its most heavily armed neighbor, France. Surprisingly, this time Sir John Simon resisted the German demands, asserting that Germany was still bound by the Treaty of Versailles. At that, the German representatives temporarily withdrew from the Disarmament Conference.

To Churchill, this withdrawal was an ominous but hardly surprising development. What shocked him, however, was the failure of the British public to support Simon's position. There were many protests from the press as well as the man on the street over what was characterized as the unfair treatment of Germany. To this, on October 17, 1932, Churchill responded in another article for the *Daily Mail*. Applauding Simon's stand, he argued that it had done "more to consolidate peace in Europe than any words spoken on behalf of Great Britain for some years." But he also pointed out that the German armaments minister had already announced that whatever the outcome of the Disarmament Conference might be,

> "A general malaise . . . had crept over both France and England—an attitude compounded of fatalism and helplessness, which, in effect, threw the nation on the mercy of any aggressor."

Germany would go its own way, doing what it thought fit. Even Simon's firm declaration, therefore, would not be sufficient to counter the growing German threat. Strong words had to be backed by a substantial arsenal.

The Simon response to Germany's demand was refreshing to Churchill, but it was soon overshadowed by the Commons' vote to consider "the fair meeting of Germany's claim to the principle of equality." Even more dispiriting was the way in which Prime Minister Baldwin defended this stance: "I think it well for the man in the street to realise that there is no power on earth that can prevent him from being bombed." It was an expression of a general malaise that had crept over both France and England—an attitude compounded of fatalism and helplessness, which, in effect, threw the nation on the mercy of any aggressor.

Churchill, who was convalescing from a debilitating bout of paratyphoid fever, summoned all his strength to respond in a speech to the House of Commons on November 23, 1932. He warned of the "war mentality" that was developing in Germany and declared that he could not "recall any time when the gap between the kind of words which statesmen used and what was actually happening in many countries was so great as it is now." He scorned the "habit of saying smooth things and uttering pious platitudes and sentiments to gain applause, without relation to the underlying facts." As for himself, he would choose a different course:

> Just as the late Lord Birkenhead used to say about India—I think it the beginning and end of wisdom there—"Tell the truth to India," so I would now say, "Tell the truth to the British people." They are a tough people, a robust people. They may be a bit offended at the moment, but if you have told them exactly what is going on you have insured yourself against complaints and reproaches which are very unpleasant when they come home on the morrow of some disillusion.

The truth to tell was of the rapid remilitarization of Germany even as Britain and its ally France disarmed. The truth to tell was this, "though it may shock the House": "I would rather see another ten or twenty years of one-sided peace than see a war between equally well-matched Powers."

> *"'Tell the truth to the British people.' They are a tough people, a robust people."*
>
> ~Speech, House of Commons, November 23, 1932

It was a frank and bold statement of national self-interest. But Churchill was statesman enough to know that self-interest alone could never ensure peace. He went on to declare his belief in "the lights of goodwill and reconciliation" throughout Europe. The way to activate these "lights" was not by rushing to disarm. Before the European democracies scurried to weaken themselves, they should first take the necessary steps to remove what Churchill called "the just grievances of the vanquished." Once this was accomplished, the causes for a new war would be reduced, if not entirely removed.

Only at this point, with war truly unlikely, should there be discussion of "the disarmament of the victors." To do otherwise, to "bring about anything like equality of armaments . . . while those grievances remain unredressed, would be almost to appoint the day for another European war—to fix it as if it were a prize-fight."

Churchill had never endorsed the punitive nature of the Treaty of Versailles, and he sincerely believed that Germany had genuine grievances, but the key was to revise the treaty from a position of strength—while British and French arms were still superior to those of Germany—rather than to appear to cave in to the demands of a resurgent enemy.

## Negotiate from Strength

Mark Twain once griped that a bank would lend you money only if you could prove you didn't need it. The sad thing is it's true. You have a much better chance of getting what you want when you negotiate from a position of strength rather than weakness, from plenty rather than want, and from adequacy rather than inadequacy. Fair play dictates that you refrain from hitting a man when he's down, but don't count on your competitors valuing fair play. Usually, it is precisely when you are down that they will hit you the hardest. The best time to enter into key negotiations is when things are going well, when you are strong and have the greatest range of options—including the option to walk away from a deal or to effectively enforce the terms of a deal. It's hard to be either persuasive or intimidating when your back's up against the wall.

It was a frank speech, stirring in its eminent good sense. Astoundingly, however, the government responded by heedlessly pressing forward with European disarmament, appealing to the House to stand behind the reduction of the Royal Air Force as an act of good faith intended to spur the rest of Europe into following suit. The under-secretary of state for air, Sir Philip Sassoon, blithely announced that the government was "prepared to accept the continuance of the serious existing disparity between the strength of the Royal Air Force and that of the air services of the other great nations" pending the outcome of the Disarmament Conference. In other words, the air force would remain weak, undermanned and under-equipped, until the failure of disarmament was a proven fact. Churchill countered that expecting France to cut its air force in half was to venture into "the region of unrealities." Without an adequate air force, he continued, no peaceful nation could hope to remain neutral or to retain its "national freedom and independence."

*"In an aerial war the greatest form of defence will undoubtedly be offence."*
~Speech, House of Commons, March 21, 1922

It was at this time, early in 1933, that Churchill, an outsider not privy to secret government intelligence, gained an ally in Desmond Morton, head of the Industrial Intelligence Unit of the Committee of Imperial Defence. Morton began feeding Churchill hard information on German war production, including the development and manufacture of aircraft, information that the government possessed but that it deliberately kept from Parliament and the people. Carefully, so as not to expose his source, Churchill deployed some of the statistics, hoping thereby to bring the House to a realization of the truth—the grave danger facing Great Britain.

In counterpoint to facts and figures was Churchill's analysis of Adolf Hitler and the current state of German government. "One of the things which we were told after the Great War would be a security for us was that Germany would be a democracy with Parliamentary institutions," he declared on April 13, 1933. Pointing to the fact that Hitler had just forced Nazi rule on all German states, completely abrogating any local authority and demolishing the last vestiges of German democratic government, he continued: "All that has been swept away. You have dictatorship—most grim dictatorship." On April 23, he turned to the public in a radio-broadcast address at a meeting of the Royal Society of St. George:

> Nothing can save England if she will not save herself. If we lose faith in ourselves, in our capacity to guide and govern, if we lose our will to live, then indeed our story is told. If, while on all sides foreign nations are every day asserting a more aggressive and militant nationalism by arms and trade, we remain paralysed by our own theoretical doctrines or plunged into the stupor of after-war exhaustion, then indeed all that the croakers predict will come true, and our ruin will be swift and final.

On October 14, 1933, Hitler made Germany's withdrawal from the Disarmament Conference permanent. To be sure, it was not a declaration of war, but it was certainly a declaration of the willingness to make war. Nevertheless, far from causing timely alarm in the upper echelons of British government, this action served only to plunge the leaders into an ever deeper state of denial. Responding to Germany's permanent withdrawal from the conference, the British government announced its redoubled resolve to continue to work toward disarmament. To this, Churchill responded by exposing more of the secret facts and figures proving ongoing German rearmament. "I cannot conceive how," he addressed the House of Commons on February 7, 1934, "in the present state of Europe and our position in Europe, we can delay in establishing the principle of having an air force at least as strong as any power that can get at us." With awful prescience, he warned that, certainly within a very few years, "the crash of bombs exploding in London and cataracts of masonry and fire and smoke will apprise us of any inadequacy which has been permitted in our aerial defences."

For this vivid imagery, Churchill was derided as an alarmist and a warmonger. He let the epithets roll off him: "There is not an hour to lose."

That, however, was not how Stanley Baldwin saw the situation. He reiterated the policy his government had doggedly pursued, even in the face of reality itself: *If—and only if—the Disarmament Conference failed would a buildup of British arms begin.* That said, Baldwin observed to the House of Commons after Churchill's February 7 speech, "I do not think we are bound to have a war."

By early 1934, the government issued a so-called parity pledge, promising that the British air force would keep pace with other air forces but would not exceed them. Churchill, standing alone—nominally a Conservative, but without the support of his party—criticized the parity policy as ignoring the "harsh realities of the European situation." He warned that a parity policy meant nothing because the Germans were capable of very rapidly building many advanced airplanes of great and formidable quality. Churchill declared that he did not want a "parity policy," but parity in fact, and very quickly, so that Britain would be in a position to match or even outrun German production. Because Baldwin had sought to hold him at arm's length by claiming that the government was obligated to defer to public opinion, Churchill now turned directly to him: "You must not go and ask the public what they think about this. Parliament and the Cabinet have to decide, and the nation has to judge whether they have acted rightly as trustees. [The prime minister] has the power, and if he has the power he has also what always goes along with power—he has the responsibility. . . . The nation looks to him to advise it and lead it. . . ."

Baldwin replied by reiterating that stepped-up production of aircraft would begin only if Britain's disarmament efforts failed. Churchill ignored this, and over the next several days, urged the doubling of the RAF.

It was a tedious, lonely battle, month after month. When the government ran out of rationally valid arguments against Churchill's position, it resorted to outright mockery. Churchill persevered, deploying more secret information when he could get it, gradually chipping away the self-delusion. Baldwin's secretary for air, Lord Swinton, presented a plan to increase the RAF's first-line strength to 1,750 aircraft by 1939. On the face of it, this sounded impressive, and the Baldwin government hoped that it would mollify—if not satisfy—the gadfly Churchill. Much to Baldwin's chagrin, however, Churchill declared that the new production goal would leave Britain "worse off in 1939 relatively than we are now—and it is relativity that counts." He portrayed the desperate reality of an arms race, pointing out that by the end of the following year, 1935, Germany would be equal in numbers to the RAF. By 1936, it would certainly overtake the British air arm.

> **"It was a tedious, lonely battle, month after month. When the government ran out of rational arguments against Churchill's position, it resorted to mockery. Churchill persevered, deploying more secret information when he could get it, gradually chipping away the self-delusion."**

Throughout the summer and fall of 1934, Winston Churchill continued to speak out on air power, telling the truth, deploying the facts in an effort to "extort more vigorous action" from the Baldwin government. The verb he used was telling. In most situations, the goal is to *persuade*. In desperate situations, it may well be to frankly *extort*, marshalling such an overwhelming preponderance of reasons and facts that the other side is compelled to capitulate. Churchill conducted his campaign of extortion by alternating the presentation of facts with statements intended to force a decision and push a choice. On November 16, 1934, he sidestepped Parliament by broadcasting a radio speech to the British public, asking the people to look ahead toward the next few years:

> I am afraid that if you look intently at what is moving towards
> Great Britain, you will see that the only choice open is the old

grim choice our forebears had to face, namely whether we shall submit or whether we shall prepare. Whether we shall submit to the will of a stronger nation or whether we shall prepare to defend our rights, our liberties and indeed our lives. If we submit, our submission should be timely. If we prepare, our preparations should not be too late. Submission will entail at the very least the passing and distribution of the British Empire and the acceptance by our people of whatever future may be in store for small countries like Norway, Sweden, Denmark, Holland, Belgium and Switzerland, within and under a Teutonic domination of Europe.

Baldwin consistently deferred to public opinion. Churchill believed this was an evasion of responsibility, but because such deference was the self-confessed modus operandi of the prime minister, Churchill decided to change public opinion rather than try simply to change the prime minister's mind. His radio speech was a prelude to a major Parliamentary offensive, liberally sown with more secret government information supplied by Morton and a young Foreign Office official named Ralph Wigram. Backed by evolving public opinion and armed with a mounting preponderance of intelligence about the activities of the enemy, Churchill was able to force Baldwin into grudgingly beginning the expansion of the RAF.

It was a victory in that it improved Britain's defenses, but it was hardly a triumph. Churchill's efforts failed to spur the government to the magnitude of effort that was really called for. In 1938, when Baldwin's successor Neville Chamberlain signed the Munich Agreement in an effort to "appease" Adolf Hitler by giving away the Czech Sudetenland, Churchill broke completely with his party to voice his opposition to what he characterized as a defeat, a shame, and a certain invitation to war. Conservative stalwarts complained of Churchill's efforts to "discredit" the Conservative administration,

Sir Harry Goschen balefully remarking that "it would have been a great deal better if he had kept quiet."

*Keep quiet!* This was impossible for a man who loved above all else two things: his country and the truth. And it was this dual love that sustained him during his decade-long sojourn in what he himself called the political *wilderness*, when he was a leader with very few followers, yet—in his heart and mind—a leader still.

**Tell the truth**—not because your mother told you to or because you know it's the right thing to do, but because it is the best way to lead any organization. The enterprise that operates without a basis of truth is fueled by delusion, which is always destructive. This is simple advice—"All the greatest things are simple," Churchill once said—but it can be hard, very hard, to follow. After all, not everyone wants to hear the truth, and telling it can send you down a road both dark and lonely.

# 11

# Navigate
# by Your Own Compass

"Nothing is more dangerous . . . than to live in
the temperamental atmosphere of a Gallup Poll, always feeling one's
pulse and taking one's temperature."
~Speech, House of Commons, September 30, 1941

The 1930s—Churchill called this decade his *wilderness years*. While his career as an author and journalist prospered during this period, he suffered political alienation and a series of personal disasters. The crash of the American stock market in 1929 took an enormous toll on his investments. Then, he was severely injured in the accident in New York. Next, as he recovered from the accident, he was stricken with paratyphoid fever, then seemed to improve, only to suffer a relapse before finally regaining his health. He was a chronic depressive, afflicted by attacks of what he termed the *black dog*. Yet—and this was the leading characteristic of Churchill the man and Churchill the leader—he was supremely resilient. Suffer he did, yet he always managed not simply to recover, but to spring back.

*"We are all worms. But I do believe that I am a glow worm."*
~Quoted in Violet Bonham Carter's *Winston Churchill
As I Knew Him (An Intimate Portrait)*, 1965

Nevertheless, throughout this long decade, Churchill was on the outs politically. The attention of Britons, like that of most people in the rest of the world, was riveted on the economic situation. In fact, the Great Depression did not hit Great Britain as hard as it did the United States and many other economies. Despite areas of unemployment and outright poverty—the coal-mine districts of Wales, parts of Scotland, and most shipbuilding communities—much of the nation actually enjoyed a modest prosperity. Despite this, the state of the British mind was an anxious one.

Winston Churchill was also anxious, but not about the economy. While his countrymen and colleagues in Parliament focused on issues of employment and investment, he watched the rise of Adolf Hitler, and he did his utmost to turn the attention of the government to it as well. The Treaty of Versailles, which had ended World War I, stripped Germany of its air force, barred its navy from building or possessing major warships and submarines, and held its army to a token force of 100,000, with neither tanks nor heavy artillery. Rising to chancellor in January 1933 under the moribund president of the German republic, Hindenburg, and then replacing him as head of state when he died in August 1934, Hitler embarked on a rearmament program that not only defied the treaty, but disregarded it utterly. Germany began building tanks in the fall of 1934. In the early spring of 1935, Hitler authorized creation of the Luftwaffe (German air force) and reintroduced conscription, beginning a vast expansion of the army. In 1935, the Anglo-German Naval Agreement allowed Germany to build submarines (which it was already secretly building in defiance of the Treaty of Versailles). By September 1938, the German army—despite the restrictions of the Treaty of Versailles—stood at more than 600,000, including forty-six infantry divisions and five full tank (panzer) divisions. The British army at this time mustered no more than 200,000 troops, many of them occupying far-flung colonial outposts. Although the

British army—thanks largely to Winston Churchill—had pioneered the development of the tank during World War I, it possessed just one more-or-less functional tank division in 1938. As to air power, another armed service forbidden Germany by treaty, the Luftwaffe possessed 3,000 modern aircraft by the autumn of 1938, dwarfing both the RAF and the French air force.

## Know When to Rock the Boat

The reason people in any organization are afraid of rocking the boat is that it makes everyone uncomfortable. That is just the point of rocking the boat. Know when to rock it. Then rock it.

The government, under Ramsay MacDonald and then Stanley Baldwin, remained resolutely focused on the economy. In great anxiety to reduce the public tax burden, defense budgets were slashed, especially funding earmarked for the air force. Churchill responded to the reductions not by asking that they be restored, but by demanding that the RAF be doubled in strength over the short term, and then doubled again over the longer term. He pointed to the rapid growth of the German Luftwaffe, which was on its way to overmatching the British air arm. When this failed to move Parliament, he took to the airwaves, broadcasting to the British people on November 16, 1934 a speech in which he sought to end public complacency by pointing out that "Only a few hours away by air there dwells a nation of nearly seventy millions of the most educated, industrious, scientific, disciplined people in the world, who are being taught from childhood to think of war and conquest as a glorious exercise, and death in battle as the noblest fate for man. There is a nation which has abandoned all its liberties in order to augment its collective might." That nation, Churchill warned, was "rearming with the utmost speed, and ready to their hands is this new lamentable weapon of the air, against which our Navy is no defense, before which women and children, the weak and frail, the pacifist and the jingo, the warrior and the civilian, the front line trenches and the cottage home, lie in equal and impartial peril."

*"He has, more than any other man, the gift of compressing the largest amount of words into the smallest amount of thought."*

~On Ramsay MacDonald, Speech,
House of Commons, March 23, 1933

The broadcast was a rare event. The BBC, a government-run monopoly, had wholly bought into the policies of the prevailing government. First and foremost among these policies was the assumption that the supreme problem Britain faced was economic, a problem that trumped all others. Under this assumption, and because the military was the single greatest drain on the public purse, the government sought to decrease military spending by two means. One was a policy of disarmament. Britain supported disarmament on an international scale and endorsed a World Disarmament Conference in 1933. When Germany summarily withdrew from the conference in October of that year, the British government responded not with alarm, but by reaffirming its own commitment to disarmament. In his 1934 BBC broadcast, Churchill took aim squarely at this instance of the denial of reality:

There are some who say—indeed it has been the shrill cry of the hour—that we should run the risk of disarming ourselves in order to set an example to others. We have done that already for the last five years, but our example has not been followed. On the contrary, it has produced the opposite result. All the other countries have armed only the more heavily; and the quarrels and intrigues about disarmament have only bred more ill-will between the nations.

When international disarmament failed, however, the British government embraced a second policy, to which Neville Chamberlain would later give a name destined to prove infamous: *appeasement*. It was now hoped that, the British example of disarmament having failed to create a world with fewer weapons, persisting on a course of disarmament would at least appease Germany and Italy, persuading them that they were not in danger from British aggression. Indeed, the British government prevailed on France to disarm as well—again, in an effort to appease the likes of Mussolini and Hitler.

This was the policy that Churchill, standing almost entirely alone, protested against. To him, it seemed an act of collective national suicide.

The great majority of the government deliberately turned its back on Churchill's warnings. There was a very real conviction that Britain simply could not afford to rearm. There was also a belief that British rearmament would only serve to spur even more military growth in Germany and Italy. Moreover, there was the fear that rearmament would incite Hitler and Mussolini to a preemptive war—for which Britain was unprepared. The tragic irony was that Britain's lack of preparation was the result of the government's refusal to prepare.

The recent horrors of the Great War served to reinforce throughout the British government a self-delusion—as Churchill saw it, it was a suicidal self-delusion—which continued a policy of deliberately weakening the British military in order to prevent war by appeasing those, namely Mussolini and Hitler, who were clearly arming for war. The policy of appeasement

**"The great majority of the government deliberately turned its back on Churchill's warnings."**

further dictated that Britain and its ally France wink at Hitler's successive violations of the Treaty of Versailles: rearmament, the militarization of the Rhineland, the annexation of Austria, and, in September 1938, the annexation of Czechoslovakia's Sudetenland.

Churchill was in a box. Out of the government, he had no direct authority to alter the course of policy. His relentless warnings and criticisms ensured that he would remain outside of government. But how could he choose to, in effect, "appease," that government by silently acquiescing in policies he deemed suicidal? He needed to find an alternative to mere criticism on the one hand and acquiescence on the other.

## Power without Authority

Just because you lack authority does not mean you possess no power. If you are on the outside, look for ways to get in, even if this means moving farther outside the normal protocols. When the usual avenues are closed to you, innovate new approaches. Make friends. Win support. Keep talking. You are not beaten until you give up.

Churchill decided to work around the official bureaucracy. The stockade of government barred to him, he could only cry in the wilderness—unless, somehow, he could gain access to information and intelligence reserved for insiders. With this, he would possess the tools of the inner circle and could use them to do what the inner circle refused to do: expose the international military situation for the grave and gathering danger that it was. Accordingly, Churchill courted certain senior members of the official class who manned the government bureaucracy and appealed to what he recognized as their own growing sense that their superiors, up to and including the prime minister himself, were adrift in perilous waters. Churchill targeted not only those who were sympathetic to his point of view, but also those who possessed the power to help him gain access to key information. Major Desmond Morton, chief of the industrial intelligence section of the Committee of Imperial Defence; Ralph Wigram and Orme Sargent, both of the Foreign Office; RAF squadron leaders Charles Anderson and Herbert Rowles; and Tank

Corps Chief Brigadier General Percy Hobart were among those who yielded to the force of Churchill's personality, character, convictions, and arguments. They risked their careers—possibly even risked prosecution for treason—by sharing with Churchill state secrets concerning the status of German war production, technological innovation, and rearmament. These were secrets the government emphatically did not want Parliament or the public to know, lest the knowledge force what was seen as a dangerous alternation in the policy of appeasement.

> *"I have watched this famous island descending incontinently, recklessly, the stairway which leads to a dark gulf. It is a fine broad stairway at the beginning, but, after a bit, the carpet ends. A little further on there are only flagstones, and, a little further on still, these break beneath your feet."*
> ~Speech, House of Commons, March 24, 1938

Thanks to the secret relationships he developed with highly placed members of the civil service and the military, Churchill was able to make his speeches to Parliament more specific, adding substantive facts and figures to bolster his warnings about the arms race that was leaving Britain in the dust. Gradually, he won support. By the time Neville Chamberlain replaced Baldwin as prime minister on May 28, 1937, government policy had shifted to a realization that Britain must improve its defensive capability. This prompted a modification of appeasement to the extent that it was no longer seen as a spur to international disarmament or as a means of permanently preventing war, but merely as a tactic to delay the outbreak of a major war until the British army, air force, and navy were better prepared to fight. While the objective of appeasement was therefore different under Chamberlain than it had been under MacDonald or Baldwin, it was still appeasement. The culmination of the policy came, of course, with the Munich Agreement of September 30, 1938, in which Chamberlain sought to "appease" Hitler by yielding to him the Czech Sudetenland in return for his pledge not to wage war and to seek nothing further in the way of territorial acquisition.

## The Moral Continuum

Can a laudable end justify the less than laudable means used to reach it? It is a question leaders of all sorts of organizations frequently face. It can be answered in every single case with an invariable statement of fact: Ends cannot be severed from means. They exist on a continuum, and it is therefore impossible to say where the one stops and the other begins. Peace was posited as the end sought by appeasement. Churchill embraced the end, but regarded appeasement as nothing more than the means to an illusion of peace, which guaranteed the very opposite of peace.

When the prime minister returned to London with the Munich Agreement, a scrap of paper clutched in his hand, he proclaimed that he had come back with "peace for our time." In response, both the public and the Parliament were lavish with praise for him. Churchill, with only a few more friends than he had had at the beginning of the decade, still stood on the far periphery of the political wilderness. From this vantage, on October 5, 1938, he rose to address the Commons: "If I do not begin this afternoon by paying the usual, and indeed almost invariable, tributes to the Prime Minister for his handling of this crisis, it is certainly not from any lack of personal regard," he began, thereby setting himself even farther apart from the majority of his colleagues. He warned them that he intended to "begin by saying the most unpopular and most unwelcome thing. I will begin by saying what everybody would like to ignore or forget but which must nevertheless be stated, namely, that we have sustained a total and unmitigated defeat, and that France has suffered even more than we have."

At this, Nancy Astor, the Viscountess Astor—first female member of Parliament in British history—responded: "Nonsense."

Churchill countered: "When the Noble Lady cries 'Nonsense,' she could not have heard the Chancellor of the Exchequer admit . . . just now that Herr Hitler had gained in this particular leap forward in substance all he set out to gain. . . . The German dictator, instead of snatching his victuals from the table, has been content to have them served to him course by course." He pressed on, suggesting that Hitler had, in effect, demanded £1 "at the pistol's point. When it was given, £2 were demanded at the pistol's point. Finally, the dictator consented to take £1 17s. 6d. and the rest in promises of goodwill for the future."

**"He warned them that he intended to 'begin by saying the most unpopular and most unwelcome thing. I will begin by saying what everybody would like to ignore or forget but which must nevertheless be stated.' "**

Nor did Churchill limit his argument to metaphor. As he had earlier augmented his speeches concerning rearmament with facts obtained through the hazardous cooperation of a few good and powerful friends, so now he endeavored to outline the specifics of the catastrophe the Munich Agreement had set into motion.

We are in the presence of a disaster of the first magnitude which has befallen Great Britain and France. Do not let us blind ourselves to that. It must now be accepted that all the countries in Central and Eastern Europe will make the best terms they can with the triumphant Nazi Power. The system of alliances in Central Europe upon which France has relied for her safety has been swept away, and I can see no means by which it can be reconstituted. The road down the Danube Valley to the Black Sea, the resources of corn [wheat] and oil, the road which leads as far as Turkey, has been opened. In fact

... it seems to me that all those countries of Middle Europe . . . will . . . be drawn into this vast system of power politics . . . radiating from Berlin, and I believe this can be achieved [without] the firing of a single shot . . . .

Churchill then brought the events of "Middle Europe"—which Prime Minister Chamberlain had famously characterized as a far-away place "of which we know nothing"—very close to home: "What I find unendurable is the sense of our country falling into the power, into the orbit and influence of Nazi Germany, and of our existence becoming dependent upon their goodwill and pleasure. It is to prevent that that I have tried my best to urge the maintenance of every bulwark of defence. . . . It has all been in vain."

> *"Nothing can save England if she will not save herself. If we lose faith in our-selves, in our capacity to guide and govern, if we lose our will to live, then, indeed our story is told."*
> ~ Quoted in Dennis Bardens's *Churchill in Parliament,* 1967

Having labored for a decade in the political wilderness, Churchill made his bitterness work for him to create a peroration as grim as it has been justly celebrated:

I do not grudge our loyal, brave people, who were ready to do their duty no matter what the cost, who never flinched under the strain of last week. I do not grudge them the natural, sponta-neous outburst of joy and relief when they learned that the hard ordeal would no longer be required of them at the moment; but they should know the truth. They should know that there has been gross neglect and deficiency in our defences; they should know that we have sustained a defeat without a war, the conse-quences of which will travel far with us along our road; they should know that we have passed an awful milestone in our history, when the whole equilibrium of Europe has been deranged, and that the terrible words have for the time being been pronounced against the Western democracies:

"Thou art weighed in the balance and found wanting."

And do not suppose that this is the end. This is only the beginning of the reckoning. This is only the first sip, the first foretaste of a bitter cup which will be proffered to us year by year unless by a supreme recovery of moral health and martial vigour, we arise again and take our stand for freedom as in the olden time.

Rhetorically donning the mantle of an Old Testament prophet, Churchill refused to join the celebration of a deluded majority or in any way to temper his lonely message of warning. Instead, he continued to follow his own moral compass to a destination both painful and necessary.

**Leaders cannot always have followers,** not when they turn down paths that, for one reason or another, are little traveled. Before you take such a turn, be certain of it. Such a path is hard and lonely. But if you are convinced that it is the right and necessary path, follow it, persuading whomever you can to share your risk as you make the way ready for others. Persist—but be impatient, no matter how long it takes those others to go your way.

# 12

# Reject the Tyrant's Bargain

"Dictators ride to and fro upon tigers which they dare not dismount.
And the tigers are getting hungry."
~ *While England Slept*, 1938

By the fall of 1938, most of the leaders of the British government were finally—and belatedly—convinced that a new European war was all but inevitable. During the administration of Prime Minister Stanley Baldwin, there was a hope—Churchill did his best to persuade the House of Commons and the British people that it was a deluded hope—for a long peace. When Neville Chamberlain succeeded Baldwin in 1937, that hope had largely vanished; however, Chamberlain believed that he needed to act to defuse tensions in Europe in order to delay the outbreak of war for as long as possible, so that Britain, which had long been in disarmament mode, could gird for battle. Accordingly, he opened negotiations with Europe's two major bellicose dictators, Italy's Mussolini and Germany's Hitler, seeking ways to "appease" both of them in the hope that war could be forestalled or at least put off.

Appeasement did not dull or diminish the voracious appetite of either dictator but, on the contrary, stimulated it. In 1938, Hitler threatened to invade Czechoslovakia in order to annex a German-speaking region of that nation known as the Sudentenland. By the terms of the Treaty of Versailles and other agreements, both Britain and France were bound to defend Czech sovereignty. The German invasion would therefore mean a new European war. Accordingly, Chamberlain flew to Munich and, on September 30, 1938, concluded an agreement with Hitler that gave him possession of the Sudetenland. Many Britons were vastly relieved, believing what Chamberlain told them, that he had brought back to Downing Street "peace with honour" and "peace for our time."

> *"All is over. Silent, mournful, abandoned, broken, Czechoslovakia recedes into the darkness. . . . We have sustained a defeat without a war."*
> ~Speech, House of Commons, October 5, 1938

"How horrible, fantastic, incredible it is that we should be digging trenches and trying on gas-masks here because of a quarrel in a far-away country between people of whom we know nothing!" Chamberlain famously remarked at the height of the Sudetenland crisis. He had a pressing reason to do whatever he could to avoid war at this point: Britain was almost wholly unprepared to fight one. Yet his remark vividly revealed the tragic limit of his vision. Whereas Chamberlain saw in the Czech crisis nothing more than a "quarrel" in a distant place with little or no connection to the interests of Great Britain, Churchill predicted that all of Czechoslovakia would soon be "engulfed in the Nazi regime," and with its loss, Britain and France would give up a valuable fortress line. With Czechoslovakia under Nazi control, Churchill pointed out in a speech to the House on October 5 that a large number of German troops would be freed up and available for Hitler to unleash upon the West.

Many people, no doubt, honestly believe that they are only giving away the interests of Czechoslovakia, whereas I fear we shall find that we have deeply compromised, and perhaps fatally endangered, the safety and even the independence of Great Britain and France. This is not merely a question of giving up the German colonies, as I am sure we shall be asked to do. Nor is it a question only of losing influence in Europe. It goes far deeper than that. You have to consider the character of the Nazi movement and the rule which it implies.

## The Trap of Expediency

Compromise is the essence of negotiation and therefore the lifeblood of business. It is, however, a grave error to confuse genuine compromise—giving up something to gain something else—with expedient surrender: giving up something under threat. Genuine compromise enables business by creating a productive relationship between parties that exchange real value for real value. Expedient surrender is always a bargain with the devil. The relationship it initiates is that between victimizer and victim, blackmailer and blackmailed. Decline to be a victim. Either avoid extortionists or confront and defeat them. You cannot bargain productively with them. They have no legitimate place in the civilized activity of business.

What it implied was unmistakable: the necessity for Britain to fight a bitter war of resistance against outright conquest. He based his prediction on the "character of the Nazi movement," which was indeed a sound basis; however, he could have based his prediction on the nature of any bargain made with a tyrant. "We should seek by all means in our power to avoid war, by analyzing possible causes, by trying to remove them, by discussion in a spirit of collaboration and good will," Chamberlain had said before he embarked on his appeasement negotiations with Hitler. "I cannot believe that such a program would be rejected by the people of this country, even if it does mean the establishment of personal contact with the dictators." What Chamberlain failed to recognize is that to negotiate with a dictator who threatens war is to bargain with a blackmailer. The likelihood—virtually the certainty—is that, given one thing, the blackmailer will return with a demand for more. There is no appeasing blackmail.

Diplomacy resembles commerce in that both assume an exchange of value for value. This is the basis of all civilized transactions. Anything else is theft, intimidation, extortion, blackmail—the stock in trade of the dictator and tyrant. To bargain with a tyrant is to set foot upon a slippery slope, as Churchill made clear to his colleagues in Parliament:

> The Prime Minister desires to see cordial relations between this country and Germany. There is no difficulty at all in having cordial relations between the peoples. Our hearts go out to them. But they have no power. But never will you have friendship with the present German Government. You must have diplomatic and correct relations, but there can never be friendship between the British democracy and the Nazi power, that power which spurns Christian ethics, which cheers its onward course by a barbarous paganism, which vaunts the spirit of aggression and conquest, which derives strength and perverted pleasure from persecution, and uses, as we have seen, with pitiless brutality the threat of murderous force. That power cannot ever be the trusted friend of the British democracy.
>
> What I find unendurable is the sense of our country falling into the power, into the orbit and influence of Nazi Germany, and of our existence becoming dependent upon their good will or pleasure. It is to prevent that that I have tried my best to urge the maintenance of every bulwark of defence. . . . It has all been in vain. Every position has been successively undermined and abandoned on specious and plausible excuses.

**"What Chamberlain failed to recognize is that to negotiate with a dictator who threatens war is to bargain with a blackmailer. The likelihood—virtually the certainty—is that, given one thing, the blackmailer will return with a demand for more. There is no appeasing blackmail."**

We do not want to be led upon the high road to becoming a satellite of the German Nazi system of European domination. In a very few years, perhaps in a very few months, we shall be confronted with demands with which we shall no doubt be invited to comply. Those demands may affect the surrender of territory or the surrender of liberty. I foresee and foretell that the policy of submission will carry with it restrictions upon the freedom of speech and debate in Parliament, on public platforms, and discussions in the Press, for it will be said—indeed, I hear it said sometimes now—that we cannot allow the Nazi system of dictatorship to be criticised by ordinary, common English politicians. Then, with a Press under control, in part direct but more potently indirect, with every organ of public opinion doped and chloroformed into acquiescence, we shall be conducted along further stages of our journey.

Chamberlain saw appeasement as a means of buying time, of giving Britain more options for defense. Churchill saw the prime minister's bargain with a blackmailer as having suddenly limited the nation's options. That is what happens when you acquiesce in theft. "I have been casting about to see how measures can be taken to protect us from this advance of the Nazi power, and to secure those forms of life which are so dear to us," Churchill explained. "What is the sole method that is open? The sole method that is open is for us to regain our old island independence by acquiring that supremacy in the air which we were promised, that security in our air defences which we were assured we had, and thus to make ourselves an island once again. That, in all this grim outlook, shines out as the overwhelming fact." The only alternative was what nineteenth-century British diplomats called *splendid isolation*, enforced by supremacy of arms. Thus, "an effort at rearmament the like of which has not been seen ought to be made forthwith, and all the resources of this country and all its united strength should be bent to that task." Claiming to have obtained "peace for our time," Chamberlain had forced Britain into a crash program of rearmament. He had forced the nation into the modern equivalent of the medieval city, which builds what it hopes will be an impregnable wall around itself and bars and guards all of the gates. Bargain with a tyrant, and you turn back the clock to the equivalent of a primitive and brutal time, to an environment in which the activities of civilized life, including diplomacy and commerce—the exchange of value for value—are impossible, a world in which all relationships are defined by force and by force alone.

**Any negotiation made in bad faith** is bound to fail. A transaction that fails to be an exchange of value for value may be theft or extortion, but it is not business. Tyrants, thieves, and extortionists are all in the same class. They demand without offering anything of genuine value. Satisfy their demand, and they demand more. The notion of bargaining with a tyrant is in all circumstances a delusion.

# 13

# Accept Uncertainty

"I cannot forecast to you the action of Russia.
It is a riddle wrapped in a mystery inside an enigma."
~Radio broadcast, London, October 1, 1939

As war clouds thickened over Europe through the spring and early summer of 1939, the Western democracies, Britain included, clung for precious comfort to what they assumed was the implacable opposition of Soviet communism to German Nazism. Joseph Stalin was no friend of democracy, of course, but, in this "age of great dictators," as it was often called, he was certainly the incontrovertible antithesis of Adolf Hitler. That much seemed certain, which meant that as long as Hitler had reason to fear Stalin and the Soviets on his Eastern Front, he would almost certainly refrain from picking a fight with the West.

*"Everybody has always underestimated the Russians. They keep their own secrets alike from foe and friends."*
~Speech, House of Commons, April 23, 1942

The problem with this overly optimistic wager on Russia was that it bet everything on the idealism of Joseph Stalin, a nonexistent commodity, as it turned out. It was quite true that Nazism was the ideological antithesis of communism. Nevertheless, Stalin was a pragmatist first, his ideological allegiance to communism coming in a distant second. Driven by pragmatism, he decided that a guarantee of nonaggression from his chief rival would put the Soviet Union in a powerful position with respect to the capitalist democracies, while also protecting his nation against German expansion. And such a guarantee would do even more. Stalin was always looking to create an ample buffer zone around his borders. Control of Polish and Finnish territory would provide a generous buffer indeed, and a guarantee of nonaggression with Germany would give the Soviet Union license to expand.

"Stalin was a pragmatist first, his ideological allegiance to communism coming in a distant second."

Not only, then, did Joseph Stalin consider making a treaty with Adolf Hitler, but he initiated the process by approaching him with a proposal for a German-Soviet nonaggression pact.

Hitler proved highly receptive. He had his own designs on Eastern Europe, most immediately Poland. If he could secure a guarantee that the Soviets would not interfere with his plans, he could with perfect confidence make his next move: divide Poland with the Soviets—Germany, of course, retaining the bigger piece. In addition, a set of Franco-Soviet military pacts loomed over Hitler's plans. A nonaggression treaty with Stalin would, in a single stroke, neutralize these, taking France out of the picture.

Thus, the apparent polar ideological opposites were strongly motivated to make an agreement, and, on August 23, 1939, the German-Soviet Nonaggression Pact, also known as the Hitler-Stalin Pact, was concluded in Moscow. The whole world—but especially Western politicians and political thinkers—was stunned. Stalin made no excuses, although apologists for his regime pointed out that the treaty with Germany was just one of several nonaggression pacts the Soviet Union had signed with various powers. This treaty went well beyond nonaggression, however. It was linked to a trade agreement, by which Germany undertook to export manufactured goods to the Soviets in return for strategic raw materials, materials required for war production.

"*Like carrying a large lump of ice to the North Pole.*"
~On a visit to Stalin in 1942, from *The Second World War,* 1948–53

That was the public part of the treaty. Unknown outside the inner circles of the German and Soviet governments was a secret protocol that provided for the partition of Poland between Germany and the USSR. The secret protocol cleared the way for both a joint German-Soviet invasion of Poland and for Soviet occupation of the Baltic states, especially Finland. Many in the West feared that the pact was a prelude to war. Had they also known about the secret protocol, they would have understood that it was a veritable prescription for war.

The nature of the secret protocol was effectively revealed when, as Churchill acknowledged in a broadcast of October 1, 1939, Russian troops entered Poland, not as "the friends and allies of Poland," but as invaders, along with the armies of Germany. The democracies universally perceived the Russian invasion as an act of utmost treachery that portended an outright military alliance with Germany. Churchill, in his October 1 broadcast, did not deny the enormity of the Soviet action, but he sought to understand it and, by understanding it, grasp and possibly exploit its strategic significance.

"Russia," Churchill explained, "has pursued a cold policy of self-interest." That sounded like bad news, but, even more, it sounded like the truth, and because it came across as frank and unflinching, it gave everything else Churchill had to say the mighty weight of scrupulously honest authority and good judgment.

He continued: "We could have wished that the Russian armies should be standing on their present line as the friends and allies of Poland instead of as invaders." More truth, and more apparently bad news, but, having established his clear-sighted credibility, Churchill provided a far more hopeful and more positive context in which the Soviet action could be interpreted: "But that the Russian armies should stand on this line was clearly necessary for the safety of Russia against the Nazi menace. At any rate, the line is there, and an Eastern Front has been created which Nazi Germany does not dare assail." Thus, Churchill concluded, "Nazi designs upon the Baltic States and upon the Ukraine must come to a dead stop."

> "Churchill . . . did not deny the enormity of the Soviet action, but he sought to understand it and, by understanding it, grasp and possibly exploit its strategic significance."

For the moment, then, Russia's apparent treachery against Poland and the Western democracies might legitimately be seen as a check on Nazi aggression—to be sure, not the pro-Western alliance Britain and France would have liked, but a check nevertheless. What, however, would be the Soviets' next move? "I cannot forecast to you the action of Russia," Churchill admitted, and then continued with a figure of speech that became instantly famous: "It is a riddle, wrapped in a mystery, inside an enigma; but perhaps there is a key."

> That key is Russian national interest. It cannot be in accordance with the interest of the safety of Russia that Germany should plant itself upon the shores of the Black Sea, or that it should overrun the Balkan States and subjugate the Slavonic peoples of south-eastern Europe. That would be contrary to the historic life-interest of Russia.

Confronted with the appearance of total catastrophe, Churchill looked into it for some legitimate good. Confronted with a mystery, he fell back on common sense and historical precedent to make an educated guess as to motives and likely outcome. His object was not to create national self-delusion or to attempt to evade harsh reality. Rather, it was to avoid destructive panic—the panic that comes from acting either on appearances or in response to the murky unknown. Churchill embraced the unknown—admitted the mystery—but he refused to become lost within it.

## Assume the Absolute Supremacy of Self-Interest

Do people and organizations ever act irrationally or even self-destructively? Of course, they do. Far more often, however, they act from what they at least perceive as their rational self-interest. They do not always act as we would like them to, but, from the point of view of self-interest, they usually act rationally and even predictably. When the intentions of another are unclear or impossible to determine precisely, assume the operation of a motive of self-interest, and then make your own plans based on that assumption. It is unlikely that you will go very far wrong, and, in most situations, action based on educated guesswork is far preferable to random acts born of panic or total paralysis born of fear.

Having established Russia's self-interest and having introduced the assumption that Russia would continue to act from self-interest, Churchill was able to make an even more positive leap, arguing that in southeastern Europe, the "interests of Russia fall into the same channel as the interests of Britain and France."

None of these three Powers can afford to see Rumania, Yugoslavia, Bulgaria, and above all Turkey, put under the German heel. Through the fog of confusion and uncertainty we may discern quite plainly the community of interests which exists between England, France and Russia—a community of interests to prevent the Nazis carrying the flames of war into the Balkans and Turkey. Thus, my friends, at some risk of being proved wrong by events, I will proclaim tonight my conviction that . . . Hitler, and all that Hitler stands for, have been and are being warned off the east and the southeast of Europe.

By the end of the war's first month, the armies of Nazi Germany had ravaged and totally conquered Poland. Worse, Stalin's Russia openly collaborated in this. Together, these events must have seemed to most friends of democracy ample reason for panic and despair, or, at the very least, for succumbing to the dark fear that is born of mystery. Instead of fleeing from it, Churchill seized upon it, treating it as an asset rather than a liability. If the unknown held the prospect for bad things, it also held the prospect for good. Reasoning from common sense and historical precedent, he sought to fill the vacuum of uncertainty with the most positive interpretation he could credibly muster, seeking in this way to maintain hope and morale without denying reality or encouraging self-delusion. In the worst possible circumstances, it was leadership at its very best.

**The sculptor has clay,** the painter paint, and the writer words. For the leader, reality is the medium, and if, at a given point in time, reality is not known, then the unknown becomes the medium with which a leader must work. She cannot reject it. She must not fear it. Instead, she must accept it, if only because it is all she has. She must use it as best she can.

# 14

# Offer the Privilege
# of Sacrifice

"I have nothing to offer but blood, toil, tears and sweat."
~ Speech, House of Commons, May 13, 1940

On May 10, 1940, Winston Churchill succeeded Neville Chamberlain, and, four days later, on May 13, he addressed Parliament for the first time as prime minister. To the government and people of his country, he offered everything he had, which amounted to just this: "blood, toil, tears and sweat." Surely, no leader of state ever entered office with such an offer. Surely, none ever gave such a speech.

The chronology of events that led up to it was as grim and desperate as the direst imagination might conceive. In 1935, Benito Mussolini, seeking to expand Italy's African empire, invaded Ethiopia. Ignoring the pleas of its exiled emperor, Haile Selassie, the democracies of the Western world did nothing to oppose Italy's aggression. Emboldened by this demonstration of a collective absence of will among the democracies, Adolf Hitler, on March 7, 1936, sent 22,000 soldiers to occupy the Rhineland in blatant violation of the Treaty of Versailles, which barred German troops from the western portion of Germany. As Hitler had predicted, the democracies again offered no opposition. "It's none of our business, is it?" an editorial in the *Times* of London rationalized. "It's their own back-garden they're walking into."

Perceiving the likes of Britain and France to be weak and Germany to be strong, Mussolini, on July 11, 1936, acquiesced in Hitler's demand that Austria, Italy's northern neighbor, be deemed a "German state." On October 25, Italy entered into a formal "entente" with Germany, creating what Mussolini described on November 1 as "a vertical line" connecting Berlin and Rome, a line, he said, "that is not a partition but is rather an axis around which all European states can collaborate." Later in the month, on November 25, the empire of Japan concluded an Anti-Comintern Pact with Germany. When Italy signed on to this the following year, the Rome-Berlin-Tokyo Axis was born. It became the springboard from which Hitler leapt into Austria on March 13, 1938, to form the Anschluss, the annexation of Austria to Germany in a government known as the Third Reich.

Again, Britain and France did nothing.

Almost immediately following the Anschluss, Hitler issued a demand for the annexation of the Sudetenland, the German-speaking portion of Czechoslovakia. Britain, like France, was bound by the terms of the Treaty of Versailles and other agreements to defend Czech sovereignty. Instead of honoring the nation's obligation, Britain's prime minister Neville Chamberlain, trademark bowler hat in hand, called on Hitler, first at his Alpine chalet, Berchtesgaden, on September 15, and then, during September 29–30, 1938, more formally, at Munich. His purpose was to implement what he called a policy of *active appeasement*, giving Hitler all that he demanded in exchange for his pledge to make no more territorial demands in Europe. His objective was to avoid war, even if that meant sacrificing Czechoslovakia.

> "His purpose was to implement what he called a policy of *active appeasement*, giving Hitler all that he demanded in exchange for his pledge to make no more territorial demands in Europe."

## A Little Evil

The folly of appeasement is agreeing to a relatively little evil for the purpose of averting a great evil. Ethically considered, ends are never separable from means, and in no instance is this truer than when evil is proposed as a means of avoiding evil. Ethical conduct unfolds along a continuum, in which origin and result, means and ends, cannot be separated. A process that commences with a wrong must conclude with one.

Returning from Munich and landing at an airport outside of London, Chamberlain descended the ladder stair of the aircraft that had carried him back from Munich and triumphantly waved the Munich Agreement, a private stationery-size sheet of paper, before the newsreel cameras. He took the document back with him to his office at 10 Downing Street, from which he made an impromptu speech: "My good friends, this is the second time in our history that there has come back from Germany to Downing Street peace with honor. I believe it is peace for our time. I thank you from the bottom of our hearts. And now I recommend you go home and sleep quietly in your beds."

Winston Churchill did not sleep. Britain and France had betrayed the Czechs. "England," Churchill declared before his fellow members in the House of Commons, "has been offered a choice between war and shame. She has chosen shame and will get war."

*"An appeaser is one who feeds the crocodile—hoping it will eat him last."*
~Generally attributed to Churchill, *c.* January 1940

Churchill went on to declare that the nation had suffered its worst military defeat ever, and without a shot having been fired. He was hardly surprised when, on March 16, 1939, Hitler violated the Munich Agreement by occupying Prague and swallowing up what was left of Czechoslovakia. Neither Britain nor France tried to stop him. Nor could they do anything other than express their dismay when Hitler and Stalin signed the August 23, 1939, Nonaggression Pact that was all but an outright union of the world's most formidable totalitarian states.

The aggressive action of Hitler and Mussolini plus the passive inaction of those who led the European democracies made war inevitable. It began at half past four o'clock on the morning of September 1, 1939, when a vast German war machine rolled into and over Poland. (Soviet forces would invade eastern Poland on September 17.) Now, at the worst possible moment, with Germany fully mobilized, Britain and France had no choice but to acknowledge that a war was being fought. They demanded that Germany withdraw from Poland, and when it did not, they declared war.

Warsaw surrendered on September 27, and Poland was completely conquered by October 5. Through it all, except for the fact of declaring war, neither France nor Britain did anything. It was as if Europe west of Germany and Austria had descended into a state of suspended animation. Churchill called it the "Twilight War," whereas American newspapers gave it the name by which the period from the fall of 1939 to the spring of 1940 remains best known, the "Phony War."

Almost immediately after Britain declared war on Germany, Prime Minister Chamberlain reached out to the man who had been his harshest critic. He telephoned Churchill to offer the same post he had occupied in the early months of World War I, First Lord of the Admiralty. Churchill accepted, hung up the receiver, turned to his wife, Clementine, and said simply, "We're back."

Churchill saw the Phony War for what it was—inaction—and that, he reasoned, was a gift, the gift of victory, for Hitler. No sooner did he take office, therefore, than he urged Chamberlain to end the Phony War by mounting an offensive. The result was a counter-

Off

invasion of Norway to contest Germany's invasion of the Scandinavian country, beginning in April 1940. This assault, however, had to be abandoned in June as the main thrust of the German offensive thundered into Holland, Belgium, and then France.

In the predawn hours of May 10, those three nations came under attack. No one woke Prime Minister Chamberlain to give him the news. Following the German invasion of Norway, there had been increasing Parliamentary agitation calling

> **"He telephoned Churchill to offer the post he had occupied in the early months of World War I, First Lord of the Admiralty. Churchill accepted, hung up the receiver, turned to his wife, Clementine, and said simply, 'We're back.'"**

on Chamberlain to step down, and Chamberlain was on the verge of doing so. But when he finally awakened on May 10, he reconsidered.

He had no desire to be seen as walking away from a crisis, even a crisis his own appeasement policy had precipitated.

For his part, Admiralty Lord Churchill was up before dawn on the tenth and by six in the morning was meeting with the secretary of state for war and the secretary of state for air to discuss the best way to meet the offensive. Sir Samuel Hoare, the air secretary, recalled that Churchill's "spirit, so far from being shaken by failure or disaster, gathered strength in a crisis." He exuded confidence, Hoare recalled, "and the news could not have been worse. Yet there he was, smoking his large cigar and eating fried eggs and bacon, as if he had just returned from an early morning ride."

At seven, Churchill's son Randolph telephoned his father to relay to him the latest radio reports and to hear what his father knew.

"Well," father replied to son, "the German hordes are pouring into the Low Countries."

Randolph asked about the likelihood that he would now be named prime minister.

"Oh, I don't know about that. Nothing matters now except beating the enemy."

At eight, Chamberlain summoned Churchill and the other members of his War Cabinet to a meeting on Downing Street. He announced to them his intention to remain as prime minister until the "French battle was finished."

> *"Nothing matters now except beating the enemy."*
> ~ Quoted in Martin Gilbert's *Churchill: A Life,* 1991

The announcement was greeted by Churchill's fellow Conservatives with outrage. They now demanded that Chamberlain resign and Churchill be named prime minister before the end of the day. Kingsley Wood gently counseled his longtime friend Chamberlain that the only man capable now of creating a "National Government," a government with the kind of unity necessary to fight the war, was Winston Churchill. Chamberlain heard his friend out, then, at eleven, convened the War Cabinet for a second meeting, at which Churchill suggested that Chamberlain dispatch Sir Rogers Keyes to Belgium in an effort to rally the Belgian king to resist Hitler's advance. Chamberlain agreed. At four thirty, the War Cabinet was convened a third time. Reports had just been received that German paratroops had seized the Rotterdam airfield and that Holland would likely fall very soon. No sooner was this message read out to the War Cabinet than a messenger delivered another. German paratroops were in Belgium. As it turned out, they were about to capture the "impregnable" Fort Eben Emael, thereby throwing open the vital bridges that provided passage to France. The War Cabinet discussed the necessity of issuing to all British troops a warning to beware of imminent attack by German parachute units.

As a discussion of the gravest sort continued, yet another messenger entered the cabinet room. Chamberlain took the message he offered, read it, and then sat in silence, allowing the talk to continue for many minutes before interrupting. He announced that he had just received answers to two questions he had posed yesterday afternoon concerning continued support for him from the Labour Party. Glancing down at the message, he told the cabinet that the members of that party—rivals of the Conservatives—declared their unwillingness to serve any longer under "the present Prime Minister." That was the answer to his first question. They were willing, Chamberlain continued, to serve under a new prime minister. And that was the answer to his second question. What it meant was that the Labour Party was willing to serve under a Conservative prime minister, provided that the prime minister was not Neville Chamberlain.

Before the hour was out, Chamberlain presented himself at Buckingham Palace to tender his resignation to George VI. Accepting, the king asked Chamberlain for advice. He gave it to him: "Winston was the man to send for."

Early that evening, the king sent for him.

"I suppose you don't know why I have sent for you?" he smiled.

Churchill took the bait.

"Sir, I simply couldn't imagine why."

At this, the monarch now laughed out loud. "I want to ask you to form a Government."

He was thoroughly prepared to do just that and reeled off a list of names of prominent figures capable of constituting neither a Conservative nor a Labour government, but what he called a *Grand Coalition*, an all-party government.

> *"We thought of him, so faithful in his study and discharge of State affairs, so strong in his devotion to the enduring honour of our country; so self-restrained in his judgments of men and affairs; so uplifted above the clash of party politics, yet so attentive to them; so wise and shrewd in judging between what matters and what does not."*
>
> ~Eulogy broadcast on King George VI, February 7, 1952

Much later in the war, but still in the midst of war, another leader would come suddenly into office. On April 12, 1945, U.S. president Franklin Delano Roosevelt died of a cerebral hemorrhage. Two hours and twenty-four minutes later, at 7:09 p.m., Harry S. Truman was sworn in as the new chief executive. The next day, he gathered the White House press corps around him. "Boys," he said, "if you ever pray, pray for me now. I don't know whether you fellows ever had a load of hay fall on you, but when they told me yesterday what had happened, I felt like the moon, the stars, and all the planets had fallen on me." It was vintage Truman, utterly disarming in its candor. Like Truman, Churchill was an unswervingly candid man, and as we can take Truman at his word when he confessed to feeling overwhelmed by his new responsibilities, so we can believe Churchill fully when he wrote that the night he became prime minister, he went to bed feeling no anxiety whatsoever, but, on the contrary, experiencing "a profound sense of relief. At last I had authority to give directions over the whole scene." Ever since the catastrophe of the Dardanelles invasion in 1915, the simultaneous possession of responsibility *and* authority had been Churchill's great ambition. He felt, he said, as if he "were walking with destiny," that his whole "past life had been but a preparation for this hour and this trial."

## Martyrdom Is Not Leadership

It is often said that to be a leader is to accept responsibility. True, but not true enough. To be a leader is to accept responsibility *and* to possess authority. Both elements are required for genuine leadership. To bear responsibility without authority is martyrdom, not leadership. To wield authority without responsibility is tyranny, not leadership.

Those who knew Winston Churchill best—family, friends, longtime political supporters—felt, even at this worst of times, a sense of salvation akin to joy. They wanted to celebrate his elevation to office. But how would Winston Churchill sell himself to those who did not know him so intimately, to those to whom he was practically a stranger?

On the afternoon of May 13, he called a meeting of all his ministers at Admiralty House. These men were the new government, the Grand Coalition of which he would often speak. Locking eyes with each of them, Churchill declared that he had "nothing to offer but blood, toil, tears and *sweat*." A few hours after this meeting, he addressed the House of Commons. "I beg to move," he began, "that this House welcomes the formation of a Government representing the united and inflexible resolve of the nation to prosecute the war with Germany to a victorious conclusion." He laid out for the Commons the nature of the coalition, one intended to represent "the unity of the nation."

> To form an Administration of this scale and complexity is a serious undertaking in itself, but it must be remembered that we are in the preliminary stage of one of the greatest battles in history, that we are in action at many other points in Norway and in Holland, that we have to be prepared in the Mediterranean, that the air battle is continuous and that many preparations . . . have to be made here at home. In this crisis I hope I may be pardoned if I do not address the House at any length today. I hope that any of my friends and colleagues, or former colleagues, who are affected by the political reconstruction, will make allowance, all allowance, for any lack of ceremony with which it has been necessary to act. I would say to the House, as I said to those who have joined this government: "I have nothing to offer but blood, toil, tears and sweat."

And so Winston Churchill sold himself to Parliament and the people of Britain exactly as he had sold himself to his innermost circle. At both venues, his offer was not the usual offer of a politician—general prosperity and a pledge that everything would be all right—but sacrifice, sacrifice of life, of limb, of rest, of leisure, of happiness, of anything remotely recalling the ease of peacetime existence. He drove home his point yet harder: "We have before us an ordeal of the most grievous kind," he said. "We have before us many, many long months of struggle and of suffering."

> *"The British nation is unique in this respect. They are the only people who like to be told how bad things are, who like to be told the worst, and like to be told that they are very likely to get much worse in the future."*
>
> ~Speech, House of Commons, June 10, 1941

The politicians of peace—of "peace for our time"—had made the people a very different offer. It was the notion that dictators, armed to the teeth, could be "appeased." It was, in fact, an offer of collective sleepy self-delusion. Churchill's faith that it was much better to offer the truth, even if the truth meant sacrifice, pain, and loss, lay at the very heart of his genius as a leader. He never doubted that the English people would not only accept his offer, hard and harsh though it was, but would embrace it; he would not, however, ask them to embrace sacrifice without the compensation of a worthy goal as expressed in a new and vigorous national policy.

You ask, what is our policy? I can say: It is to wage war, by sea, land and air, with all our might and with all the strength that God can give us; to wage war against a monstrous tyranny, never surpassed in the dark, lamentable catalogue of human crime. That is our policy. You ask, what is our aim? I can answer in one word: It is victory, victory at all costs, victory in spite of all terror, victory, however long and hard the road may be; for without victory, there is no survival. Let that be realised; no survival for the British Empire, no survival for all that the British Empire has stood for, no survival for the urge and impulse of the ages, that mankind will move forward towards its goal.

There is a quality of fine music in this great speech. It begins in a minor key as a dirge with just four heavy notes: *blood, toil, tears, and sweat.* The form of this tune is perfectly suited to the dark crisis at hand. But then, beginning with the question, *You ask, what is our policy?*, the music modulates from minor key to major, and, rhythmically, it steps up from dirge to march, welling in magnificent crescendo to conclude with the fugitive strains of what sounds very nearly like an ode to joy: "But I take up my task with buoyancy and hope. I feel sure that our cause will not be suffered to fail among men. At this time, I feel entitled to claim the aid of all, and I say, 'come then, let us go forward together with our united strength.'"

**You can choose to be a politician,** or you can choose to be a leader. A politician sells whatever is obviously and superficially appealing. The merchandise offered varies from time to time and place to place, but the *benefit* is always the same—an easier life. In contrast, a leader sells the counterintuitive—never the obvious, selfish benefit, but a most unlikely item: the privilege of sacrifice. This is not a case of peddling pain to a masochist; for a competent leader never offers sacrifice for the mere sake of sacrifice. The proposed bargain is invariably made in a much larger context—the greater good—and the leader must therefore make the case for sacrifice by showing how, even though it entails risk and loss, sacrifice is an investment rather than an expenditure. It holds the promise of profit, the acquisition of a great benefit—not the easier life a politician promises, but, collectively, a better life.

# 15

# Make Good Use
# of Adversity

"There are men in the world who derive as stern an exaltation from the prox-
imity of disaster and ruin, as others from success."
~ *The Story of the Malakand Field Force*, 1898

For the title of the book he based on his Harvard University senior
thesis, an analysis of the British government's failure to prevent
World War II, John F. Kennedy paraphrased the title of a prescient
book Winston Churchill had published in 1938, on the eve of that
war. Kennedy called his book *Why England Slept*, and Churchill had
titled his *While England Slept*. In both, the most insightful word is the
verb. As the clouds of war gathered, England, France, and the other
democracies, the United States included, were somnolent, sleep-
walking through a period of history defined by the violent
dynamism of Adolf Hitler, which culminated in Blitzkrieg—German
for "Lightning War"—the juggernaut invasion of Poland in the
East and Belgium, France, and the other nations of the West,
the "small countries," as Churchill called them in a letter to
Franklin D. Roosevelt, which "are simply smashed up, one by one,
like matchwood."

The Blitzkrieg through Western Europe did not happen immediately. If England and other democracies had slept in the years,
months, and days before Hitler invaded Poland on September 1,

1939, thereby beginning the war, they returned to a kind of slumber following the invasion. Instead of moving aggressively against Germany, Britain and France settled into watchful waiting, neither nation actually coming to the aid of invaded Poland.

> *"Poland has again been overrun by two of the great Powers which held her in bondage for 150 years but were unable to quench the spirit of the Polish nation. The heroic defence of Warsaw shows that the soul of Poland is indestructible, and that she will rise again like a rock, which may for a spell be submerged by a tidal wave, but which remains a rock."*
>
> ~Radio broadcast, London, October 1, 1939

At 4:15 on the morning of April 9, 1940, Hitler's soldiers walked into Denmark and were met with virtually no resistance. Norway was a different story. Immediately after Britain's declaration of war in September 1939, Prime Minister Neville Chamberlain tapped Winston Churchill, who had been out of the government for most of the 1930s, to resume his World War I post as first lord of the Admiralty. Itching to end the Phony War with a bold offensive stroke, he goaded Chamberlain into authorizing a counter-invasion of Norway. Despite some success, the British, together with French units, were forced to withdraw as Hitler launched *Fall Gelb*, "Operation Yellow," a general invasion of Western Europe.

> *"In war, the clouds never blow over; they gather unceasingly and fall in thunderbolts."*
>
> ~ *The World Crisis*, 1923–31

It began at dawn on May 10, 1940, when the German army crossed into Luxembourg, Belgium, and the Netherlands, violating their neutrality and drawing out of France, as Hitler knew it would, the troops of the British Expeditionary Force (BEF), the army Britain had sent to the Continent at the outbreak of the war. This left France exposed and vulnerable; however, that nation's generals took comfort from their faith that the Maginot Line was, if not absolutely impregnable, sufficiently so to delay any invasion and provide time to build up forces. An elaborate string of fortifications, the Maginot Line covered the border between France and Germany, except for the Ardennes region, which was so densely forested that French planners assumed no modern army could ever invade through it. As it turned out, invasion through the Ardennes was precisely what Operation Yellow called for.

### Never Be Predictable

Often, the greatest advantage you have over a competitor is what the rival assumes you can and cannot do. To the degree that you can violate his assumptions, you will own the element of surprise, attacking where the rival is least prepared to defend, compensate, or counterattack. Avoid predictability. Achieve surprise, even if doing so presents difficulty.

As French high command placed its faith in a defensive strategy centered on the Maginot Line, the British government soothed itself with the notion that the French army, a force of about five million men, was certainly capable of stopping the German juggernaut. This assessment was compounded more of wishful thinking than careful analysis. The quality of the French military leadership at every level was poor and, even more damaging was the extent to which a defeatist malaise had infected the entire force, from top to bottom. Neither the French military nor the civilian government had created a strong vision of the nation's war objectives.

The swiftly moving panzer (armored) divisions that constituted the principal component of the German invasion force tore through the "impenetrable" Ardennes. The plan was to drive through the great open plain of France, all the way to the English Channel, cleaving the French forces in the south from the English forces in the north, fragmenting the defenders so that they could be defeated in detail and mopped up. Breaking through the Ardennes and over-running Belgium meant that the invaders essentially bypassed the vaunted Maginot Line. Historians would later write of the "failure of the Maginot Line." In fact, it did not so much fail as it was simply rendered irrelevant.

Army Group B of the invasion force made a decoy move in the north, which lured Allied forces to counter it. Simultaneously, the much larger Army Group A burst through the Ardennes for the main invasion. In the meantime, south of both of these army groups, a smaller German force under Marshal Wilhelm Ritter von Leeb pinned down the defenders of the Maginot Line, ensuring that some 400,000 French troops manning the line would be kept out of the principal battle. Instead of functioning as a defensive asset, therefore, the Maginot Line had itself to be defended, creating a massive drain on precious manpower.

And there was even worse. Whereas the armored divisions of the main German invasion were brilliantly led by Heinz Guderian, the prime architect of German tank technology and tactics, and by Erwin Rommel, soon to earn legendary renown as a tank com-mander, the uniformly mediocre French commanders were conven-tional and, therefore, predictable. Falling for the decoy attack, French general Maurice Gamelin left the sector between the border region towns of Namur and Sedan thinly defended. It was here that Army Group A pushed through.

As grim as this situation was, General Gamelin made it worse when he ordered the French Seventh Army, commanded by one of his best generals, Henri Giraud, to withdraw from its position as a mobile reserve force near Dunkirk, on the North Sea coast near the Belgian border, to Breda in the Netherlands, for the purpose of bol-stering the Dutch army. As a mobile force, the Seventh Army had been ideally situated to attack the invaders when they were most vulnerable, with their supply lines stretched thinner and thinner the farther they penetrated into French territory. By moving the mobile reserve out of position, however, Gamelin effectively invited a deeper invasion.

While the Allied war on the ground sputtered, combat in the air was also failing miserably. Britain had good aircraft, but relatively few stationed on the Continent. As for the French air force, it was equipped mostly with obsolescent aircraft, which were thoroughly outclassed by the advanced planes of the German Luftwaffe. To make matters worse, leadership of the French air arm was so dispersed among various field commanders that the entire force was all but paralyzed.

By nightfall on May 12, seven panzer divisions had advanced as far as the east bank of the River Meuse. This was reality, yet Allied commanders persisted in their belief that crossing the Meuse in strength would require five, even six days. They therefore operated on the assumption that they had until May 17 to organize a strong resistance. On May 13, however, Guderian suddenly vaulted across the river and erected pontoon bridges for a general advance. With the Meuse breached at Dinant, Guderian and Rommel launched an attack on Sedan and its environs, sweeping aside two entire French armies, the Second and the Ninth.

Prime Minister Churchill did not stand idly by. On May 16, he flew across the English Channel in the hope that his personal presence might infuse the French leadership with a greater will to resist. He counseled that now was no time for passive defense, but, rather, the moment had come to counterattack, to deploy the vast French mobile reserve against the overextended invaders, chewing up as many of the enemy as possible.

It was a bold and feasible plan—to which, however, the French high command replied that the "mobile reserve" no longer existed. A large portion of it had been thrown away in piecemeal actions, and the rest, including Giraud's Seventh Army, was cut off in positions from which it was of no use. Even Winston Churchill, the indomitable, felt his heart sink.

Whatever else he may have been, Paul Reynaud, the French premier, was hardly indomitable. He had for all practical purposes given up days earlier, and it was at this moment, even as Churchill tried in vain to inspirit his nation's ally, that Reynaud publicly pronounced the Battle of France lost. The declaration descended upon Churchill as if it had been a physical blow, doubly painful coming, as it did, just after the revelation that the mobile reserve, in whose existence Churchill had invested so much hope, was no more. The worst thing about Reynaud's capitulation was not that the assessment behind it was probably all too true, but that surrender was utterly premature. The British and French soldiers in the field were not giving up. They were still fighting and dying.

The contrast between Reynaud and Churchill could not have been more dramatic. The prime minister returned to London on May 17, deeply depressed, yet, on May 19, he made his first broadcast to the British nation as prime minister—having ascended to the office just nine days earlier—posing to the people the question: "Is this not the appointed time for all to make the utmost exertions in their power?" Reciting the litany of "shattered States and bludgeoned races; the Czechs, the Poles, the Norwegians, the Danes, the Dutch, the Belgians," he warned that upon them all "the long night of barbarism will descend, unbroken even by a star of hope," paused, and then allowed his sentence and his thought to turn: "unless we conquer, as conquer we must; as conquer we shall."

As armies of men crumbled beneath him, Churchill recruited an army of words, words commanded, as it were, by the all-powerful concept of *unless*. *Unless* we conquer, all will be swallowed up in one long and terrible night. Then there was the mighty verb, which he repeated, tolling it three times as if it were some great bell of unimaginable weight and resonance: *conquer, conquer, conquer*. And not just repeating it, but transforming through an irresistible progression of English grammar, syntax, and definition: *unless* we conquer, as conquer we *must*, as conquer we *shall*. *Unless, must, shall*—the meaning marched forward as the literal

**"As armies of men crumbled beneath him, Churchill recruited an army of words."**

armies, at this time and in this place, could not. They advanced from a conditional statement (*unless*) and through a statement of admonition (*must*), arriving in final triumph at a statement of inevitable victory (*shall*).

---

### The Reality of Words

You can achieve in language what you cannot always achieve in physical fact. If the enterprise falters, suffers reverses, and passes through a difficult time, use words to show what a better time will look like, what benefits it will bring, and how it may be achieved. Use words not to escape reality as it is, but to model reality as you would like it to be or become.

---

It was as if the new prime minister had found a way to redefine defeat as victory. A frightened nation took courage from the broadcast. For that, Winston Churchill was thankful, but he who knew the power and potential of words had limits. The very night of his broadcast, he ordered the Admiralty to assemble a large fleet of small vessels and make them ready to "proceed to ports and inlets on the French coast." He knew very well how to read a map. The German advance had cut off the main portion of the BEF (British Expeditionary Force), along with a large number of French troops, forcing them into a pocket that backed up on Dunkirk and opened to nothing but the sea. With each passing hour, the pocket was becoming smaller as Guderian's panzers closed in. Words, even great words, were one thing. Churchill was preparing to evacuate the British army.

The terrible fact was that the conquest of France had not only proceeded far more swiftly than Churchill or the French could have imagined, but it also moved much faster than even the German planners had dared to contemplate. Guderian's tanks rolled out far in advance of the slower infantry units that supported them. A bold and supremely self-confident commander, Guderian was not disturbed by this exposure of his armored assets. Not so his superiors, however, first among them Adolf Hitler. They all fretted that, separated from the infantry, the tanks and other vehicles were vulnerable to counterattack. On May 15 and again on May 17, the German high command ordered Guderian to pause in order that the infantry could catch up. He protested vehemently that every halt gave the English and French an opportunity to regroup and even to counterattack. But his superiors were inflexible.

They might have taken satisfaction in the fact that no counterattack was forthcoming. Battered and bleeding, the Allies were too exhausted, depleted, and demoralized to strike back. With what seemed an almost limitless capacity to make a desperate situation even worse, it was at this moment, on May 20, that French high command relieved General Gamelin and replaced him with the superannuated General Maxime Weygand. The transfer of command consumed valuable time, further delaying the attempt to organize a counterattack.

So it was that, despite the delays imposed by Hitler and his top military advisers, Guderian's 2nd Panzer Division managed to reach the French coastal town of Abbeville on May 19. This advance drove a wedge between the surviving Allied armies, herding almost all of the BEF, together with a number of French units, up against the sea. These forces, some 400,000 men, had no place to go—except into the saltwater.

On May 20, Churchill learned that Joseph P. Kennedy, United States ambassador to the Court of St. James's, observing the desperate situation of the BEF, informed President Roosevelt that the

British government was almost certain to seek terms from Hitler, to reach a negotiated peace—in short, to surrender. At this time, the president was pondering whether to lend Britain fifty World War I–vintage U.S. destroyers, which the Royal Navy desperately needed as convoy escorts. It would be a grave error to deliver them only to have Britain capitulate and turn them over to Hitler. So FDR hung fire, waiting to see what Churchill—and Hitler—would do. Seeking to counteract Ambassador Kennedy's defeatism and free up the destroyers, Churchill wrote to FDR: "Our intention is, whatever happens, to fight on to the end in this Island, and provided we can get the help for which we ask, we hope to run them very close in the air battles in view of individual superiority." Once again, the prime minister plunged into the very heart of a critically desperate situation and extracted from it not just hope, but the opportunity for positive action. Yes, France would fall. Yes, Germany would almost certainly invade England. But both of these catastrophes at least provided an opportunity to fight the invader and to fight him to the very last.

> **"Once again, the prime minister plunged into the very heart of a critically desperate situation and extracted from it not just hope, but the opportunity for positive action."**

After thus reframing desperation as opportunity, Churchill directly addressed the issue that he knew kept Roosevelt from authorizing the immediate release of the destroyers. "Members of the present Administration would likely go down during this process should it result adversely," Churchill acknowledged frankly, "but in no conceivable circumstances will we consent to surrender." He did not hesitate to dig to rock bottom: "If members of the present Administration were finished and others came in to parley amid the ruins, you must not be blind to the fact that the sole remaining bargaining counter with Germany would be the Fleet, and, if this country was left by the United States to its fate, no one would have the right to blame those then responsible if they made the best terms they could for the surviving inhabitants. Excuse me, Mr. President, putting this nightmare bluntly. Evidently I could not answer for my successors, who in utter despair and helplessness might well have to accommodate themselves to the German will." In this way, Churchill sought to give FDR a stake in his survival, which depended on the survival of England. He, Winston Churchill, would never surrender. But if defeat came nevertheless, he could be forced out and replaced by those who would. And for the United States, that would mean the loss of a friendly naval fleet that guarded the Atlantic separating peaceful America from a Europe in the grasp of a rapacious conqueror. Should Britain be allowed to fail, the fleet would probably be bargained away, and, with it, the security of the United States. Even at the very verge of extremity, Churchill would neither give up nor beg. In the worst case, the fleet remained a possession of absolute value, which it was in the interests of America to help defend.

**"Even at the very verge of extremity, Churchill would neither give up nor beg."**

## Use the Carrots, Use the Sticks

Positive motives (motives of attraction) are more compelling than negative motives (motives of avoidance), but most powerful of all is the combination of positive and negative motives. Want to elicit action? Show not only that the present moment is the right moment to act, but that it is the only moment in which effective action is possible.

From dealing with President Roosevelt and the United States, the prime minister returned his attention to the crisis in France.

So the BEF had its back to the wall. Well, Churchill reasoned, World War I had demonstrated that this most hazardous and uncomfortable position was one from which the British soldier tended to fight most effectively. Churchill took heart from this fact and, as France tottered on the abyss, he flew again to Paris on May 22 for a personal interview with General Weygand. He proposed an Anglo-French attack against the wedge that Guderian had driven between the two Allied armies. The objective was to throw everything possible into a pincers attack against this wedge, cutting off the Germans on the coast at Abbeville, and then linking up around the isolated enemy. It was a last-ditch bid to turn the tables on Hitler's army, an attempt by a trapped army to trap the trappers.

"I will try" was all the answer Weygand could muster.

For a short time, at least, this answer was enough for Churchill, who returned to London in good spirits. Hours later, however, the reports began to come in from the front. The French had clearly lost anything resembling a fighting spirit. On May 21, BEF elements had counterattacked to the south from Arras, making rapid inroads into the German line. But when the French failed to follow up to the north, the BEF had no choice but to retreat, and, on May 24, evacuated Boulogne. Writing from the field to the Defence Office, Major General Sir Hastings Ismay complained about French defeatism: "Of course, if one side fights and the other does not, the war is apt to become somewhat unequal."

There was nothing for it now but to make for Dunkirk on the English Channel and hope for the miracle of evacuation. That miracle, code named *Operation Dynamo*, was given urgent motivation by fresh intelligence received from a brilliant group of British code breakers—they were popularly referred to as the "bright boys"—working feverishly at Bletchley Park, a grand old estate, now converted for war work, outside of London. They had intercepted and decrypted two communications. One was a German plan to cut off the BEF and any remaining French forces from the sea. This would end any hope of evacuation. The other order, however, came directly from Adolf Hitler. As of May 24, armored forces under the command of German general Paul Ludwig von Kleist had advanced to the southern perimeter of what was now the "Dunkirk pocket," the sliver of French coast that contained what remained of the BEF, along with some of the best soldiers of the French army.

A pocket? It was really a bag, and Kleist had his hand on the drawstring. However, Hitler's order to him was the same order he had twice before given Guderian. Halt, the Führer commanded. Wait for the infantry.

Churchill and his military advisers were in agreement. Evacuation was urgent—the backdoor to the sea was about to be slammed shut—and it was also feasible, for Hitler had done what the British and French had been unable to do: he had stopped the advance of the German army. Evacuation, therefore, was a matter of now or never.

So Operation Dynamo unfolded, from May 26 through June 4, 1940. The Admiralty had cobbled together a ragtag fleet of 693 ships, including thirty-nine destroyers, thirty-six minesweepers, seventy-seven civilian fishing trawlers, and twenty-six pleasure yachts. What all the vessels had in common was a relatively shallow draft, which permitted them to come in close to shore to pick up evacuees, who were ferried out to this flotilla in an even more motley assortment of smaller craft. The evacuation was carried out under artillery fire while a valiant Anglo-French rearguard force delayed the final German advance against Dunkirk.

While the flotilla went about its hazardous work, Luftwaffe air-craft, German U-boats, and E-boats (small torpedo attack boats) pounded the small craft transferring the troops from shore to the larger ships that would take them to England. That was bad enough, but the real horror came from the bombing and shelling of the troops onshore awaiting evacuation. With no place to run, they made for easy targets. Luck at long last was with the Allies. Although the English Channel, a notoriously turbulent body of water, was unusually calm during this period, the prevailing weather conditions were cloudy, a dual circumstance that at once made the evacuation process easier even as it impeded German air operations. Moreover, the incessant bombing of Dunkirk itself may actually have aided evacuation operations. The exploding ordnance produced a lot of smoke and dust, which provided a screen from attack.

Not that the operation proceeded smoothly. Large numbers of men, exhausted and fearful, were confined to a relatively small area subject to artillery fire and strafing by aircraft. Confusion combined with friction between the British and the French to create a barely controlled chaos. Heroism was common enough, especially among the troops assigned to the rearguard. They voluntarily put off their evacuation to the last minute, and many knew they would never escape. Nevertheless, panic was common, as well, and officers sometimes had to brandish or even fire their pistols to prevent a disorderly rush to the boats. Despite the actions of the enemy and the sometimes ungovernable emotions of the troops, a total of 338,226 soldiers, including 140,000 French troops, were saved. Tanks, guns, vehicles, and other heavy equipment had to be abandoned—a serious loss—but the core of the British professional army had been rescued and would fight again, and yet again.

Each day of the evacuation had been an agony of suspense. As the operation went forward, there were those among the five members of Churchill's War Cabinet who argued for accepting Benito Mussolini's offer to negotiate peace. The prime minister shot back, pointing out that the odds of securing fair and decent terms from the likes of Mussolini and Hitler were "a thousand to one against" and that less would be lost by going down in honorable defeat than by surrendering. "Nations which went down fighting rose again," he declared, "but those who surrendered tamely were finished." Later, meeting with his full cabinet, Churchill explained that he had given much thought to "entering into negotiations with That Man." He was certain that Hitler would demand the fleet, naval bases, "and much else." Worst of all, England would become a "slave state." Surrender was, quite simply, a bad bargain because all was not yet lost. England still had "immense reserves and advantages." The prime minister met the eyes of his cabinet members. "I am convinced that every man of you would rise up and tear me down from my place if I were for one moment to contemplate parley or surrender. If this long island story of ours is to end at last, let it end only when each one of us lies choking in his own blood upon the ground."

Do or die. That was the choice, stark as it was. On June 4, the prime minister was able to report to Parliament the success of the Dunkirk evacuation, even as he admonished his colleagues to bear in mind that Dunkirk *was* an evacuation, and "Wars are not won by evacuations."

**"Surrender was, quite simply, a bad bargain because all was not yet lost."**

Through sheer force of will, determination, and continued mass mobilization, the fight would have to be taken to the enemy and positive victories won. To bask in the glow of the Dunkirk miracle would be to return to sleep, and Churchill would not allow Dunkirk to be regarded as a source of comfort, a warm bed on an icy night. He wanted it to serve instead as a springboard to new battles offering new opportunities for triumph, not on terms dictated by German efforts at conquest, but at times and in places of Britain's choosing.

> **Like gravity, adversity is a force.** Like gravity, it can pull one down. But, also like gravity, properly engineered, adversity can motivate, propel, and elevate. Interpretation is the key. This does not mean lying about problems and difficulties. This does not mean hiding reality or hiding from reality. Transforming adversity into a foundation for achievement requires interpreting, presenting, and exploiting the opportunities within reverses and catastrophes.

# 16

# Put Threats
# in Their Place

"We are waiting for the long-promised invasion. So are the fishes."
~Radio broadcast to the French people, London, October 21, 1940

Ask any CEO to list the roles she plays in the organization, and
*cheerleader* will very likely turn up among them. Some CEOs even
put this at the top of the list.

Obviously, in any organization, high morale and healthy enthu-
siasm are important, and the CEO who denies that she has any part
to play in stirring the spirit of her enterprise denies a significant
aspect of leadership. But far worse than this is the leader who literally mistakes herself for a cheerleader. Think about it. Take a mental
snapshot of a cheerleader—performing a well-rehearsed program of
stunts in order to stir the crowd into making loud, rhythmic noises.
There is no invitation to thought and nothing remotely resembling
inspiration. It is a show, really, and nothing more—an entertain-
ment, a diversion. When things are going badly for the team, cheerleading is even a diversion from reality.

The role of cheerleader is to mediate between mere spectators
and the team that is actually *in the game*. The role of a CEO, the
leader of an enterprise, is very different. Her constituency is the
players themselves, the competitors on the field, and if she is a

mediator, her role is to stand between the members of the enterprise and reality. The leader filters and shapes perception for the purpose of advancing the enterprise. To those who follow, the leader delivers nothing less than a picture of reality. In this, she cannot afford anything rehearsed, choreographed, or canned. Mere volume, rhythm, and diversion are not only insufficient to leadership—they are destructive.

It would be easy to describe Winston Churchill as the greatest cheerleader who ever lived. It would also be wrong, very wrong.

**"The leader filters and shapes perception for the purpose of advancing the enterprise. To those who follow, the leader delivers nothing less than a picture of reality."**

To be sure, he is justly remembered as the great rock, the strength, the inspiration for England in its most perilous hour and, indeed, served the same function for the entire free world in time of grave crisis. But the closer we look at how Churchill accomplished this mission of morale—of the national, spiritual, mental, and physical salvation of a people—the less it resembles anything like cheerleading. As his nation's chief executive officer, Churchill was above all else a master mediator, delivering to the world his vision of the reality that confronted it. The genius in this was that the vision always provided hope without for a moment denying peril. Churchill's vision of reality never failed to seem real. It never came across as fiction. It never rang hollow. It plunged fully into terror, destruction, and despair only to emerge, remarkably, with hope—the possibility, even the inevitability, of ultimate triumph.

Churchill's aim was always to put threats in their place, to ensure that, on the one hand, they were never slighted, let alone ignored, but, on the other, to keep fear of them from becoming inflated, unreasonable, and overwhelming. It was never a question of bravado, but one of management. Like people and other resources, threats, Churchill knew, could be—had to be—managed.

## The Art of the CEO

The ideal CEO does not just lead an organization of people, he manages the reality in which that organization operates. This requires confronting threats as well as delivering opportunities. It calls for managing failure as well as success. The effective CEO is a screen through which the people he leads experience the realities of the marketplace, of competition, of advances in research and development, of success, and of failure. He plants himself between the organization and the universe in which it operates and, every day, delivers a version of that universe to the organization. If his version is false—falsely pessimistic or falsely optimistic—it will neither endure nor, even in the short term, prove effective. The leader's art is to create a version of reality that is compounded of raw reality and reality interpreted for maximum productivity. It must be a balanced and believable version of the truth. But it must be given firm direction toward achieving the goals of the enterprise.

On June 4, 1940, he addressed the House of Commons in the aftermath of Operation Dynamo, the well-nigh miraculous evacuation of the British Expeditionary Force from Dunkirk. Churchill delivered a concise narration of the evacuation, lingering over heroic details. He spoke of how the "armored scythe-stroke" of the German forces "almost reached Dunkirk—almost but not quite. . . ."

The Rifle Brigade, the 60th Rifles, and the Queen Victoria's Rifles, with a battalion of British tanks and 1,000 Frenchmen, in all about four thousand strong, defended Calais to the last. The British Brigadier was given an hour to surrender. He spurned the offer, and four days of intense street fighting passed before silence reigned over Calais, which marked the end of a memorable resistance. Only thirty unwounded survivors were brought off by the Navy, and we do not know the fate of their comrades.

Their sacrifice, however, was not in vain. At least two armored divisions, which otherwise would have been turned against the British Expeditionary Force, had to be sent to overcome them. They have added another page to the glories of the light divisions. . . .

Despite heroism of this magnitude, Churchill admitted that, a week earlier, when "I asked the House to fix this afternoon as the occasion for a statement, I feared it would be my hard lot to announce the greatest military disaster in our long history. . . . The whole root and core and brain of the British Army, on which and around which we were to build, and are to build, the great British Armies in the later years of the war, seemed about to perish upon the field or to be led into an ignominious and starving captivity." But, despite intense and unremitting fire from the enemy, "the Royal Navy, with the willing help of countless merchant seamen, strained every nerve to embark the British and Allied troops" and created a "miracle of deliverance, achieved by valor, by persever-ance, by perfect discipline, by faultless service, by resource, by skill, by unconquerable fidelity. . . . The enemy was hurled back by the retreating British and French troops. He was so roughly handled that he did not hurry their departure seriously. The Royal Air Force engaged the main strength of the German Air Force and inflicted upon them losses of at least four to one; and the Navy, using nearly 1,000 ships of all kinds, carried over 335,000 men, French and British, out of the jaws of death and shame, to their native land and to the tasks which lie immediately ahead."

It was an exciting and heroic story. Indeed, the British nation was jubilant over the "miracle at Dunkirk." And this is precisely what Churchill feared.

He celebrated the success of Operation Dynamo, but he went on to warn the members of Parliament and the British people: "We must be very careful not to assign to this deliverance the attributes of a victory. Wars are not won by evacuations." With this adjustment to perception made, he adjusted it even more finely: "But there was a victory inside this deliverance, which should be noted. It was gained by the Air Force."

This was a great trial of strength between the British and German Air Forces. Can you conceive a greater objective for the Germans in the air than to make evacuation from these beaches impossible, and to sink all these ships which were displayed, almost to the extent of thousands? Could there have been an objective of greater military importance and significance for the whole purpose of the war than this? They tried hard, and they were beaten back; they were frustrated in their task. We got the Army away; and they have paid fourfold for any losses which they have inflicted. Very large formations of German aeroplanes—and we know that they are a very brave race—have turned on several occasions from the attack of one-quarter of their number of the Royal Air Force, and have dispersed in different directions. Twelve aeroplanes have been hunted by two. One aeroplane was driven into the water and cast away by the mere charge of a British aeroplane, which had no more ammunition. All of our types—the Hurricane, the Spitfire and the new Defiant—and all our pilots have been vindicated as superior to what they have at present to face.

When we consider how much greater would be our advantage in defending the air above this Island against an overseas attack, I must say that I find in these facts a sure basis upon which practical and reassuring thoughts may rest. I will pay my tribute to these young airmen. The great French Army was very largely, for the time being, cast back and disturbed by the onrush of a few thousands of armored vehicles. May it not also be that the cause of civilization itself will be defended by the skill and devotion of a few thousand airmen? There never has been, I suppose, in all the world, in all the history of war, such an opportunity for youth. The Knights of the Round Table, the Crusaders, all fall back into the past—not only distant but prosaic; these young men, going forth every morn to guard their native land and all that we stand for, holding in their hands these instruments of colossal and shattering power, of whom it may be said that

*Every morn brought forth a noble chance*
*And every chance brought forth a noble knight,*

deserve our gratitude, as do all the brave men who, in so many ways and on so many occasions, are ready, and continue ready to give life and all for their native land.

Churchill also acknowledged the heavy loss of men in the army—more than thirty thousand—but, seeking to adjust perception yet again, he noted that, against this loss, "we can set a far heavier loss certainly inflicted upon the enemy." Even now, he did not stop. True, the enemy had lost many men, but it was also the case that "our losses in material are enormous," nearly a thousand heavy guns, "all our transport, all the armored vehicles that were with the Army in the north. This loss will impose a further delay on the expansion of our military strength." How long the delay will last "depends upon the exertions which we make in this Island. An effort the like of which has never been seen in our records is now being made. Work is proceeding everywhere, night and day, Sundays and week days. Capital and Labor have cast aside their interests, rights, and customs and put them into the common stock. Already the flow of munitions has leaped forward. There is no reason why we should not in a few months overtake the sudden and serious loss that has come upon us, without retarding the development of our general program."

After this magnificent seesaw of loss and gain, Churchill warned: "our thankfulness at the escape of our Army . . . must not blind us to the fact that what has happened in France and Belgium is a colossal military disaster. The French Army has been weakened, the Belgian Army has been lost, a large part of those fortified lines upon which so much faith had been reposed is gone, many valuable mining districts and factories have passed into the enemy's possession, the whole of the Channel ports are in his hands, with all the tragic consequences that follow from that, and we must expect another blow to be struck almost immediately at us or at France."

*The next blow*—that, of course, was the great threat hanging over England. Churchill confronted it head-on: "We are told that Herr Hitler has a plan for invading the British Isles. This has often been thought of before. When Napoleon lay at Boulogne for a year with his flat-bottomed boats and his Grand Army, he was told by someone, 'There are bitter weeds in England.' There are certainly a great many more of them since the British Expeditionary Force returned."

He then set about carefully putting the threat of invasion into the perspective of context. Taking the historical view, he noted "that there has never been a period in all these long centuries of which we boast when an absolute guarantee against invasion, still less against serious raids, could have been given to our people. In the days of Napoleon the same wind which would have carried his transports across the Channel might have driven away the blockading fleet. There was always the chance, and it is that chance which has excited and befooled the imaginations of many Continental tyrants." In the present crisis, Churchill acknowledged, we "are assured that novel methods will be adopted, and when we see the originality of malice, the ingenuity of aggression, which our enemy displays, we may certainly prepare ourselves for every kind of novel stratagem and every kind of brutal and treacherous maneuver." Admitting this, he declared nevertheless his "full confidence that if all do their duty, if nothing is neglected, and if the best arrangements are made, as they are being made, we shall prove ourselves once again able to defend our Island home, to ride out the storm of war, and to outlive the menace of tyranny, if necessary for years, if necessary alone."

## Make the Unfamiliar Familiar

Churchill's consuming interest in history served him well as a leader. He knew that the greatest—and the most destructively paralyzing—fear was fear of the unknown. What horrors would the Germans visit upon England when (for it seemed inevitable) they invaded? Churchill did not want to minimize the threat, which was very real; however, he sought to put it in a manageable context by revealing it in the light of history. England had been threatened many times in the past, and by very powerful enemies. It had always successfully resisted invasion. Churchill understood that one of the most potent instruments a leader possesses is precedent. Select the right precedent, and you make the unknown at least more or less known. To the degree that you can reduce an unknown quantity, you also diminish the most powerful fuel that sustains fear.

When Churchill, at age thirteen, enrolled at Harrow, he was very much attracted to the school band—particularly, the kettle drum, which he longed to be allowed to play. When that was denied him, however, he declared in a 1945 speech to the boys of his alma mater, he thought he "might try to be the conductor." In his speech to the boys, Churchill joked: "Eventually, after a great deal of perseverance, I rose to be conductor of quite a considerable band. It was a very large band and it played with very strange and formidable instruments, and the roar and thunder of its music resounded throughout the world." Of course, Churchill was referring to his role as wartime prime minister, but the fact was that he really did, in adult life, become a conductor. In his greatest speeches, he summoned and shaped emotion in the manner of a maestro. Nowhere is this more in evidence than in his great speech of June 4, 1940. As he approached its end, he built to a stirring emotional climax as he spoke of outliving the menace of tyranny—then, great conductor that he was, he molded his words into a tantalizing diminuendo, drawing back from the swelling chords he had sounded—"if all do their duty . . . we shall prove ourselves once again able to defend our Island home, to ride out the storm of war, and to outlive the menace of tyranny, if necessary for years, if necessary alone"—by quietly observing: "At any rate, that is what we are going to try to do. That is the resolve of His Majesty's Government—every man of them. That is the will of Parliament and the nation." Making his musical effect smaller, quieter, had the effect of drawing the listener—even the reader—closer, so that what came next burst upon his listeners in a glorious, thundering finish:

> Even though large tracts of Europe and many old and famous States have fallen or may fall into the grip of the Gestapo and all the odious apparatus of Nazi rule, we shall not flag or fail. We shall go on to the end, we shall fight in France, we shall fight on the seas and oceans, we shall fight with growing confidence and growing strength in the air, we shall defend our Island, whatever the cost may be, we shall fight on the beaches, we shall fight on the landing grounds, we shall fight in the fields and in the streets, we shall fight in the hills; we shall never surrender, and even if, which I do not for a moment believe, this Island or a large part of it were subjugated and starving, then our Empire beyond the seas, armed and guarded by the British Fleet, would carry on the struggle, until, in God's good time, the New World, with all its power and might, steps forth to the rescue and the liberation of the old.

Grim and joyous, and utterly realistic—in short, eminently "doable." Churchill vowed to fight on, fight everywhere, fight in every conceivable way. Yet he admitted the possibility that the

British Isles might nevertheless be lost. Should that happen, however unlikely, even *then*, even in this worst possible case, the fight would continue by other means, and it would be carried on until the moment (which he presented as inevitable) that the United States—still neutral in 1940—came to the rescue of Britain and the rest of Europe. Churchill ended on a glorious note, but by no means on a note requiring a miracle to carry and sustain it. The summons to duty and hope and glory at the end of this speech were also a serious and sober assessment of the current dire crisis and its likely triumphant resolution. Winston Churchill was first and last a leader, but never, not for a moment, a mere cheerleader.

> **The words *leader* and *cheerleader*** have the root word *leader* in common, but that is where the similarity ends. A big part of a leader's job is to mediate reality for the members of the enterprise he leads. This means continually presenting the situation—the marketplace, the competitive environment, the state of the art in a particular industry, and so on—in the most productive light possible. It does not mean distorting reality, and it certainly does not mean falsifying reality. It means recognizing and explaining threats as well as opportunities. It means presenting the situation in a way that exhibits all of the potential for advance, advantage, and profit, as well as risk and outright menace. It means presenting reality such that the enterprise can actively and successfully engage it, work with it, shape it, contribute to it, compete in it, and ultimately win in it.

# 17

# Put the Highest Value
# on Rock Bottom

"The British nation is unique in this respect.
They are the only people who like to be told how bad things are,
who like to be told the worst."
~ Speech, House of Commons, June 10, 1941

After less than six weeks in combat, France surrendered to
Germany on June 17, 1940. What made it worse—if such a thing
could be made worse—was the identity of the figure who tendered
the surrender, Marshal Henri Philippe Pétain, the hero of World
War I who had immortalized himself by his defiant defense of
Verdun in 1916, declaring his resolution to resist the German
onslaught with the phrase, *Ils ne passeront pas* ("They shall not pass").
Churchill wasted no time in broadcasting the news to the British
people: "The news from France is very bad," he began, and what he
chose to say next could have taken his message in any direction. A
lesser leader would have wailed in protest against this turn of events
that left Britain standing alone against the German juggernaut.
Instead, he focused on the "gallant French people who have fallen
into this terrible misfortune." And then he moved on: "Nothing will
alter our feelings towards them or our faith that the genius of France
will rise again." And he moved on yet further:

What has happened in France makes no difference to our actions and purpose. We have become the sole champions now in arms to defend the world cause. We shall do our best to be worthy of this high honour. We shall defend our island home, and with the British Empire we shall fight on unconquerable until the curse of Hitler is lifted from the brows of mankind. We are sure that in the end all will come right.

At rock bottom, Winston Churchill found the solid ground from which he could lead the fight. In this brief broadcast of "very bad" news, he sought to show the British people just how sure their footing now was. The great thing about rock bottom is that you cannot sink deeper.

On the day after he delivered this broadcast, Churchill addressed a packed House of Commons. His very first sentence ratified the unspoken bargain he had made with the

**"The great thing about rock bottom is that you cannot sink deeper."**

British government and the British people—to tell them the truth, even when he was obliged to speak from the depths: "I spoke the other day of the colossal military disaster which occurred when the French High Command failed to withdraw the northern armies from Belgium at the moment when they knew that the French front was decisively broken at Sedan and on the Meuse." Then he plunged into the gory details:

This delay entailed the loss of fifteen or sixteen French divisions and threw out of action for the critical period the whole of the British Expeditionary Force. Our Army and 120,000 French troops were indeed rescued by the British Navy from Dunkirk but only with the loss of their cannon, vehicles and modern equipment. This loss inevitably took some weeks to repair, and in the first two of those weeks the battle in France has been lost.

He continued with more of the particulars:

When we consider the heroic resistance made by the French Army against heavy odds in this battle, the enormous losses inflicted upon the enemy and the evident exhaustion of the enemy, it may well be the thought that these twenty-five divisions of the best-trained and best-equipped troops might have turned the scale. However, General Weygand had to fight without them. Only three British divisions or their equivalent were able to stand in the line with their French comrades. They have suffered severely, but they have fought well. We sent every man we could to France as fast as we could re-equip and transport their formations.

I am not reciting these facts for the purpose of recrimination. That I judge to be utterly futile and even harmful. We cannot afford it. I recite them in order to explain why it was we did not have, as we could have had, between twelve and fourteen British divisions fighting in the line in this great battle instead of only three.

The details added to the heartbreak—the aspect of *what-might-have-been-if-only*. Having stated this, acknowledged this, and explained this, Churchill refused to wallow in it. Instead, he set the whole catastrophe out of the way: "Now I put all this aside. I put it on the shelf, from which the historians, when they have time, will select their documents to tell their stories. We have to think of the future and not of the past."

## In a Storm

Good leaders learn from the past. Great leaders learn from the past, and then leave it behind. Experience should serve as a guide, not an anchor. Use what you learn not in a vain effort to replay the past—it can't be done—but to shape the future. As any competent sailor knows, in a storm, some cargo is valuable enough to keep on board while some has to be jettisoned. The trick is in knowing which is which.

There is one great truth about rock bottom. You cannot, you *must* not, stay there. Hit the cellar, and there is only one thing to do. You rise. "Of this, I am quite sure, that if we open a quarrel between the past and the present, we shall find that we have lost the future." And so he proceeded to the future: "The disastrous military events which have happened during the past fortnight have not come to me with any sense of surprise. Indeed, I indicated a fortnight ago as clearly as I could to the House that the worst possibilities were open; and I made it perfectly clear then that whatever happened in France would make no difference to the resolve of Britain and the British Empire to fight on, 'if necessary for years, if necessary alone.'"

**"There is one great truth about rock bottom. You cannot, you must not, stay there. Hit the cellar, and there is only one thing to do. You rise."**

Defiance and determination were cornerstones of the Churchill doctrine of war fighting, but he never allowed it to appear as if he were tilting at windmills. *Will* must be backed by *means*. Churchill explained that "seven-eighths of the troops we have sent to France since the beginning of the war—that is to say, about 350,000 out of 400,000 men—are safely back in this country. . . . a very large and powerful military force. This force comprises all our best-trained and our finest troops, including scores of thousands of those who have already measured their quality against the Germans and found themselves at no disadvantage. We have under arms at the present time in this Island over a million and a quarter men. Behind these we have the Local Defense Volunteers, numbering half a million. . . ." Churchill admitted that there were not enough weapons to arm all of these volunteers immediately, but "very large additions to our weapons" would be coming "in the near future." From this discussion, he went on to take an inventory of the Royal Navy, which, he pointed out, was confident in its "ability to prevent a mass invasion." He then addressed the "great question of invasion from the air, and of the impending struggle between the British and German Air Forces."

> It seems quite clear that no invasion on a scale beyond the capacity of our land forces to crush speedily is likely to take place from the air until our Air Force has been definitely overpowered. In the meantime, there may be raids by parachute troops and attempted descents of airborne soldiers. We should be able to give those gentry a warm reception both in the air and on the ground, if they reach it in any condition to continue the dispute. But the great question is: Can we break Hitler's air weapon?

As the members of the House well knew, Churchill had frequently appealed to Parliament to build an air force to match the expanding air force of Germany. This had been the burden of many of his speeches during the late 1930s, when he languished outside of the Baldwin and Chamberlain governments. He could very well have savored an I-told-you-so moment, but he pointedly avoided doing so:

> Now, of course, it is a very great pity that we have not got an Air Force at least equal to that of the most powerful enemy within striking distance of these shores. But we have a very powerful Air Force which has proved itself far superior in quality, both in men and in many types of machine, to what we have met so far in the numerous and fierce air battles which have been fought with the Germans.

The prime minister was at pains to demonstrate—by personal example—that now was no time for partisan finger pointing.

## I Told You So

Few things are sweeter than the arrival of an I-told-you-so moment. And few occasions demand greater self-restraint. Resist the temptation to rub another's nose in the fruits of his error. Leadership is not about beating down colleagues and competitors. It is about carrying the common enterprise forward productively. Keep your mouth shut and your eye on that prize.

Churchill went on to explain the advantages of defending one's homeland, of fighting on and flying over friendly soil. Nevertheless, he did not overlook "the danger of bombing attacks, which will certainly be made very soon upon us by the bomber forces of the enemy." He conceded that "the German bomber force is superior in numbers to ours," but he pointed out that "we have a very large bomber force also, which we shall use to strike at military targets in Germany without intermission." He declared that he had no intention of underrating "the severity of the ordeal which lies before us; but I believe our countrymen will show themselves capable of standing up to it, like the brave men of Barcelona, and will be able to stand up to it, and carry on in spite of it."

*"The RAF is the cavalry of modern war."*
~ Quoted in Peter Stansky's *Churchill: A Profile,* 1973

Churchill wanted above all else to give "the House and the country some indication of the solid, practical grounds upon which we base our inflexible resolve to continue the war." He pointed out that there were some very brave people who declared, "Never mind. Win or lose, sink or swim, better die than submit to tyranny—and such a tyranny." And he agreed with them—but only to a point. He assured his listeners "that our professional advisers of the three Services unitedly advise that we should carry on the war, and that there are good and reasonable hopes of final victory." He was not proposing a last stand, gallant and futile. It was not *do and die* but *do and win*. But how? How, with France and every other friendly European power fallen to Hitler? How could there be a *reasonable* hope for final victory?

We may now ask ourselves: In what way has our position worsened since the beginning of the war? It has worsened by the fact that the Germans have conquered a large part of the coast line of Western Europe, and many small countries have been overrun by them. This aggravates the possibilities of air attack and adds to our naval preoccupations. It in no way diminishes, but on the contrary definitely increases, the power of our long-distance blockade. Similarly, the entrance of Italy into the war increases the power of our long-distance blockade. We have stopped the worst leak by that. We do not know whether military resistance will come to an end in France or not, but should it do so, then of course the Germans will be able to concentrate their forces, both military and industrial, upon us. But for the reasons I have given to the House these will not be found so easy to apply. If invasion has become more imminent, as no doubt it has, we, being relieved from the task of maintaining a large army in France, have far larger and more efficient forces to meet it.

With France out of the war, Churchill argued, we have more of our troops available to defend England. That was certainly one way of looking at it. But what of Hitler's war machine?

If Hitler can bring under his despotic control the industries of the countries he has conquered, this will add greatly to his already vast armament output. On the other hand, this will not happen immediately, and we are now assured of immense, continuous and increasing support in supplies and munitions of all kinds from the United States; and especially of aeroplanes and pilots from the Dominions and across the oceans coming from regions which are beyond the reach of enemy bombers.

Churchill went on to speak of the strain Germany was under to occupy and defend all of the vast territory it had captured. Moreover, we "must not forget that from the moment when we declared war on the 3rd September it was always possible for Germany to turn all her Air Force upon this country, together with any other devices of invasion she might conceive, and that France could have done little or nothing to prevent her doing so." What this means is that Britain has lived under the danger of invasion, "in principle and in a slightly modified form, during all these months"– months in which "we have enormously improved our methods of defense, and we have learned what we had no right to assume at the beginning, namely, that the individual aircraft and the individual British pilot have a sure and definite superiority." Adding all of this up on a "dread balance-sheet and contemplating our dangers with a disillusioned eye, I see great reason for intense vigilance and exertion, but none whatever for panic or despair."

*"Our defeats are but stepping stones to victory, and his [Hitler's] victories are but stepping stones to ruin."*

~Speech, Edinburgh, October 12, 1942

The fact nevertheless remained, Churchill admitted, that the Battle of France had been lost and that the Battle of Britain was about to begin. As we will see in the next chapter, Churchill saw this not as a doom but as an opportunity for the British people to live "their finest hour."

It was the hour in which the ascent from rock bottom begins, the point from which there is only a single alternative to inaction: a move up. Expressed this way, it was not an hour of doubt, but one of certainty. And, Churchill understood, the virtue of certainty was that it, by definition, vanquished fear of the unknown—of all fears the very greatest. Rock bottom? Winston Churchill intended to make the very most of being there.

> **Pollyanna, the star of early** twentieth-century children's literature whose incurable optimism made her see bad as good and disappointment as delight, would have made a very poor leader, not to mention an insufferable one. Churchill was no Pollyanna, but he did see the advantage of disadvantage. Unlike Pollyanna, he did not mistake defeat for victory, but he did his utmost to exploit defeat as a means to victory. Rock bottom makes a foundation so strong that the loftiest structures can be raised upon it.

# 18

# Practice the Craft
# of Conscience

"Let us . . . so bear ourselves that if the British Empire
and its Commonwealth last for a thousand years, men will still say:
'This was their finest hour.'"
~ Speech to the House of Commons, June 18, 1940

*Conscience* is one of those words with a quaint, even archaic ring. We use it as parents talking to our children, and then, chances are, when our children are grown and have left the house, we put it away. We don't know quite what to do with the word or the concept the word denotes. Ostensibly, conscience is a good thing, of course, an honorable faculty of mind that keeps us ethical. Yet, if we are completely honest with ourselves, there are times when having a conscience seems much the same as carrying just so much excess baggage. It slows us down. Who doesn't (at least at times) imagine what it would be like to be "free" of conscience? In business, especially, there is much talk about ethics, but it is the ruthless, even amoral CEOs and entrepreneurs who are often most envied, if not admired. We often speak of a "killer instinct" peculiar to very successful people. Let's face it, in many business environments, a conscience is regarded as dead weight.

Much the same has been true in certain governments and certain nations. It seems, for example, absurd to speak of Adolf Hitler's conscience. Indeed, all of the Nazi leaders deliberately sought to displace the conventional conscience—call it human decency—with a doctrine of conquest and racial destiny. In assigning members of his infamous SS to carry out the so-called Final Solution, the mass murder of Jews in extermination camps, Heinrich Himmler spoke of the necessity of conquering "normal" human feelings—the conscience—in order to better serve the needs of the state.

## Ethical Ends Require Ethical Means

There is a foolproof way of assessing the ethics of any objective. Assess the ethics of the means necessary to achieve that end. Any enterprise that tolerates, let alone requires, unethical acts is an unethical organization, however ethical it may believe its purposes and its goals are. Conscience does not simply materialize at the end of a process. It is active throughout the process. It cannot be suspended without sacrificing ethics. If you set ethical goals for your organization, they can only be reached by ethical means.

The history of the Nazi regime proves that it is possible to pervert anything. It is possible not merely to portray possession of a conscience as useless, but even as downright treasonous, a crime against the state. There is a temptation in war, especially at a critical juncture of war, when defeat looms as a very real possibility, even for ethical leaders to counsel ruthlessness, an abandonment of decency, a jettisoning of conscience. Certainly, Churchill's nation faced such a crisis early in World War II. What possible use could conscience be in a confrontation with the twentieth-century equivalent of a barbarian invasion?

"If we are completely honest with ourselves, there are times when having a conscience seems much the same as carrying just so much excess baggage. It slows us down."

*"All the greatest things are simple, and many can be expressed in a single word: Freedom: Justice: Honour: Duty: Mercy: Hope."*
~ Speech, Royal Albert Hall, London, May 14, 1947

As it turned out, the question, for Winston Churchill, was not rhetorical. For him, the answer was both obvious and of urgent importance. In the fight against Hitler, *conscience* would be the ultimate weapon.

As Churchill conceived of it, conscience was no Sunday school lesson, pleasant but disposable. It was the heart of the identity he shared with his people. He had grown up steeped in a concept of what must be termed *Britishness*, an intimate and all-pervasive identification with certain national values compounded of courage, essential decency, indomitable tenacity, and a commitment to duty. His sense of this identity formed his conscience. More than a personal conscience, it was a collective conscience, what he, as an Englishman, believed and what he believed he stood for. There are some feelings we have that seem to set us apart from others, and there are some feelings that connect us to others. The very strongest feeling Churchill possessed was clearly of the latter kind. He was confident that the structure and content of his own individual conscience were those of the British nation as a whole. He identified completely with his country, and his country—to a remarkable degree—identified with him.

This shared conscience, a shared identity, is the reason why the themes of duty and sacrifice resounded so effectively in Churchill's wartime speeches. Animated by the impulses that drove these themes, Churchill in the deepest sense spoke the language of his people, and because he spoke it so powerfully, he expressed the national identity more thoroughly and more meaningfully than did the very people to whom and for whom he spoke.

When Churchill addressed the House of Commons on June 18, 1940, in the aftermath of Dunkirk and in the full expectation of a massive German invasion, he did not hesitate to describe the outcome of the Battle of France as "disastrous." He spoke of bombing attacks as something that "will certainly be made very soon upon us" and invasion as "imminent." He wanted to be absolutely clear: The British people were facing the worst crisis in their modern history, perhaps in all their history. His purpose in this was not to instill fear, but to present reality—and, because he knew that he shared a very special conscience with his people—he sought to present the danger as an opportunity.

> **"His purpose in this was not to instill fear, but to present reality—and, because he knew that he shared a very special conscience with his people— he sought to present the danger as an opportunity."**

Noting the grim and simple fact that the "Battle of France is over," Churchill launched into one of his most celebrated perorations: "I expect that the Battle of Britain is about to begin. Upon this battle depends the survival of Christian civilization. Upon it depends our own British life, and the long continuity of our institutions and our Empire."

A leader defines the values of the enterprise. For Churchill, these values came in a cluster of close equivalents:

> *Christian civilization*
> *Our own British life*
> *The continuity of our institutions*

In sum, the values of the British enterprise were the "Britishness" embodied in the conscience of each and every Briton. It was this identity that was now in peril and very much at stake.

How would Hitler attack these cherished values? Churchill answered in a single sentence: "The whole fury and might of the enemy must very soon be turned on us." The reason for this, he explained, was that "Hitler knows that he will have to break us in this Island or lose the war." As Churchill saw it, Hitler was well aware of how hard it would be to "break" a people possessed of so strong a conscience—a conscience powerful enough to drive Britons not merely to save themselves, but to save the free world: "If we can stand up to him, all Europe may be free and the life of the world may move forward into broad, sunlit uplands."

*"The great struggles in history have been won by superior will-power wresting victory in the teeth of odds or upon the narrowest of margins."*
~ Speech, House of Commons, June 25, 1941

Hitler would unleash his fury upon Britain precisely because it was a righteous nation animated by a powerful moral identity, a great collective conscience. The challenge Churchill next issued to Parliament and the British people was less a question of whether or not they could defeat Hitler as it was whether or not they would be worthy of acting on what they knew to be the dictates of their own conscience. The consequence of failing to be worthy was nothing less than the onslaught of chaos—the absence of values, a great and horrible void where once the British identity had been: "But if we fail, then the whole world, including the United States, including all that we have known and cared for, will sink into the abyss of a new Dark Age made more sinister, and perhaps more protracted, by the lights of perverted science."

*"I have not become the King's First Minister in order to preside over the liqui-dation of the British Empire."*
~ Speech, Mansion House, London, November 10, 1942

A leader must sell the members of his enterprise on a chosen course of action. To do this, he must on the one hand vividly render the benefits of the course he promotes, and, on the other hand, with equal vividness, he must paint the consequences of failing in that chosen course. This done, there is nothing left but to point the direction *away* from failure. For Churchill, it was to run into the embrace of conscience itself: "Let us therefore brace ourselves to our duties, and so bear ourselves that, if the British Empire and its Commonwealth last for a thousand years, men will still say, 'This was their finest hour.'"

How to defeat Hitler? How to save Britain and the world? Churchill's answer was simply *to be British*—to act in accordance with the dictates of a conscience born of a profound national identity, a weapon so powerful that Adolf Hitler himself knew to fear it.

**Winston Churchill felt a special power** in the British identity, which he exploited to lead his nation through survival and into victory by appealing to the manifestation of that identity as a collective national conscience. In truth, there was nothing magical about "Britishness." Any worthwhile enterprise is driven by certain values that constitute its identity and, therefore, the conscience of its members. Effective leadership requires a keen awareness of this identity and calls for skill in the craft of conscience, motivating and guiding the organization in accordance with the connection each member has with its core values. The effective leader does not rely on conscience in some abstract or generalized sense, but targets a specific commitment to the organization, an identification with its values. It is this identification that drives a willingness to do one's *duty*, to perform voluntarily and enthusiastically the deeds each individual owes to the common enterprise. In any truly high-stakes endeavor, conscience is not an appendix—useless, annoying, better shed—but a vital organ.

# 19

# Defy Them

"You do your worst—and we will do our best."
~ Churchill to Hitler and his "grisly gang,"
in a speech at County Hall, London, July 14, 1941

Winston Churchill was a romantic, who saw in war a vast theater for the cultivation and display of glory and courage. At the very same time and in the very same degree, he was a realist, who regarded war as an obscenity productive of nothing more than devastation and heartbreak. The romantic in him looked to the past for inspiration, to ages of bygone chivalry. The realist looked to the present and to the future. Churchill loved to read the science fiction of H. G. Wells, who, in the 1920s, had forecast war waged from the skies. He leavened this reading by consultation with a close friend, an Oxford University professor named Frederick Lindemann, who, during World War I, had worked at the Royal Air Force Laboratory at Farnborough, and went on to study the potential and possibilities of aerial warfare, especially high-explosive bombardment. In 1924, Churchill asked Lindemann to review some of his own ideas on aircraft and bombs. The result was an article Churchill wrote for a popular magazine, *Nash's Pall Mall*, in which he described a "bomb no bigger than an orange," which might "possess a secret power to destroy whole blocks of buildings—nay to concentrate the force of a thousand tons of cordite and blast a township at a stroke." He went on to speculate that even the explosives currently available could someday be "guided automatically in flying machines by wireless or other rays, without a human pilot, in ceaseless procession upon a hostile city. . . ."

*"War, which used to be cruel and magnificent, has now become cruel and squalid. In fact it has been completely spoilt. It is all the fault of Democracy and Science."*

~ *My Early Life,* 1930

Sixteen years after he published the article, from August 1940 to May 1941, the horrific future he predicted began to arrive, as the German air force, the Luftwaffe, rained bombs on London and other English cities night and day. Less than four years after this first round of what Londoners and others took to calling the *Blitz*—short for the German word *Blitzkrieg,* "Lightning War"—Churchill's visionary prediction became even more literally a reality, as Hitler hurled against England pilot-less bombs and rockets, the V-1s and V-2s. Yet another element of the *Pall Mall* article also became fact before World War II ended: the creation and use of a single bomb possessing a "secret power" that gave it the force of thousands of tons of ordinary explosives, enough to "blast a township at a stroke." Fortunately, for London, it was used not by the Germans, but by the Americans, and the targets were the Japanese cities of Hiroshima and Nagasaki.

But the bombing of the first Blitz, from August of 1940 to May of 1941, using piloted aircraft and ordinary high-explosive bombs, was terrible enough. The intention of the campaign was to demoralize the British people and erode their will to continue to make war. The cost was staggering. Some 43,000 civilians were killed and another 139,000 injured. Infrastructure damage was catastrophic, with an estimated 20 percent of London reduced to ruins. The Germans learned to combine high-explosive bombing with incendiary attacks, the high explosives creating rubble, the incendiary bombs setting it ablaze, so that great fires consumed large portions of the city. On the night of May 10/11, 1941, the worst night of the Blitz, 550 enemy bombers dropped 100,000 bombs on London, killing some 1,500 people. The Houses of Parliament—the building known as the Palace of Westminster—was hit fourteen times during the Blitz, and on the night of May 10/11, 1941, the chamber of the House of Commons was completely destroyed, killing three people there. Buckingham Palace, seat of the king and queen, was also seriously damaged in the raids, though it was London's poorer and working-class neighborhoods that seemed always to get the very worst of it. In addition to London, the key industrial and port cities of Southampton, Birmingham, Liverpool, Bristol, Plymouth, and Coventry were heavily bombed. The celebrated Coventry Cathedral, built between the late fourteenth and early fifteenth centuries, was almost totally flattened in the Coventry Blitz of November 14, 1940. Only the Cathedral's tower, spire, and outer wall survived.

> **"The Germans learned to combine high-explosive bombing with incendiary attacks, the high explosives creating rubble, the incendiary bombs setting it ablaze, so that great fires consumed large portions of the city."**

Day after day, night after night, the raids continued. In his June 18 speech to Parliament, two months before the Blitz began, Churchill had sought to steel his countrymen to what he knew would be a rain of ruin from the skies, "the . . . bombing attacks, which will certainly be made very soon upon us by the bomber forces of the enemy." He assured the Commons and the nation, "I do not at all underrate the severity of the ordeal which lies before us," but he continued: "I believe our countrymen will show themselves capable of standing up to it . . . and will be able to stand up to it, and carry on in spite of it, at least as well as any other people in the world. Much will depend upon this; every man and every woman will have the chance to show the finest qualities of their race, and render the highest service to their cause." Churchill himself remained in London throughout the Blitz. At every opportunity, he visited neighborhoods that had been bombed. He made certain that his fellow Londoners saw him as one of them. They knew he would have been justified in removing himself and his family from the danger. They also knew that he chose not to do that, but to stay in the beleaguered city with those who suffered and died.

> **"Churchill himself remained in London throughout the Blitz. At every opportunity, he visited neighborhoods that had been bombed. He made certain that his fellow Londoners saw him as one of them."**

But, throughout the Blitz, Churchill did much more than comfort the suffering and the families of the dead. He told Londoners—and the people of the other English cities under attack—that they were not merely struggling to survive; they were helping to win the war. Churchill knew that the raids on England's cities were exacting a high cost on the German Luftwaffe, which lost about 600 bombers, mostly shot down by the skillful and daring fighter pilots of the RAF. This loss rate represented only about 1.5 percent of the bombing sorties flown, but it was substantial nevertheless. Far more important, as Churchill knew, was this: To the extent that Hitler devoted his air force to bombing cities, he sacrificed his chance to destroy RAF bases and aircraft on the ground. By concentrating on civilian targets, he left key military targets intact, and as long as there were British planes and pilots to oppose the Luftwaffe, Churchill believed, the Luftwaffe would lose. By enduring the raids, horrific as they were, Londoners and others were encouraging the German air force to spend itself without achieving the result it sought: the destruction of England's ability to resist an invasion. The failure to destroy the RAF was a strategic blunder from which neither the Luftwaffe nor the German war effort would ever recover.

## Sacrifice and Strategy

Symbolism is important, but strategic purpose must never be subordinated to it. Hitler made the mistake of trying to take personal vengeance on the people of England, thus sacrificing the most important military objectives. Churchill, in contrast, never called for sacrifice without strategic purpose. The defiant attitude of Londoners carried great symbolic importance, but far more important was the fact that by defying German bombs, the heroic people of Britain, encouraged and guided by their prime minister, lured Hitler into exhausting his air force. The Blitz inflicted great suffering and loss, but unquestionably contributed to the Allied victory over Nazi Germany.

And there was an even greater cost to Germany. The world saw the massive bombing of civilians as terrorism of the most brutal kind. In neutral nations—especially the United States—the spectacle greatly increased sympathy for the British cause. Reporters on the scene, including, most famously, broadcast journalist Edward R. Murrow, delivered eyewitness reports from the heart of the Blitz—Murrow's broadcasts always beginning with the trademark line, "*This* is London"—and portrayed both the suffering and the indomitable spirit of the British nation, which seemed to be concentrated in the person of its leader, Winston Churchill. In the very midst of apparent victimization and even defeat, the prime minister of a government unable to keep its citizens from harm, Churchill nevertheless led Britain to a moral victory that also produced the strategic result of winning support from the United States.

> *"Learn to get used to it. Eels get used to skinning."*
> ~ On being bombed, from notes for a June 20, 1940, speech

On July 14, 1941, after what proved to be the end of the first Blitz, Churchill delivered a speech from London's County Hall. It was intended as a tribute to the heroism of Londoners, but it was far more than mere praise. It was an assessment of achievement and a prescription for victory. He began by defining the Blitz not as some great offensive operation, but as a craven act born of the desperation of failure: Hitler, "defeated in his invasion plans by the RAF, . . . declared his intention to raze the cities of Britain to the ground." This opening put the terror of the Blitz in an entirely new light. Churchill revealed it not as a legitimate, rational tactic of war, but as a crime committed by a desperate and doomed criminal. Yet Churchill's genius as a communicator never relied on merely denigrating an enemy. His speech showed that he was fully cognizant of the very real enormity of Hitler's campaign of terror from the air.

First and foremost was the fear of the unknown. "None of us," Churchill admitted, "quite knew what would be the result of a concentrated and prolonged bombardment of this vast centre of population." He went on to paint a picture of eight million inhabitants of the Thames Valley, all of them "dependent from day to day upon light, heat, power, water, sewerage, and communications on the most complicated scale." He recounted with perfect candor how anxiety concerning "Public order, public health . . . all the essential services . . . the shelter of millions of men and women, and the removal of the dead and wounded from the shattered buildings; the care of the wounded when hospitals were being ruthlessly bombed, and the provision for the homeless—sometimes amounting to many thousands in a single day, and accumulating to many more after three or four days of successive attacks" had at first "seemed overwhelming." He admitted that, before the war, plans had been made to move the government out of London and that many officials saw "a very great danger that a sudden wave of panic might send millions of people crowding out into the countryside along the roads."

These fears were real, but, Churchill implied, they were fears of the unknown. When the worst actually happened, when the bombings actually began, and when the unknown was transformed into very real devastation, something arose to displace the fear. "Well," he told his London audience, "when you are doing your duty and you are sure of that, you need not worry too much about the dangers and consequences."

## Define the Enterprise

The leader of any enterprise constantly works to define the enterprise, to shape the perception of the people who are a part of it. Effective leaders do not shove, force, push, yank, pull, berate, or manhandle. They guide, firmly, yet also gently enough, so that those who are guided feel that they are also acting in response to their own will.

Again, vintage Churchill. As a leader, he communicated the reality of the problems, the dangers, the consequences, the very real pain and loss, and he communicated these frankly, vividly, and unsparingly. But he always and invariably found and revealed the counterweight to the horror and the fear. Here, he expressed it in the single word *duty*.

Yet he did not claim that duty magically vanquished all anxiety and doubt. Churchill understood that words were powerful, but he also knew that they could very easily become hollow and brittle if you forgot or, worse yet, denied the realities that lay behind them. He admitted that, even armed with a sense of duty, which he believed he shared with the rest of the British people, he had still suffered doubt and anxiety. "I must admit that I greatly feared injury to our public services, I feared the ravages of fire, I feared the dislocation of life and the stoppage of work, I feared epidemics of serious disease or even pestilence. . . ." He made it real, as real as his own life, as real as his own experience:

I remember one winter evening travelling to a railway station—which still worked—on my way north to visit troops. It was cold and raining. Darkness had almost fallen on the blacked-out

streets. I saw everywhere long queues of people, among them
hundreds of young girls in their silk stockings and high-heeled
shoes, who had worked hard all day and were waiting for bus
after bus, which came by already overcrowded, in the hope of
reaching their homes for the night. When at that moment the
doleful wail of the siren betokened the approach of the German
bombers, I confess to you that my heart bled for London and
the Londoners.

He continued: "All this sort of thing went on for more than four
months with hardly any intermission. . . . There were grievous com-
plaints about the shelters and about conditions in them. Water was
cut off, railways were cut or broken, large districts were destroyed by
fire, twenty thousand people were killed, and many more thousands
were wounded." Death, devastation, terror, horror—"the whole fury
of the Hun" loosed upon London. "But"—and upon this conjunc-
tion, Churchill lifted both his speech and the fate of his nation—

But there was one thing about which there was never any doubt.
The courage, the unconquerable grit and stamina of the
Londoners showed itself from the very onset. Without that all
would have failed. Upon that rock, all stood unshakable. All the
public services were carried on, and all the intricate arrangements, far-reaching details, involving the daily lives of so many
millions, were carried out, improvised, elaborated, and perfected
in the very teeth of the cruel and devastating storm.

As he gave this speech in July 1941, Churchill and his audience
were well aware that the war was far from over, and they had every
reason to believe that the Blitz, despite the present lull, would
resume. The speaker did not ignore this. "If the storm is to renew
itself," he declared, "London will be ready, London will not flinch,
London can take it again."

*London can take it again.* It was an expression of confidence as well
as an exhortation to endurance, but it was no appeal to masochism.
It was, rather, Churchill's effort to mine a source of energy he had
discovered long ago in himself and, in the very teeth of the Blitz,
among his fellow Britons. It was defiance.

> We ask no favours of the enemy. We seek from them no com-
> punction. On the contrary, if tonight our people were asked to
> cast their vote whether a convention should be entered into to
> stop the bombing of cities, the overwhelming majority would cry,
> "No, we will mete out to them the measure, and more than the
> measure, that they have meted out to us." The people with one
> voice would say: "You have committed every crime under the
> sun. Where you have been the least resisted there you have been
> the most brutal. It was you who began the indiscriminate
> bombing. We will have no truce or parley with you, or the grisly
> gang who work your wicked will. You do your worst—and we will
> do our best." Perhaps it may be our turn soon; perhaps it may be
> our turn now.

Wielding the great power of words, Churchill remained wary of
their hollowness the instant they were divorced from reality. As he
admitted the darkest side of that reality at the outset of his speech,
so he returned to it at its conclusion. "We live in a terrible epoch of
the human story," he acknowledged, "but we believe there is a broad
and sure justice running through its theme. It is time that the enemy
should be made to suffer in their own homelands something of the
torment they have let loose upon their neighbours and upon the
world." From horrific crime, through resolution, through defiance,
through the reality of terror, Churchill led his listeners—and his
nation—to a vision of hope, which he then bolstered with the reality
of the changing military situation: "We believe it to be in our power
to keep this process going, on a steadily rising tide, month after

month, year after year, until they are either extirpated by us or, better still, torn to pieces by their own people."

It is asking a great deal of a people to stay strong and keep the faith when they are on the receiving end of high explosives and vicious incendiaries dropped in vast quantity from the sky. Churchill knew this, and having constructed a platform of hope, he reinforced it with some of the hard military particulars. Even as he did this, however, he had more danger and death to offer and more sacrifice to ask for. Defiance would mean victory, he insisted, but defiance would have a price. "It is for this reason that I must ask you to be prepared for vehement counter-action by the enemy." This time, though, Churchill promised that it would not be so one-sided. "Our methods of dealing with them have steadily improved. They no longer relish their trips to our shores." Nevertheless—

> "From horrific crime, through resolution, through defiance, through the reality of terror, Churchill led his listeners—and his nation—to a vision of hope, which he then bolstered with the reality of the changing military situation."

We do not expect to hit without being hit back, and we intend with every week that passes to hit harder. Prepare yourselves, then, my friends and comrades, for this renewal of your exertions. We shall never turn from our purpose, however sombre the road, however grievous the cost, because we know that out of this time of trial and tribulation will be born a new freedom and glory for all mankind.

**Isaac Newton's analysis of motion** in the physical universe—for every action there is an equal and opposite reaction—applies as well to the conduct of human affairs. An action against a people will produce a reaction. Churchill was anxious to ensure that the reaction would be powerful, if possible powerful out of all proportion to the action that provoked it. For this, he needed a source of energy, which he found by tapping into the defiant spirit of the English people. Like any other force, however, defiance is useless, even dangerous, unless it is managed. Churchill was a master at mining sources of human will and then managing the result.

# 20

# Greet Hardship
# as Opportunity

"Do not let us speak of darker days; let us speak rather of sterner days.
These are not dark days: these are great days—the greatest days our country
has ever lived; and we must all thank God that we have been allowed . . . to
play a part in making these days memorable in the history of our race."
~ Speech, Harrow School, London, October 29, 1941

On October 29, 1941, Prime Minister Winston Churchill visited his
alma mater, Harrow School, to address the boys struggling to do their
lessons in a time of desperate war when England stood alone, fighting
against a terrible tyranny, fighting for its life and for the survival of
civilization itself. During the preceding decade, Churchill had
preached preparedness for war, appealing largely in vain to a
Parliament stricken with a malaise of fatalistic anxiety and stubborn
denial. If adults, the nation's leaders no less, could be so paralyzed by
fear as to be unable to respond appropriately to that fear, what must
mere boys have felt in the terrifying early months of World War II?

> *"What he [Adolf Hitler] has done is to kindle a fire in British hearts, here
> and all over the world, which will glow long after all traces of the conflagra-
> tions in London have been destroyed."*
> ~ Quoted in Guy Eden's *Portrait of Churchill,* 1950

When he stood before the boys of Harrow, Churchill endeavored to put himself in their state of mind and to directly address their concerns, speaking not as the prime minister and war leader of Great Britain, but as if he were their sympathetic teacher. He delivered a lesson that was both gentle and firm, beginning with that favorite tactic of the classroom, comparison and contrast:

> Almost a year has passed since I came down here at your Head Master's kind invitation in order to cheer myself and cheer the hearts of a few of my friends by singing some of our own songs. The ten months that have passed have seen very terrible catastrophic events in the world—ups and downs, misfortunes— but can anyone sitting here this afternoon, this October afternoon, not feel deeply thankful for what has happened in the time that has passed and for the very great improvement in the position of our country and of our home? Why, when I was here last time we were quite alone, desperately alone, and we had been so for five or six months. We were poorly armed. We are not so poorly armed today; but then we were very poorly armed. We had the unmeasured menace of the enemy and their air attack still beating upon us, and you yourselves had had experience of this attack; and I expect you are beginning to feel impatient that there has been this long lull with nothing particular turning up!

From this, he turned to the next lesson that had to be learned, and, like a good teacher, he expressed complete confidence that everyone would be capable of learning it well:

> But we must learn to be equally good at what is short and sharp and what is long and tough. It is generally said that the British are often better at the last. They do not expect to move from crisis to crisis; they do not always expect that each day will bring up some

noble chance of war; but when they very slowly make up their minds that the thing has to be done and the job put through and finished, then, even if it takes months—if it takes years—they do it.

And then to yet "another lesson":

Another lesson I think we may take, just throwing our minds back to our meeting here ten months ago and now, is that appearances are often very deceptive, and as Kipling well says, we must ". . . meet with Triumph and Disaster. And treat those two impostors just the same."

Quite a lesson, this last one. Triumph and disaster, victory and defeat, progress and hardship—*all* could be treated as opportunities, provided that you learn the greatest "lesson" taught by "what we have gone through in this . . . period of ten months": "never give in, never give in, never, never, never, never—in nothing, great or small, large or petty—never give in except to convictions of honour and good sense."

### Manage Information

A leader manages people, money, and other resources, but the most important asset a leader manages is information. Deliver bad news as catastrophic news, and you promote catastrophe in your organization. Deliver that same information as the outline of a challenge, in which opportunity resides, and you bring to the enterprise the possibility not merely of survival and recovery, but genuine advance. Some may dismiss information management as "spin," others, more directly, as lying. It need not be either. To manage information is to discover and open the potential for profit in any event. Disaster speaks for itself. Opportunity often requires an advocate to identify and promote it.

Ten months earlier, Churchill reminded the boys, circumstances could not have been more calamitous. "We stood all alone . . . and to many countries it seemed that our account was closed, we were finished." But: "Very different is the mood today." Because, ten months earlier, "there was no flinching and no thought of giving in, . . . we now find ourselves in a position where I say that we can be sure that we have only to persevere to conquer." The British people had transformed disaster into triumph—or, rather, as Kipling had written, found the seeds of future triumph in present disaster.

**"The British people had transformed disaster into triumph—or . . . found the seeds of future triumph in present disaster."**

"You sang here a verse of a School Song," the speaker continued. "You sang that extra verse written in my honour, which I was very greatly complimented by and which you have repeated today." It went like this:

> Not less we praise in darker days
> The leader of our nation,
> And Churchill's name shall win acclaim
> From each new generation.
> For you have power in danger's hour
> Our freedom to defend, Sir!
> Though long the fight we know that right
> Will triumph in the end, Sir!

"But there is one word in it I want to alter," Churchill announced. "I wanted to do so last year, but I did not venture to. It is the line: 'Not less we praise in darker days.' I have obtained the Head Master's permission to alter *darker* to *sterner*. 'Not less we praise in sterner days.'"

Do not let us speak of darker days: let us speak rather of sterner days. These are not dark days; these are great days—the greatest days our country has ever lived; and we must all thank God that we have been allowed, each of us according to our stations, to play a part in making these days memorable in the history of our race.

Here ended the lesson—a lesson, Winston Churchill well knew, that would resonate far beyond the quad at Harrow, that would be heard by the British people, by the American people—still neutral in the fall of 1941—by the imprisoned people of the occupied lands, and even by the German and Italian people. He knew as well that it would also be heard by their leaders.

> **Shakespeare asked, "What's in a name?"** Churchill asked, "What's in a label?" The answer to the second question can be *everything*. Something happens. A situation develops. You have a choice of labeling it a disaster and treating it as such, or as an opportunity and leading the members of your enterprise in its fullest realization. Look very hard at the possibilities before you slap a label on any event. Make it your business to make the very best of whatever happens to you and your organization.

# 21

# Provide Perspective,
# Create Priorities

"Now this is not the end. It is not even
the beginning of the end. But it is, perhaps,
the end of the beginning."
~ Speech, Mansion House, London, November 10, 1942

Whatever else a leader does, Churchill believed, he must provide perspective and create priorities for his constituents. In no other situation was this function more important than in war, with all its complexity, confusion, and potential for uncertainty and panic. Churchill made perhaps his most famous assessment of perspective on November 10, 1942, when, speaking at the Lord Mayor's Luncheon in London, he hailed General Bernard Law Montgomery's victory over German general Erwin Rommel at El Alamein in North Africa. It was the first significant Allied ground victory of the war. "The Germans have received back again that measure of fire and steel which they have so often meted out to others," the prime minister observed. "Now this is not the end. It is not even the beginning of the end. But it is, perhaps, the end of the beginning." Anxious neither to oversell nor undersell the achievement, he formulated a crystal-clear definition of this particular victory at this particular time and place. It was an assessment that gave the triumph full weight but not an ounce more.

## Assess Reality with the Greatest of Care

Because the vision of the chief executive has such an impact on the organization, it is crucially important that every assessment be made with the greatest of care. Inflation is a potential problem, creating false expectations and, ultimately, generating disappointment. But chronically underrating or undervaluing achievements is also destructive to the morale of individuals as well as the enterprise as a whole. What is more, habitual underestimation of achievements paints the CEO as ungrateful and impossible to please. An accurate assessment gives direction to the organization and builds credibility for the leader.

Far less familiar was an even more critical effort to fix perspective and set priorities in World War I, long before Churchill became prime minister. On January 19, 1918, when he was minister of munitions, Churchill issued an appeal to Prime Minister David Lloyd George. In November of the preceding year, a Bolshevik government had come to power in Russia and announced its intention to make a "separate peace" with Germany. Churchill knew that once Russia pulled out of the war, the Germans would be free to release hundreds of thousands of soldiers from the Eastern Front and throw them against the West. After nearly four years of combat, this would give the Germans instantaneous numerical superiority over the Allies on the Western Front. At this point, the Royal Navy was enjoying priority in recruitment of manpower. Churchill believed it was urgent to shift the priority to the army, which was about to face a vastly reinforced enemy.

> To me this [the naval priority] is incomprehensible. The imminent danger is on the Western front; & the crisis will come before June. A defeat here will be *fatal*.

Please don't let vexation against past military blunders (which I share with you to the full) lead you to underrate the gravity of the impending campaign, or to keep the army short of what is needed. You know how highly I rate the modern defensive compared with offensive. But I do *not* like the situation now developing and do not think all that is possible is being done to meet it.

Up to this point, the minister of munitions expressed his opinion concerning priorities. Next, he invited the prime minister to "Fancy if there was a bad break!"—that is, to imagine what would happen if the Germans managed to break through the British lines. To prod Lloyd George's imagination, Churchill cited an example: "Look what happened to Italy. One night may efface an army. . . ." In the Battle of Caporetto, fought from October 24 to November 9, 1917, near the modern Slovenian town of Kobarid, Austro-Hungarian forces, stiffened by German units, smashed through the Italian front line and routed the Italian army, killing 11,000, wounding 20,000, and making prisoners of a staggering 275,000. The defeat came close to knocking Italy out of the war. The chief weakness in the Italian front was an absence of a mobile reserve. Once the line was broken, there was nothing to stop the enemy's advance.

Having planted this picture in Lloyd George's mind, Churchill continued, imploring the prime minister to furnish more "men at once—at all costs," taking them "from Navy, from Munitions, from Home Army, from Civil Life." Moreover, war production needed to be ramped up. "Stint food and commercial imports to increase shells, aeroplanes & tanks," Churchill urged. "Wire and *concrete* on the largest possible scale."

"The priority need was not only for men and matériel," but also for a "good plan for counter blows all worked out beforehand to relieve pressure at the points of attack when they manifest themselves."

*"You must look at facts because they look at you."*
~Speech, House of Commons, May 7, 1925

Having in no uncertain terms laid out the immediate priorities and put them into perspective by the example of Caporetto, Churchill ended by hammering his point home—using a heavy rhetorical sledge: "If this went wrong everything would go wrong. . . . The Germans are a terrible foe, & their generals are better than ours." He even made bold to admonish the prime minister (who was, after all, a friend): "Ponder & then *act*."

For his part, Churchill, having already pondered, acted in accordance with the priorities he himself had established. He rode herd on the air minister—the man in charge of aircraft requirements—not to allow new aircraft engine orders to fall below 4,000 units per month. Churchill even let him know that the Ministry of Munitions would approve an increase to 5,000 or 6,000. He also made a personal—and highly hazardous—tour of the entire British-held front, discussing face to face with all field commanders what they needed in terms of tanks, ammunition, and mustard gas. He did not stop with the officers, but advanced into the front-line trenches to inspect the soldiers and the battlefield for himself.

The result of his front-line tour was twofold. On the one hand, it prompted him to redouble his efforts to add to the defensive forces that held the line. On the other, however, it turned his ultimate strategic vision from defense to offense. Up to this time, Churchill's strategic priority had been defensive. As he wrote to Sir Archibald Sinclair after the conclusion of the Third Battle of Ypres, which had spanned July into early November 1917, "Thank God our offensives are at an end."

Let them [the Germans] make the pockets. Let them traipse across the crater fields. Let them rejoice in the occasional capture of placeless names & sterile ridges: & let us dart here & there armed with science & surprise & backed at all points by superior artillery. That is the way to break their hearts & leave them bankrupt in resources at the end of the 1918 campaign.

This shunning of offensive strategy was not defeatism, but the recognition that the weapons technology then in use inevitably favored defenders. Two men dug into a trench and manning a machine gun could wipe out an entire company of attackers. Heavy artillery was more effective than any advance by masses of infantry. Yet when he saw the deteriorating condition of British soldiers defending the trench lines, Churchill immediately reordered his vision of priorities, appealing to the War Cabinet (of which, as minister of munitions, he was *not* a member) to formulate a new *offensive* strategy for the coming year, 1919. Now, more than ever before, Churchill championed the perfection of the "land cruiser"— the tank—which, with the airplane, he saw as the technological means of breaking the Western Front stalemate. Tanks could rumble over trenches and barbed wire, machine-gun bullets ricocheting off their thick armor. Airplanes could fly high above those same trenches and obstacles, raining ruin from above. Together, used in sufficient numbers—which the Ministry of Munitions would have to supply—these two weapons could end what Churchill now regarded as the "waste and slaughter sagging slowly downwards into general collapse." Acting on his own revised perception, Churchill set up a Tank Board, assigning to it the goal of building 4,459 tanks by April 1919. Simultaneously, he asked the air minister to double Britain's air force by that same time.

> "He . . . made a personal— and highly hazardous— tour of the entire British-held front, discussing face to face with all field commanders what they needed in terms of tanks, ammunition, and mustard gas. He did not stop with the officers, but advanced into the front-line trenches to inspect the soldiers and the battlefield for himself."

Churchill is often portrayed as a stubborn man: the English bulldog. Determined, dauntless, and indomitable he surely was, but stubborn he was not. He possessed the mental agility to shift priorities when he perceived this as necessary, and he possessed the passionate eloquence to persuade others to see the situation from his perspective and follow whatever system of priorities he developed. Doubtless, he was right about the necessity of shifting from a massive defense to an overwhelming offense. However, by the time the shift was in motion, the Germans had finally exhausted themselves in a series of desperate offensives intended to break the Allied lines before American troops could be put on the line in sufficient numbers to make a major impact on the war. Failing to break through with these costly offensives, the German army began to give way. Its position on the Western Front first weakened, and then buckled, before finally crumbling. The armistice of November 11, 1918, ended the war before the grand offensive Churchill contemplated for the spring of 1919 could be organized, let alone launched.

**To lead an organization** is to provide the perspective from which its members view the universe in which it operates and, from this perspective, to formulate the priorities of the enterprise and communicate these effectively. Churchill was adept at creating priorities, which he communicated both clearly and with passion. He never let his passion solidify into dogma, but remained flexible, altering priorities in response to changing situations and fresh insights.

# 22

# Be Indomitable

"The V sign is the symbol of unconquerable will."
~Speech, County Hall, London, July 14, 1941

The people of the twentieth century considered themselves to have reached a very lofty stage of evolution, in which rational thought had largely displaced emotion, prejudice, mythology, and other atavistic modes of perception and behavior. Two cataclysmic world wars and innumerable "lesser" armed conflicts during that century should probably be sufficient to discredit this assessment. If mass and massive violence bears any relation to the evolution of rationality, it is surely inverse. So, based on the evidence, there is very little reason to suppose that humanity in the twentieth century was any more rational than at any other time. On the contrary, the evidence of the world wars and so much else suggests that modern men and women retain powerful connections with visceral, primal impulses and instincts that arise from somewhere other than rationality.

Despite the evidence, many modern political and business leaders have persisted—and still persist—in appealing only to the rational, intellectual, "reasonable" level of their constituents, as if fearful of, embarrassed by, or simply wishing to deny the primal wellsprings of behavior. This is understandable. Atavism, urge, and instinct are intimidating, especially in large organizations, where a very great deal is always at stake. Yet the leader who turns his back on this level of motivation does so at his peril and that of the entire enterprise.

[ 219 ]

Many in the generation that witnessed the rise of Adolf Hitler were astounded at how so unprepossessing a man—not handsome, adorned with a "cookie-duster" mustache that called to mind Charlie Chaplin's celebrated "Little Tramp" movie persona, the author of a garbled amalgam of political theory and racist rant (his memoir-manifesto *Mein Kampf*), pos-

**"Atavism, urge, and instinct are intimidating, especially in large organizations, where a very great deal is always at stake. Yet the leader who turns his back on this level of motivation does so at his peril and that of the entire enterprise."**

sessing (some said) the stilted manners of a restaurant waiter—could possibly have moved a nation with such catastrophic results. It was certainly not by an appeal to reason. Whatever else the Nazi movement was, it was a vast spectacle, an elaborately staged pageant of symbols: torchlight parades, mass rallies, Roman salutes, a blend of Nordic and Crusader mythologies, a mysticism of race and blood, all somehow contained in the iconic black swastika within a white circle on a red background—quite possibly the most powerful symbol since the Christian cross. Hitler, his propaganda minister Josef Goebbels, and his chief lieutenant and SS head Heinrich Himmler were all deeply engrossed in symbolism, unembarrassed by the power of symbols, and expert at exploiting them to move the masses.

*"A monster of wickedness, insatiable in his lust for blood and plunder."*
~Characterization of Hitler, delivered
in a radio broadcast of June 26, 1941

After Hitler came to power in 1933, Germany rearmed at a rapid pace. The European democracies, Britain and France—demoralized by World War I, despite their victory—neither resisted this rearmament nor took timely steps to counter it by matching it. If, in the interwar arms race, the democracies were virtually nonstarters, they fell even further behind in the escalation of symbolism. Against the frenzied rise of torchlight parades, mass rallies, and the swastika, symbols that incited rather than inspired, Britain, France, and the United States relied on the treasured if tired old standbys, the Union Jack, the Tricolor, and the Stars and Stripes.

When war came in September 1939, France remained oddly somnolent. Its soldiers fought and died, but most of its leaders failed to summon a credible defense against German aggression, let alone an effective resistance to conquest. As for the United States, it did its utmost to remain neutral. Throughout the 1930s, before the war, Winston Churchill agitated and appealed for rearmament, only to find himself a voice crying in the wilderness, all but alone. The British government and a vast majority of the British people were fearful that rearming would in itself bring on a new war. Immediately after the war began, however, Chamberlain appointed Churchill to his War Cabinet as First Lord of the Admiralty. From this post, then as prime minister, he presided over a crash program of war production.

## Symbols and Bombers, Too

The only thing worse a leader can do than neglect symbolism or deny its power is to rely on symbols and neglect the nitty-gritty realities of the job at hand. Churchill wanted symbols and bombers, too.

Churchill also embarked on a campaign that targeted the hearts, the minds, the will, the very soul of the British people. Through some of the greatest speeches any leader has ever composed and delivered, he made his appeal to a level of behavior, resolve, and motivation that lay both beneath and beyond mere rationality. He also seized upon a simple and curiously powerful symbol that, as it were, went toe to toe with the swastika and the Roman salute.

In his electrifying "Blood, Toil, Tears, and Sweat" speech—as prime minister, his very first speech to the House of Commons—on May 13, 1940, Churchill offered as answer to the question he himself posed—"You ask, what is our aim?"—a one-word answer: "It is victory, victory at all costs, victory in spite of all terror, victory, however long and hard the road may be; for without victory, there is no survival." Thanks to Churchill, that word and that concept became the underlying as well as the overarching theme of the war, repeated so often that it was ingrained into the British psyche as a kind of mantra. To enhance and complete its transformation into a living symbol, Churchill began to flash a hand sign, the index finger and middle finger upraised in the form of the letter "V"—sometimes with the ubiquitous Churchill cigar lodged between them. Soon, Churchill was seen in photograph after photograph, newsreel after newsreel, public appearance after public appearance, flashing the V sign. As Hitler and Nazism were intimately associated with the swastika, so, very soon, Churchill and democracy were linked to the V for Victory.

For many years since World War II, commentators have speculated on the origin of the V sign. One very appealing interpretation traces it back to thirteenth-century England and the most famous battle of the Hundred Years' War, Agincourt, in which, on October 25, 1415, fewer than 6,000 men under King Henry V of England decisively defeated a much larger French force (perhaps as many as 30,000 foot soldiers and knights) under one of King Charles VI's lieutenants. Henry's secret weapon was his legion of longbowmen, who constituted the majority of his greatly outnumbered army. The Anglo-French historian Jean Froissart (c. 1337–1404), author of the epic European history the *Chronicles*, wrote of how English soldiers waved their fingers at the French. Froissart did not specify whether or not these soldiers were archers, nor did he specify which fingers they waved or exactly how they waved them; however, a legend nevertheless evolved to the effect that, during the Battle of

Agincourt, French knights repeatedly charged through the ranks of the English longbowmen in an effort to hack off their hands or, at least, the two fingers—index and middle—with which they drew back their bows. In response, the archers defiantly issued a two-finger salute, taunting the knights by waving their second and third digits at them. Winston Churchill, of course, was a historian and a great reader of history, including Froissart and other accounts of Agincourt. Understandably, a modern legend has arisen, identifying the classic battle pitting outnumbered common English bowmen against mounted French nobles as Churchill's origin of the V-for-Victory sign. Not only did it embody a rich historical reference to a key English victory, immortalized by Shakespeare in *Henry V*, but it was also a sign of defiance and the determination to be indomitable.

> *"Give me the facts, Ashley, and I will twist them in the way I want to suit my argument."*
>
> ~Spoken to his historical research assistant,
> Maurice P. Ashley

It is no wonder that people have sought such a compelling source for so pervasive and powerful—so "Churchillian"—a gesture. Unfortunately, however, there is no evidence that the prime minister had Agincourt in mind when he began using the gesture. In fact, the V for Victory seems not to have even originated with him at all, but with a Belgian refugee living in London. On January 4, 1941, Victor De Lavelaye, a lawyer who worked as a program organizer for the BBC, broadcast to his countrymen in Nazi-occupied Belgium an idea for a new form of resistance: "I am proposing to you as a rallying emblem the letter V, because V is the first letter of the words '*Victoire*' in French, and '*Vrijheid*' in Flemish: two things which go together, as Walloons and Flemings are at the moment marching hand in hand, two things which are the consequence one of the other, the Victory [*Victoire*] which will give us back our freedom [*Vrijheid*], the Victory of our good friends the English. Their word for Victory also begins with V." Coming from a man with the first name of Victor, the idea is not all that surprising. Certainly, the BBC embraced it, and Douglas Ritchie, director of the BBC European Service, came up with the idea of regularly broadcasting an audible V sign, using the Morse code for V (dot-dot-dot-dash); as finally adopted by the broadcast service, this sound bite was followed up with the opening chords of Beethoven's *Fifth Symphony*: three staccato notes preceding a momentous sustained chord, which came across as a perfect emulation of the Morse code. The identification of the *Fifth Symphony*'s opening motif with V for Victory was further reinforced by the fact that the number five is written as the Roman numeral V. (So pervasive became the association of the *Fifth* with the idea of victory that, ever since World War II, the composition has often borne the nickname *Victory Symphony*.) The British and other Allies also greatly relished appropriating this iconic work of an iconic German composer to signify victory over Germany. To gild the symbolic lily, contemporary commentators additionally pointed to Beethoven's own purported explanation of his symphony's arresting opening notes, that it represented "fate knocking on the door," and they said that soon, very soon, fate would come knocking on the Nazis' door, in the form of massive bombardment, retaliation, and Allied conquest. On July 20, 1941, after consultation with Churchill, the BBC broadcast to every occupied country as well as resistance groups an explicit instruction to use the visual V sign and its audio equivalents to express their own defiance of the Nazi occupation.

The "Victory campaign" caught on in a big way, as people in the occupied territories began chalking the V sign on walls and even painting it over swastikas on official posters and signs. Locomotive engineers blasted the Morse code signal on their whistles, and schoolteachers clapped their hands—dot-dot-dot, *dash*—to summon children to their lessons. Even one friend casually visiting another might knock on the door with three staccato taps followed by a final decisive rap. De Lavelaye and his BBC managers believed the campaign would do much to erode the morale of every single German occupier, who, De Lavelaye explained, would repeatedly encounter the V sign and thereby come to "understand that he is surrounded, encircled by an immense crowd of citizens eagerly awaiting his first moment of weakness, watching for his first failure."

## Symbolic Weapons

Effective symbols are powerful for both the user and those against whom they are used. The V for Victory was intended not only to inspire the British and their allies, including those individuals and groups carrying on the resistance movement in occupied lands, but also to intimidate and demoralize the enemy.

Among the very first to take up the BBC Victory campaign, Winston Churchill quickly made it his own. At every public opportunity, whenever he found himself before a camera lens, he flashed the V sign with his fingers. At first, he was indifferent as to whether his palm faced inward, toward his body, or outward, toward others. His private secretary, John Colville, discreetly pointed out to him that the inward-facing form of the gesture was unsavory, even obscene. As Colville delicately noted in his diary in September 1941, "The PM will give the V-sign with two fingers in spite of representations repeatedly made to him that this gesture has quite another significance." Colville was referring to the so-called bow finger or two-fingered salute commonly used by members of the British working class in precisely the same way that Americans (and others) today gesture with the middle finger. It has often been suggested that Churchill, an aristocrat, was initially unaware of the bow finger and changed over to the consistent use of the gesture palm outward

[ 225 ]

only after being informed of the meaning of the palm-inward gesture among the "lower classes." Perhaps. But the fact is that Churchill, who had commanded and served among "common" soldiers in India, South Africa, and in World War I, could hardly have been unfamiliar with the two-fingered salute. It is far more likely that, consciously or not, he wanted to charge the V-for-Victory sign with a double entendre, as if to sharpen the point of his message of defiance and contempt of Hitler and his henchmen. In the course of the war, he may have thought better of this, transforming the sign from one primarily signaling an exuberantly vulgar defiance to a more noble message of indomitable will. In 1944, for example, about to depart Naples after a visit, he flashed the V-sign to a group of cheering Italians on the pier. He turned to an Englishman on board his ship. "D' you think they like that?" he inquired. "Yes," his companion answered, "though I believe the sign also has an improper connotation in the Mediterranean lands." Churchill replied: "I know that, but I have superseded that one—V for Victory." This suggests that, by 1944, the transformation was complete. By this time, Churchill was confident that he owned the symbolic gesture, V for Victory, and freely bestowed it on the world.

Perhaps the greatest measure of the success of Churchill's attempt to create a symbol of indomitable will, a kind of benediction intended to empower others to be as indomitable as he, was the Nazi efforts to counteract the V-for-Victory campaign by preempting it with their own "V for *Viktoria*" project. It never caught on, but, in 1944, after German engineers perfected the Fieseler Fi 103/FZG-76, the pilotless "buzz

> "Perhaps the greatest measure of the success of Churchill's attempt to create a symbol of indomitable will, a kind of benediction intended to empower others to be as indomitable as he, was the Nazi efforts to counteract the V-for-Victory campaign by preempting it with their own 'V for Viktoria' project. It never caught on."

bomb," Hitler personally approved calling it the Vergeltungswaffe-1, meaning "vengeance weapon" or "reprisal weapon," because it was to be used in retaliation for the intensive campaign of Allied strategic bombing that was pounding German cities into rubble. Propaganda minister Josef Goebbels instantly seized on the *Vergeltungswaffe* idea and appropriated the initial "V" for what was a weapon purely of terror, mostly targeted against civilian London. Used beginning in June 1944, the V-1 was joined by the more advanced V-2 rocket in September of that year in what became known as the second Blitz.

**A talisman is any object,** usually marked with magical signs, believed to confer some great power or protection on one who bears or wears it. Of course, as rational residents of the twenty-first century, we associate such an object with a bygone age or a primitive culture. That, however, is a mistake. Effective leaders understand and exploit the power of symbols, including talismans—symbols intended to make us feel indomitable. Churchill found the ideal talisman in the V-for-Victory sign. You may find yours in a logo, a motto, or a principle. Any symbol that can be made meaningful to the members of an enterprise may serve to embolden, encourage, and empower. Appeal to reason and rationality, by all means, but never neglect the soul and the imagination—the need to believe in the power, even the mystical power, of an enduring value or profound goal.

# 23

# Gather
# Good Partners

"At last—we've gotten together."
~ Franklin D. Roosevelt, welcoming Churchill
aboard the USS *Augusta*, August 9, 1941
"We have."
~ Churchill (nodding), in reply

On August 31, 1939, Franciszek Honiok, a German Silesian imprisoned by the Nazi government for his outspoken sympathies with
Poland, was taken from one of Adolf Hitler's concentration camps,
forced to don the uniform of a Polish soldier, transported to the
German town of Gleiwitz (present-day Gliwice) on the Polish
border, and shot in the back. Honiok was the first casualty of World
War II. Heinrich Himmler, chief of Adolf Hitler's elite SS, wanted to
make Germany look like the victim of Polish aggression. The official
German claim was that this man was part of an attack on the radio
station in Gleiwitz, and everything that followed—the blitzkrieg
invasion of Poland and the most destructive war in history—flowed
from this counterfeit attack.

After the German army and air force crossed the Polish border,
Neville Chamberlain protested, Hitler ignored him, and, on Sunday,
September 3, at 11:15 a.m., Chamberlain broadcast to the British
people the terrible fact that their nation was now at war with Germany.

*"[I was] conscious of a profound sense of relief. I felt as if I was walking with destiny, and that all my past life had been but a preparation for this hour and this trial."*

~Remark on May 10, 1940, after being named prime minister

Immediately after the message, air-raid sirens screamed in London. Churchill, who had listened to the prime minister's broadcast with his wife, Clementine, responded to the alert by going outside to scan the sky. His bodyguard, Police Inspector W. H. "Tommy" Thompson, persuaded him to withdraw to a basement shelter, which, reluctantly, he did, brandy bottle in hand. As we have already noted, it was later that very day that Chamberlain appointed Churchill—his most unsparing critic—First Lord of the Admiralty, the post he had held early in World War I. Churchill was at the office by 6 p.m. that evening.

## Pitch In

When Prime Minister Neville Chamberlain, long a political adversary, asked Churchill to serve in his cabinet as First Lord of the Admiralty, Churchill accepted gratefully and unconditionally. He reported for work that very evening and never was so ungracious as to drop even the slightest hint of I-told-you-so.

Britain, Churchill knew, needed all the help it could get, and from his new government post, he began courting the United States—or, more precisely, the *president* of the United States, Franklin D. Roosevelt. For Churchill knew what any great CEO knows: that vast enterprises never really do business with other vast enterprises, but that a leader within one enterprise does business with a leader in another. Great as this war was certain to be—a world-engulfing conflict—its "business" had to be, first and foremost, a matter of relations between one leader and another. Britain needed an ally, which meant that Churchill needed a partner.

Throughout World War II—beginning months before Pearl Harbor forced America into the war—Churchill used brilliant personal correspondence and face-to-face meetings to court Roosevelt much as an ardent beau might court a prospective lover who was by turns shy and haughty. Yet what first unmistakably drew Roosevelt to Churchill's side was the prime minister's *public* performance. The leadership stance

**"Churchill knew what any great CEO knows: that vast enterprises never really do business with other vast enterprises, but that a leader within one enterprise does business with a leader in another."**

he crafted was heroic and defiant, yet coldly realistic. His speeches to the British people—which, via broadcast, Churchill knew would also be heard by America and the whole world—were, as we have seen throughout this book, sublimely inspirational and sublimely frank. Inspiration and reality suffused with absolute confidence— that was the Churchill message, and, as Eleanor Roosevelt remarked, the prime minister's speeches were "a tonic to us here in the United States." In some ways, she observed, Churchill "was more blunt with the people of Great Britain than my husband ever was with us."

Churchill understood that to woo FDR as a partner, a personal appeal was absolutely necessary, but, alone, it was not sufficient. In everything he did and said in public, Churchill made it his business to present himself as the embodiment of the indomitable British spirit arrayed in righteous confidence. Yet even as Churchill voiced his certainty that Britain, not Nazi Germany, would emerge the victor, France was falling, and the British troops there, the bulk of Britain's professional army, were being pushed toward the English Channel at Dunkirk. From London, U.S. Ambassador Joseph Kennedy sent the president a cable on May 27, 1940: "Only a

**"The leadership stance he crafted was heroic and defiant, yet coldly realistic. His speeches . . . were . . . sublimely inspirational and sublimely frank."**

miracle can save the BEF [British Expeditionary Force] from being wiped out or, as I said yesterday, surrender." He went on to observe that the possibility, even the desirability, of British surrender was everywhere in the air. Whereas Churchill and a few others "want to fight to the death . . . other members [of the Cabinet] realize that physical destruction of men and property in England will not be a proper offset to a loss of pride."

FDR had begun to sense that his ambassador was a defeatist (he would be fired in good time), but even the president had to admit that the odds against Britain were stacked high. Nor were the American people eager to get into yet another "European war." Fearful that any ships and planes he might turn over to Britain would quickly fall into enemy hands when that island nation was conquered—and reluctant to act against the will of the majority of the American people—FDR continued to delay, seeking congressional authorization for the release of the matériel Churchill asked for.

Churchill refused to be discouraged, and on May 26, 1940, the miracle Ambassador Kennedy had certainly believed impossible began unfolding. Carried in an ad hoc fleet of warships, merchant vessels, fishing boats, and pleasure yachts, a total of 338,226 soldiers, including some 140,000 French troops, reached the safety of England by June 4. On that very day, Winston Churchill, having replaced Neville Chamberlain as prime minister on May 10, 1940, delivered to the House of Commons his most celebrated speech:

> We shall fight on the beaches, we shall fight on the landing grounds, we shall fight in the fields and in the streets, we shall fight in the hills; we shall never surrender, and even if, which I do not for a moment believe, this island or a large part of it were subjugated and starving, then our Empire beyond the seas, armed and guarded by the British fleet, would carry on the struggle,

until, in God's good time, the new world, with all its power and might, steps forth to the rescue and the liberation of the old.

The British nation took heart, and Franklin Roosevelt got the message. A month later, on June 10, the day Italy declared war on England and France, he gave the commencement address to the University of Virginia Law School Class of 1940, promising to "extend to the opponents of force the material resources of this nation" while simultaneously girding at home so "that we ourselves in the Americas may have equipment and training equal to the task of any emergency and every defense."

Churchill heard the president's speech on radio and the next day cabled FDR that it came as "a strong encouragement in a dark but not unhopeful hour." Churchill was even more gratified when the president sent Prime Minister Paul Reynaud of France a telegram promising aid and expressing solidarity, but when Churchill urged FDR to make the telegram public, the president demurred. He was still unwilling to appear as if he were stepping boldly toward war.

When France surrendered to Germany on June 22, 1940, Britain was left very much alone. Unknown to Churchill, the U.S. departments of War and the Navy had advised the president to send no more matériel to Britain, warning that continuing to do so would "weaken our present state of defense."

But the president could not resist the pull of Churchill's defiant conviction and confidence. Roosevelt maintained the flow of equipment. Nevertheless, he sought independent corroboration of his intuitive response to the prime minister. No longer willing to rely on the reports of Ambassador Kennedy, he sent to London in July Colonel William "Wild Bill" Donovan, the man who would soon create the Americans' key wartime intelligence agency, the OSS (Office of Strategic Services). After meeting with Churchill, Donovan was effusive in his praise, expressing complete confidence that, with this prime minister's leadership, the British nation would prevail.

FDR was pleased by the confirmation of his own instincts, but, in the midst of an election year, running for an unprecedented third term against Republican Wendell Wilkie, whose platform included a powerful pledge that "no American boys [would] ever be sent to the shambles of the European trenches," he continued to withhold full commitment.

Churchill pursued a course of patience and persistence. As a politician, he understood that the reelection of his American counterpart would be imperiled if the president appeared to rush headlong into war. Churchill was also keenly aware that fifty World War I–vintage U.S. destroyers, desperately needed as convoy escorts, hung in the balance, and he would have understood if FDR had held off releasing the ships until after the election. For his part, Roosevelt was persuaded that the British could not afford to wait for the escorts, and in September, in the midst of the reelection campaign, the president urged Congress to approve a destroyers-for-bases deal, whereby the United States would give Britain the fifty ships in return for the use of British naval bases in the Western hemisphere. He did delay taking the next step until after the election: the push to enact Lend-Lease, the policy of supplying the Allies with war materials without cash payment.

Churchill sent FDR a congratulatory cable on the day after the American elections: "I did not think it right for me as a Foreigner to express my opinion upon American politics while the Election was on, but now I feel you will not mind my saying that I prayed for your success and that I am truly thankful for it." He was careful to avoid giving the impression of dragging Roosevelt into marriage at the point of a shotgun. Thankfulness for Roosevelt's victory "does not mean that I seek or wish for anything more than the full, fair and free play of your mind upon the world issues now at stake in which our two nations have to discharge their respective duties." But: "Things are afoot which will be remembered as long as the English language is spoken in any quarter of the globe, and in expressing the comfort I feel that the people of the United States have once again cast these great burdens upon you, I must avow my sure faith that the lights by which we steer will bring us all safely to anchor."

*"A pessimist sees the difficulty in every opportunity; an optimist sees the opportunity in every difficulty."*

~ Conversational remark, frequently quoted

Churchill understood that he had not yet made a faithful personal friend of Franklin Roosevelt, but he was absolutely confident that the president was a faithful friend to democracy, and the prime minister would rely on that to bind two great democracies during the greatest crisis democracy had ever faced. For his part, FDR continued to approach the prospect of an Anglo-American alliance gingerly. Around Christmas 1940, he remarked to his longtime aide and confidant Harry Hopkins that "a lot . . . could be settled if Churchill and I could just sit down together for a while." Hopkins instantly grasped that a direct meeting between Roosevelt and Churchill was desirable but out of the question, politically and diplomatically, at this moment. He therefore volunteered to meet with Churchill in the president's place.

If the trip to war-torn Britain was politically and diplomatically impossible for FDR, it should have been physically impossible for Harry Hopkins. A trans-Atlantic journey through U-boat-infested waters to a city under nightly bombardment would tax even the healthiest of men, and Hopkins was far from healthy. A cancer operation had removed most of his stomach in 1937 and left him chronically ill. Nevertheless, he undertook the mission to function as a remote extension of the president's eyes, ears, and instincts.

*"Churchill is the gov't in every sense of the word. This island needs our help now Mr. President with everything we can give them."*

~ Harry Hopkins, to President
Franklin D. Roosevelt, January 3, 1941

When he was first told that Hopkins was coming, Churchill knew nothing of the role he played in the Roosevelt administration, but he made it his business to find out, and, once he learned the truth, the prime minister warmly greeted the president's emissary with exuberant flattery of his boss, which put Hopkins in a most receptive mood as he observed the prime minister in action over the next few weeks. Hopkins wasted no time in cabling the president: "This island needs our help now Mr. President with everything we can give them." At dinner with Churchill, Hopkins addressed the prime minister: "I suppose you wish to know what I am going to say to President Roosevelt on my return. Well, I'm going to quote you one verse from that Book of Books . . . . : 'Whither thou goest, I will go; and where thou lodgest, I will lodge: thy people shall be my people, and thy God my God.'" He paused, and then added: "Even to the end."

## Do Job Number One

If all business is people business, it follows that job number one is to identify those people within an organization who have the power and authority to help you, to give you and your enterprise what you need. Identifying such people means finding out who they are, what they do, to whom they report, and what it is *they* want. Never ask for anything. Instead, define areas of common concern and common benefit. Transform the pronouns *you* and *I* into *we*.

At this, Winston Churchill wept, in part, perhaps, with relief. He had understood that winning an alliance with the United States meant earning the confidence of the president, and *that* required winning over Harry Hopkins. The mission had been accomplished.

On January 19, 1941, having had a full report from his emissary and confidant, the president handed his recent electoral rival, Wendell Wilkie, who was about to leave for England, a note to give the prime minister. Its substance consisted of verses FDR had committed to memory from Longfellow's "The Building of the Ship":

> I think this verse applies to your people as it does to us.
>> Sail on, O Ship of State!
>> Sail on, O Union, strong and great!
>> Humanity with all its fears,
>> With all the hopes of future years,
>> Is hanging breathless on thy fate!
>
>> As ever yours,
>> Franklin D. Roosevelt

The "ship of state," as it turned out, was more literal than metaphoric. On Sunday morning, August 3, 1941, FDR embarked on the presidential yacht *Potomac* for what was billed to the press as a few days of fishing. Hours later, off Martha's Vineyard and in absolute secrecy, the president and a small party were transferred from the *Potomac* to the U.S. Navy cruiser *Augusta*, which steamed toward Placentia Bay, Newfoundland, and a rendezvous with the British warship HMS *Prince of Wales*. Aboard her was Prime Minister Winston Churchill.

The secrecy surrounding the meeting was crucial for two reasons. First, a majority of Congress and a majority of the people of the United States remained fearful of being drawn into war. Second, the Atlantic Ocean was swept by German surface raiders and U-boats, which routinely sank thousands of tons of British shipping. If it were even suspected that the prime minister was crossing the ocean, no ship would escape targeting.

The *Augusta* and the *Prince of Wales* drew toward one another as August 9 dawned over the deceptively peaceful bay. At about eleven, Churchill boarded a launch and motored across the bay to the anchored American ship. Dressed in the dark blue uniform of a Royal Navy officer, the prime minister clambered aboard and faced the president of the United States, who stood, in the suit of a civilian, leaning on the arm of his son Elliott, the heavy steel braces that supported FDR hidden beneath his trouser legs. The two men stood facing each other as the national anthems of both nations were played.

As they looked toward one another, President Roosevelt must have been well aware of the great risk Churchill had taken in making the trip. For his part, the prime minister had a keenly sympathetic admiration for the personal courage of a chief executive who insisted on standing, painfully supported by unyielding braces, on the rising and falling deck of a ship at anchor.

## Go the Distance

"By their deeds you shall know them," Saint Matthew wrote. Words are important, but driven by deeds, they are downright compelling. Churchill braved the war-torn Atlantic to show FDR what his partnership meant to him. Take every opportunity to demonstrate your commitment to your allies and partners.

The anthems concluded, Churchill stepped forward, bowed slightly, and presented Roosevelt with a letter from King George VI. Extending his hand, the president said, "At last—we've gotten together."

"We have," Churchill nodded.

The two men established immediate rapport, though it was also apparent that Churchill took the lead in pushing for a partnership founded on personal friendship. This was partly due to the urgency of Britain's perilous situation, and was partly the product of Churchill's personal need to win the heart of the American president. When U.S. Ambassador to the Soviet Union W. Averell Harriman passed through London some weeks later, Churchill met with him and asked, referring to FDR, "Does he like me?"

If Churchill saw the creation of the most important alliance of the war as a personal friendship between leaders, Roosevelt never fully yielded himself. To the people of the United States, FDR seemed all at once a brother, a father, an uncle, and a friend. He had brought America through the Great Depression with Fireside Chats that seemed personally directed to each and every listener. Yet those who knew him better, who worked with him daily, found something cooler and more remote in the president. Publicly self-confident, genial, and indefatigable in his optimism, FDR always held something back on a person-to-person level. Harry S. Truman thought him both "a great man" and an "old fakir."

**"If Churchill saw the creation of the most important alliance of the war as a personal friendship between leaders, Roosevelt never fully yielded himself."**

It was abundantly clear that Roosevelt admired Churchill, and it was also clear that Roosevelt had wanted to meet Churchill face to face almost as much as Churchill had wanted to meet him. But whereas Churchill felt an imperative to form a bond of personal friendship with the New World leader, FDR's goal was not so much to make a friend of the prime minister as it was to charm him, the way a politician might charm any one of his leading constituents.

Churchill willingly made himself emotionally vulnerable to cement an Anglo-American alliance. He believed this alliance was just too important to become nothing more than a relation of one nation to another. It had to be a joining of one mind, heart, and soul to another. FDR, in contrast, conceded nothing to vulnerability. Thus, the relationship between the two leaders was unequal from the start, yet nevertheless personal from first to last. In August 1941, Britain obviously needed the United States. Less obvious to many was America's need of Britain, but, already, FDR was working to make that need clear to the American people. "The best immediate defense of the United States," he said at a press conference on December 17, 1940, "is the success of Great Britain defending itself." He explained that "from a selfish point of view of American defense . . . we should do everything to help the British Empire to defend itself." Yet military and political necessity was never enough for either Churchill or Roosevelt. In this unprecedented crisis threatening to engulf the entire world, these two men—in different degrees—felt the need to become more than diplomatic partners.

The first day of the conference between Churchill and Roosevelt had taken place aboard the American ship. The second day, Sunday, commenced with divine services on the British vessel. The president was transported from the *Augusta* to the *Prince of Wales* on board the destroyer *McDougal*. FDR painfully walked across the gangplank, Elliott steadying him. "Every step," Churchill later wrote, was "causing him pain." He was rewarded, however, by a moving service, which included the singing of "Onward, Christian Soldiers." Churchill wept openly. Roosevelt, as usual, was more reserved, but, tellingly, he remarked in private to Elliott: "If nothing else had happened while we were here, that would have cemented us. 'Onward, Christian Soldiers.' We *are*, and we *will* go on, with God's help." Both Roosevelt and Churchill were chief executives whose concept of leadership rose far above the level of mere administration. They understood the power of symbols, and they knew how to use and manipulate them, whether the symbol in question was a flag, a national anthem, or a hymn that grew from a shared faith.

## Symbols Should Never Be Empty

Effective leaders value symbols and use them without ambivalence or embarrassment. The best symbols—the most powerfully communicative—are simple, direct, and unambiguous. They emphasize values an enterprise or allies hold in common. All great symbols are magnets, drawing a team together, reminding them of the unity of their purpose. A symbol is meaningless unless its freight of meaning is shared.

Much more than ceremony was conducted at the Atlantic Conference. Although the United States was not yet a combatant, the two leaders concluded the closest thing possible at the time to a formal alliance. It was codified in the Atlantic Charter, which they signed on August 14, 1941, and which proclaimed (in the words of the charter) "certain common principles in the national policies of [the leaders'] respective countries on which they base their hopes for a better future for the world."

**At the head of a great nation in a monumental war,** struggling to master massive and bewildering forces, Winston Churchill maintained one principle above all others: *Whatever enterprise you command, your business is a business of people.* Historians would write of an alliance between the United Kingdom and the United States, but this, Churchill knew, was an illusion. The alliance was first and foremost a partnership between two people: Winston Churchill and Franklin Roosevelt. Running a nation while fighting a war was, like any other endeavor of consequence, first and last a human affair built on individual relationships.

Job number one, Churchill believed, was to identify the partners his nation needed and then to recruit and win them. He approached only those who had the power to help his nation in its time of need, then, instead of asking for anything, he defined areas of common concern and common benefit, beginning a process in which the pronouns *you* and *I* are transformed into *we*.

Churchill built a personal relationship with his key partner, FDR. With him, he confronted threats head on, never sugar coating the truth or dodging the bad news, of which there was plenty. Although he built a political and military alliance on the basis of something approaching a personal friendship, he made it a practice always to separate issues from egos, to identify the work necessary to create the common good, and to pitch in—directly—to get this work done.

Churchill forged a personal relationship not only with Roosevelt, but also with his own people. Churchill was a legendarily inspiring speaker, but the source of his ability to persuade and to move did not rest on eloquence alone. His most inspiring speeches were firmly founded on fact. The grimmer the fact, the more inspiring the speech. He was at all times frank—frankly inspirational.

All effective leaders accept risk, but few leaders embraced risk more enthusiastically than Winston Churchill. He did so, however, only after making certain that the stakes were worth winning, and then he persuaded powerful partners to share the risks in pursuit of rewards that were beyond question worth gaining.

# 24

# Suit the Tune to the Time and the Place

"The message of the sunset is sadness;
the message of the dawn is hope."
~ *My Early Life,* 1930

Each of the six volumes of Winston Churchill's magnum opus, *The Second World War,* begins with an epigraph titled "Moral of the Work":

*In War*: Resolution
*In Defeat*: Defiance
*In Victory*: Magnanimity
*In Peace*: Goodwill

*Moral,* in the sense of the lesson or principle taught by, implied by, or contained in a story or an event, is a word we learn early in life, when our parents and teachers take great pains to show us that what we read and what we experience have enduring meaning beyond the words or the events of specific moments. No experience was bigger, more complex, more chaotic, more destructive, or more horrific than World War II, and no man was more closely associated with its entire course, from origin to outcome, than Winston Churchill. His massive, Nobel Prize-winning history of the war was written from a distinctly personal point of view. Churchill managed to distill from his own experience of the war a moral that is a valuable formula for leadership and, more generally, the conduct of life.

**"Each significant situation we encounter calls for a different tune in a key perfectly suited to it."**

The four parts of Churchill's moral add up to more than their sum by implying a fifth part, an additional moral. It is this: Suit the tune you play to the time and place of its playing.

Each significant situation we encounter calls for a different tune in a key perfectly suited to it. Like all profound morals, Churchill's is very simple, yet also very difficult. Being resolute in war, with all of its pain, loss, and terror, is hard. Responding to defeat with defiance is harder still, though no more difficult than acting with magnanimity toward the defeated. Hardest of all, perhaps, is maintaining goodwill to preserve the peace when you are blessed with peace.

Hard, all of this. But for a genuine leader, keying all decisions, pronouncements, and actions to changing circumstances is essential. The ability to carry this off not only sets the genuine leader apart from those incapable of leading effectively—it also sets her apart from the mere dictator or tyrant. Whereas a genuine leader possesses and exercises the ability to change and the capacity to conform her actions, thought processes, and decisions to the changing demands of various situations, the dictator or tyrant is at all times what he is, regardless of the situation. His personality, his attitude, and his processes of thought and of making decisions are frozen in a single mode. His effort is always to force circumstances and other people into conformity with his own rigid will rather than to adapt his will to circumstances and other people.

[ 244 ]

> *"Small people, casual remarks, and little things very often shape our lives more powerfully than the deliberate, solemn advice of great people at critical moments."*
>
> ~ *Thoughts and Adventures,* 1932

In the case of Winston Churchill, the most memorable of the four qualities he listed in his "moral" to his World War II history were the first two. He presented himself to the British people and to the people of the world, friends, neutrals, and enemies alike, as the very model of resolution, not only in speech after speech, but in policy. From the very first day of World War II, he spoke not merely of survival, but always of victory, total and absolute. It was still early in the war, from January 14 to 24, 1943, that Churchill and Roosevelt met at Casablanca on the still-contested battlefield that was at the time North Africa and mutually agreed that the Allied war aim would be to obtain nothing short of the unconditional surrender of all of the Axis powers. The resolution, therefore, was toward absolute victory.

It was a position not without problems. Although it provided an overriding and unambiguous directive to everyone fighting the war—and such stark simplicity is a powerful leadership tool—the policy of adhering to unconditional surrender excluded the possibility of a negotiated end to the war. Critics, including a number of recent historians, have argued that, while the policy may have raised the Allied morale and focused the Allied effort, it did much the same for the Axis. Without hope of a negotiated settlement, the Germans and Japanese were emboldened to fight to the death in the belief that they had nothing to lose. A number of writers have suggested that, had Allied policy allowed for a conditional surrender on the part of the Axis powers, for something less than abject capitulation, the war might have ended sooner than it did. In Europe, the option of a negotiated peace might well have galvanized the resolve of the substantial anti-Hitler faction within the German high command to overthrow the Führer in order to salvage something of Germany. In the Pacific war, it must be remembered, Japan's objective in attacking Pearl Harbor on December 7, 1941, had been to force the United States to negotiate terms after its fleet had been destroyed. Had the Allies offered terms some three years later, when they held the upper hand, it is possible that war on this front would have ended as well.

The prospect of an early end to all the bloodshed and heartbreak was a powerful incentive to concede certain conditions to the other side and end the war considerably short of total victory. For better or worse, Churchill, Roosevelt, and Stalin all shared the same resolve not to do this, but to persevere until the Axis agreed to surrender without condition. Germany did yield in this way, on May 7–8, 1945, but Japan did not. In the end, after dropping two atomic bombs on the Japanese, FDR's successor, Harry S. Truman, granted a condition. He agreed to allow Emperor Hirohito to retain his throne, with the stipulation that his authority would be subject to that of the supreme Allied commander, General Douglas MacArthur. As some had criticized Churchill and his fellow leaders for their adherence to the doctrine of unconditional surrender, so others now criticized Truman for allowing Hirohito to remain Japan's emperor. Many believed he should not only have been removed, but also prosecuted as a war criminal.

*"The true guide to life is to do what is right."*
~ Speech, University of Huddersfield,
West Yorkshire, October 15, 1951

The second quality, defiance in defeat, was also richly demonstrated in the career of Winston Churchill. From the beginning of the war in 1939 until well into 1942, the British experience overwhelmingly consisted of a series of defeats. To each of them, Churchill responded with increasing defiance. On July 14, 1941, after enduring months of devastating air raids on London and other cities in the first Blitz, Churchill addressed Hitler and his henchmen directly. "You do your worst," he invited, "and we will do our best." Other inspiring leaders have taken this approach, of course. On September 23, 1779, the British warship HMS *Serapis* tangled with the USS *Bonhomme Richard* in the North Sea at the Battle of Flamborough Head. When the skipper of the *Serapis* called out to ask if the *Bonhomme Richard* was ready to surrender, Captain John Paul Jones—a figure Churchill much admired—famously replied, "I have not yet begun to fight." Similarly, Ulysses S. Grant, in his Overland Campaign during the Civil War, suffered one defeat after another at the hands of Robert E. Lee, responding each time not with the expected withdrawal, but with a defiant advance farther south. As General George S. Patton Jr. wrote in his field notebook, "You are not beaten until you admit it. Hence, don't."

## Cut Your Losses?

Some say that the clearest proof of insanity is doing something, failing, and then doing it again and again, in exactly the same way. For his defiance in the face of defeat, Churchill is accounted a hero. In the December 1862 Battle of Fredericksburg during the Civil War, General Ambrose Burnside led fourteen assaults on the Confederate position, suffering a catastrophic repulse each time. For this, he is often accounted the worst commander in the Civil War. Resolution and defiance do not require the repetition of tactics and strategies that have proven unsuccessful. Retreating, regrouping, and taking a new tack—all of these may be done without giving up. In any effort, there comes a time when the best course is to cut your losses. The purpose of this, however, is not to give up, but to stay in the game, surviving to fight another day. Never confuse maneuver with surrender. Resolution and defiance do not require insanity.

Less well identified with Churchill are the last two maxims of his moral:

*In Victory*: Magnanimity

*In Peace*: Goodwill

However, both of these aphorisms formed a part of his leadership approach, the willingness and ability to adapt policy to the situation. After World War I was ended by armistice, Churchill, like President Woodrow Wilson, favored a conciliatory rather than a punitive peace. Churchill did not propose exercising magnanimity for the sake of magnanimity alone, but because he recognized that a *defeated* Germany might well rejoin the family of nations as a peaceful democracy, provided that it was treated with justice and even mercy, but a defeated and *punished* Germany, humiliated and financially ruined by a harsh treaty, would emerge as a vengeful nation. Like Wilson, Churchill hoped that the Great War would bring an end to war itself. A magnanimous treaty would promote that end, whereas a punitive treaty would virtually ensure the outbreak of another war.

> *"The inscrutable and undecided judge upon whose lips the lives of millions hung."*
> ~On Woodrow Wilson, from *The World Crisis*, 1923–31

Tragically, in the end, the Treaty of Versailles was unremittingly punitive and did create in Germany precisely the climate of vengeance that Churchill had feared. Cast out of the British government during the 1930s, Churchill devoted most of the decade to a campaign of speeches and articles warning Parliament and the people about the danger of Hitler's rise and his rearming of Germany. Although the government of Prime Minister Stanley Baldwin persistently denied the possibility of another war and stubbornly pursued a self-destructive course of disarmament, Churchill persisted with his message, always insisting that Germany was driven by a powerful motive of revenge. Belatedly, Britain did begin to rearm and prepare for a new war, but the years lost in willfully ignoring the Nazi threat cost the nation dearly in blood and treasure.

When World War II approached its end in Allied victory, Churchill urged that the mistakes of the Treaty of Versailles not be repeated. He insisted on the unconditional surrender of the Axis, but, once that had been obtained, he advocated granting the defeated enemy magnanimous terms intended to foster the rebuilding of the Axis countries as genuine democracies. He was also an eloquent and enthusiastic champion of America's postwar Marshall Plan, the massive financial assistance scheme to enable the recovery of all Europe, friend and former foe alike (see Chapter 25).

**"For Churchill, magnanimity in victory was closely related to goodwill in peace. Everyone who worked with Winston Churchill, political allies as well as political opponents, remarked on his decency and absence of malice."**

As we saw in Chapter 5, when a major industrial strike threatened production in World War I, Minister of Munitions Churchill met with labor leader David Kirkwood. Kirkwood had every reason to expect a harsh and ill-tempered confrontation. Instead, Churchill began the meeting by suggesting, "Let's have a cup of tea and a bit of cake together." The resulting meeting ended the strike.

## All Business Is People Business

Corporations never do business with one another. It is the people who manage the corporations who do business with one another. All business is based on human relationships—people talking to other people, people making deals with other people, and people treating one another fairly or not. The language of business is money, it is true, but behind that language are feelings, attitudes, and other products of human relationships. Whatever business you are in—making shoes, designing software, or advising on investments—you are in the people business. You may say that you partner with a business, that you sell to a business, or buy from one. You may even run a business-to-business company. In the end, however, your customers, clients, partners, vendors, and competitors are people, not businesses. And people, not businesses, crave goodwill and generally respond to it in kind.

For Churchill, peacetime foreign policy was founded on the very same goodwill that drove his relationships with political colleagues as well as political opponents. He understood that nations do not practice diplomacy with nations, but that the leader of one nation creates a relationship with the leaders of another, and then they agree to call it diplomacy. The greatest alliance of World War II—perhaps the greatest alliance in history—is characterized as that of the United States and Great Britain. Actually, it was forged, on Churchill's initiative, not between two nations or even two governments, but between two men, Winston Churchill and Franklin D. Roosevelt. This great military and political relationship was sparked by, guided by, and maintained by the person-to-person goodwill that existed between the prime minister and president.

**"[Churchill] understood that nations do not practice diplomacy with nations, but that the leader of one nation creates a relationship with the leaders of another, and then they agree to call it diplomacy."**

The phrase "It's business, not personal" is a familiar one. Insofar as it keeps us from acting on motives of personal vindictiveness, personal prejudice, or even personal affection, it is a pretty good maxim. But it can also be seriously misleading. At its core, all business—all politics, all diplomacy—*is* personal, and the most effective leaders are the ones who have always realized this.

**Effective leadership requires** a fine balance between inflexibility—an iron backbone when it comes to values, ethics, and issues of core identity—and adaptability, the judgment and capacity to adapt approach and policy to time, place, and situation. It is this kind of flexibility that distinguishes a genuine leader from a mere tyrant.

## 25

# Win

"Victory, victory at all costs, victory in spite of all terror, victory however long
and hard the road may be; for without victory there is no survival."
~ Speech, House of Commons, May 13, 1940

From the beginning of World War II, when Great Britain was battered and at bay, standing alone against the Axis, and most of the
world considered its defeat and conquest only a matter of time—
very little time—Prime Minister Winston Churchill declared the
nation's war aim.

It was victory.

It was also sheer audacity, coming as it did when many in the
British government were talking about how to negotiate surrender
to Germany as an alternative to annihilation. And it was all the
more audacious because of the way Churchill presented it—not as a
desperate dream or empty boast, but as a fact, nothing more and
nothing less.

Victory became the theme of Churchill's war. As the prime minister and President Franklin D. Roosevelt agreed at the Casablanca
Conference of January 1943, victory would mean the unconditional
surrender of all the Axis powers. There would be no compromise,
and none of the major Allies—at the time, the United States, Great
Britain, and the Soviet Union—would make a separate peace. All
would fight, in unity, until total victory had been achieved.

With all of the dangers the Allies faced in a war unprecedentedly vast in scope, the goal of victory was a weapon of singular importance. It cut through the complexities, eliminated all ambiguity, and erased any ambivalence. The concept of unconditional victory did not simplify World War II, but it did give the Allies—every civilian, every soldier—something to hang on to, a sturdy handle, a purpose. Speak with virtually any of the rapidly dwindling number of Americans and Britons who lived through World War II, whether as soldiers or as civilians, and, even if they speak of grief, loss, fear, and pain, they also invariably speak with nostalgia for what has been called the "good war." It is remembered this way because it was presented by Churchill and other Allied leaders as a contest of democracy against tyranny, civilization against barbarism, good against evil, and it was framed—especially by Churchill—not in negative terms, as a struggle for survival, but in terms wholly positive, as a fight clear through to absolute victory.

**"Victory became the theme of Churchill's war . . . all would fight in unity."**

If no other American war of the twentieth century is remembered with anything approaching such positive sentiments, it is because none has ever been so clearly and positively defined as World War II. Korea, Vietnam, Iraq—all have been murky, at best half-hearted insofar as they were prosecuted to achieve limited objectives, and at worst wholly misbegotten: Korea, a war fought with inadequate resources in fear of igniting a larger conflict; Vietnam, a civil war misinterpreted as a battle in a contest of global domination; Iraq, the wrong war with the wrong enemy in the wrong place. In these conflicts, it was impossible to define victory without ambiguity and ambivalence, and so they were fought more or less as forlorn hopes, doomed to be costly and incomplete, and to leave a legacy of bitterness and division.

## For Every Endeavor an Absolute Goal

Page 1, Chapter 1 of *Leadership 101*: "A leader sets goals." If ever a sentence fell into the category of *it goes without saying*, this one would seem to be it. But the truth is that many CEOs and managers fail to set goals. Either they assume that the members of their organization all share the same implicit goals, which therefore may be taken for granted, or they just don't give the subject much thought. Even those leaders who do articulate a set of overall goals for their enterprise often embark on particular programs, campaigns, and projects without defining specific goals for them. Every traveler needs a destination, and every archer a target. So every participant in a collective enterprise needs a goal, unambiguously articulated and of eloquently defined value. If, for a given endeavor, you find it impossible to create a goal on these terms, abandon the project before you commit any significant resources to it. By definition, it is doomed.

Although it was tremendously difficult to achieve in the reality of flesh, blood, and steel, victory was starkly simple in concept. It meant the total military defeat of the enemy, period. As a goal, it was therefore entirely quantifiable. It was also so elementary that it could be reduced to a single symbol—the celebrated V-for-victory sign that was ubiquitous during the war and that Churchill himself transformed into a personal trademark, a public greeting, and the punctuation of his wartime speeches: two fingers upraised in the shape of the letter V.

> *"Death and sorrow will be the companions of our journey; hardship our garment; constancy and valour our only shield. We must be united, we must be undaunted, we must be inflexible."*
> ~ Speech, House of Commons, October 8, 1940

[ 255 ]

Victory was also the property of the people. Churchill always strove to make that clear. Victory was not something *he* wanted, or the *king* wanted, or the *government* wanted. It was what the *people* needed and demanded. It was what the people would have to earn, wresting it with *their* blood, toil, tears, and sweat from the jaws of defeat and the grasp of the enemy. On May 8, 1945, V-E Day, the day Germany surrendered unconditionally, Churchill and other members of the government appeared on the balcony of the Ministry of Health in London. What could be said at such a moment, so long awaited, so hard won, the moment of absolute victory? Winston Churchill knew exactly what to say:

> God bless you all. This is your victory! It is the victory of the cause of freedom in every land. In all our long history we have never seen a greater day than this. Everyone, man or woman, has done their best. Everyone has tried. Neither the long years, nor the dangers, nor the fierce attacks of the enemy, have in any way weakened the independent resolve of the British nation. God bless you all.

**"No sooner had the prime minister pronounced the words 'This is your victory!' than the crowd gathered in the street below the balcony shouted back, 'No, it is yours!' It was the perfect leadership moment, the moment at which leader and followers were revealed as one in purpose and values."**

Churchill gave the victory to those he deemed its rightful owners, and they, in turn, sought to give it back to him. No sooner had the prime minister pronounced the words "This is your victory!" than the crowd gathered in the street below the balcony shouted back, "No, it is yours!" It was the perfect leadership moment, the moment at which leader and followers were revealed as one in purpose and values. It is the point of balance every great enterprise strives to attain.

*Victory*, difficult as it had been in fact,

was simple in concept. But *winning*, that would be far more compli-cated, and for this reason, in most of his public pronouncements, in the great wartime speeches, Churchill brought the concept of victory to the fore and held the subject of winning in abeyance, a dis-cussion for another day.

Winning was what had to be done *after* victory. As World War II drew to a close, people talked about winning the war without losing the peace. They spoke from tragic experience. The conclusion of World War I had been an Allied victory in war followed by an Allied defeat in peace—the humiliating Treaty of Versailles provided fertile ground for the growth of a warmongering dictatorship. Having emerged victorious in *this* war, Churchill and the other Allied leaders resolved to win *this* peace.

## Make a Sale, Create a Customer

A good salesman makes a sale. A great salesman creates a cus-tomer. He does not merely part coin from client, but creates a relationship between the customer and the company, a rela-tionship defined by a series of sales—directly from this cus-tomer and, through word of mouth, from other customers, as well. Making the sale is victory. Creating a customer is winning. Victory is an event, whereas winning is a relationship.

Every business—and all leadership—is a selling business. If you are a shoe salesman, you sell shoes. If you are a teacher, you sell ideas. If you are a politician, you sell the benefits of your leadership. Any salesman can lie to make a sale. In doing so, he has created a victim rather than a customer. His business is doomed. If you want to stay in business and, even more, prosper in business—sell more shoes, turn out better students, attain higher office—you need to do more than sell. Whatever you are selling, you need to create customers. That is winning.

It was, however, far more difficult to nail down the meaning of *winning* than it had been to define *victory*. The greatest single complicating factor was not the defeated enemy, but one of the triumphant allies. Churchill was among the first of the Western leaders to recognize that Joseph Stalin, leader of the Soviet Union, intended to grab as much control over Eastern Europe as he could, quite possibly with the same goal as Hitler: the eventual domination of the West. Early in 1945, Churchill wondered aloud what would happen when RAF Bomber Command had completed the destruction of Germany: "What will lie between the white snows of Russia and the white cliffs of Dover?" And when the soldiers of the Red Army entered Poland more as conquers than as liberators, Churchill remarked to his friend Sir John Colville, "I have not the slightest intention of being cheated over Poland, not even if we go to the verge of war with Russia."

In the end, there would be no real peace with the Soviet Union, which, in the Cold War that almost immediately followed World War II, did not so much metamorphose from ally to enemy as it did, more ambiguously, from ally to former ally. While standing with the United States in its efforts to contain the expansion of the Soviet sphere of influence, Britain—under the premiership of Churchill, then Clement Attlee (from July 1945 to October 1951), and then Churchill once again—supported American-led efforts to rebuild Europe. This program, the centerpiece of which was the Marshall Plan, was dedicated not only to rebuilding the material infrastructure of Europe, in Allied and former enemy nations alike, but also to restoring its economic and political structure. The goal was to create an enduring positive relationship between the nations of the Continent and Britain and the United States, a relationship founded on democratic ideals. Thus, winning was ultimately defined as the physical, economic, and political recovery of Europe on a democratic basis. Because the democratic stipulation alienated

the interests of the Soviet Union, the definition of winning had to be
further defined to include victory in the Cold War. For the foresee-
able future, this meant containing the aggressive expansion of
Soviet communism. In preventing Stalin and his successors from
gaining control of Europe, the creators of the Marshall Plan hoped
that in the fullness of time (no one knew when), the success of
democracy would in itself be sufficient to defeat communism
entirely, without resorting to an apocalyptic world war. In a world
armed with nuclear weapons, the Cold War would be limited, often
frustratingly constrained, a species of shadow conflict that would be
a far cry from the unambiguous "good war" that had preceded it.

*"A hard-boiled egg of a man. . . . At once a callous, a crafty and an
ill-formed man."*

~ On Joseph Stalin, quoted in
Piers Brendon's *Winston Churchill,* 1984

In a celebrated speech he delivered to an audience at tiny
Westminster College in Fulton, Missouri, on March 5, 1946,
Churchill evoked a gloomy image of Cold War Europe:

A shadow has fallen upon the scenes so lately lighted by the
Allied victory. Nobody knows what Soviet Russia and its
Communist international organisation intends to do in the
immediate future, or what are the limits, if any, to their expansive
and proselytising tendencies. . . . From Stettin in the Baltic to
Trieste in the Adriatic, an iron curtain has descended across the
Continent. Behind that line lie all the capitals of the ancient states
of Central and Eastern Europe. Warsaw, Berlin, Prague, Vienna,
Budapest, Belgrade, Bucharest and Sofia, all these famous cities
and the populations around them lie in what I must call the
Soviet sphere, and all are subject in one form or another, not only

to Soviet influence but to a very high and, in many cases, increasing measure of control from Moscow.

Despite the gloom, Churchill did not think for a moment of abandoning the goal of winning the peace. "I do not believe that Soviet Russia desires war," he went on to explain. "What they desire is the fruits of war and the indefinite expansion of their power and doctrines." That desire, clearly, would have to be curbed by the democratic nations, but not by war: "We have to consider here to-day while time remains . . . the permanent prevention of war and the establishment of conditions of freedom and democracy as rapidly as possible in all countries." Nor even less could it be countered by "a policy of appeasement." No, Churchill explained, "What is needed is a settlement, and the longer this is delayed, the more difficult it will be and the greater our dangers will become."

In the absence of war on the one hand and appeasement on the other—both of which would surely mean losing the peace—Churchill outlined a third course:

> From what I have seen of our Russian friends and Allies during the war, I am convinced that there is nothing they admire so much as strength, and there is nothing for which they have less respect than for weakness, especially military weakness. For that reason the old doctrine of a balance of power is unsound. We cannot afford, if we can help it, to work on narrow margins, offering temptations to a trial of strength. If the Western Democracies stand together in strict adherence to the principles of the United Nations Charter, their influence for furthering those principles will be immense and no one is likely to molest them. If however they become divided or falter in their duty and if these all-important years are allowed to slip away then indeed catastrophe may overwhelm us all.

Then he recited the hard lessons of experience:

Last time I saw it all coming and cried aloud to my own fellow-countrymen and to the world, but no one paid any attention. Up till the year 1933 or even 1935, Germany might have been saved from the awful fate which has overtaken her and we might all have been spared the miseries Hitler let loose upon mankind. There never was a war in all history easier to prevent by timely action than the one which has just desolated such great areas of the globe. It could have been prevented in my belief without the firing of a single shot, and Germany might be powerful, prosperous and honoured to-day; but no one would listen and one by one we were all sucked into the awful whirlpool. We surely must not let that happen again. This can only be achieved by reaching now, in 1946, a good understanding on all points with Russia under the general authority of the United Nations Organisation and by the maintenance of that good understanding through many peaceful years, by the world instrument, supported by the whole strength of the English-speaking world and all its connections. There is the solution which I respectfully offer to you in this Address to which I have given the title "The Sinews of Peace."

After victory came winning, and in the complicated, nearly heart-breaking postwar world, winning was indeed difficult, yet essential, and by no means impossible.

Churchill's strategy for winning was to create a permanent relationship among the democratic nations, founded on shared ideological, moral, and political values, and a specific commitment to maintaining military strength. The ideology would hold the democratic nations together, and their combined military strength would serve as a deterrent to Soviet aggression. In the Cold War, winning the peace paradoxically required maintaining the threat of war. It was a hard course Churchill outlined in Fulton, Missouri—in some ways even harder than the course of blood, toil, tears, and sweat he had outlined in London during the Blitz—but the goal was the goal beyond victory itself. It was *winning*, winning the peace of the world. It was the single goal that could give enduring meaning to victory. It was the goal of civilization itself.

**The goal of any enterprise is to win,** which means to create an environment of relationships that sustain and prosper the organization. Winning is not synonymous with victory. Victory is an event necessary to winning; however, winning is not an *event* in time, but a *relationship* between your enterprise and the world, which includes customers, partners, investors, colleagues, and competitors. As a simple, direct, and unambiguous concept, victory can be a powerful motivator of success in a particular endeavor, project, or campaign, but the creation of a successful enterprise requires the usually simple concept of victory to be subordinated to the typically more complex concept of winning. Each individual victory should contribute to the creation of profitable relationships. That is the winning strategy, the strategy of sustainable success.

# BIBLIOGRAPHY

The following selections from among the veritable library of works devoted to Winston Churchill include the sources for this book as well as suggestions for further reading.

Bardens, Dennis. *Churchill in Parliament.* New York: A. S. Barnes, 1969.

Bartlett, John, Justin Kaplan ed. *Bartlett's Familiar Quotations.* 16th Edition. Boston: Little, Brown and Company, 1992.

Best, Geoffrey. *Churchill: A Study in Greatness.* New York: Hambledon and London, 2001.

Blake, Robert, and William Roger Louis, eds. *Churchill.* New York: W. W. Norton, 1993.

Bonham Carter, Violet. *Winston Churchill: An Intimate Portrait.* New York: Harcourt, Brace, and World, 1965.

Brendon, Piers. *Winston Churchill.* London: Secker & Warburg, 1984.

Bullock, Alan, ed. *Blood, Toil, Tears and Sweat: The Speeches of Winston Churchill.* Boston: Houghton Mifflin, 1989.

Churchill, Winston S. *Great Contemporaries.* London: Thornton Butterworth, 1937.

Churchill, Winston S. *My Early Life: A Roving Commission.* New York: Simon and Schuster, 1996.

Churchill, Winston S. *The River War.* London: Longmans, Green, 1899.

Churchill, Winston S. *The Second World War.* 6 vols. Boston: Houghton Mifflin, 1948–53.

Churchill, Winston S. *The Story of the Malakand Field Force: An Episode of Frontier War.* New York: W. W. Norton, 1989.

Churchill, Winston S. *Thoughts and Adventures.* London: Thornton Butterworth, 1932.

Churchill, Winston S. *The World Crisis, 1911–1918.* 2 vols. London: Oldhams Press, 1938.

Churchill, Winston S. *While England Slept: A Survey of World Affairs, 1932–1938.* New York: G. P. Putnam's Sons, 1938.

Churchill, Winston S. *His Father's Son: The Life of Randolph Churchill.* London: Weidenfeld and Nicholson, 1996.

Churchill, Winston S. (grandson), ed. *Never Give In! The Best of Winston Churchill's Speeches.* New York: Hyperion, 2003.

Colville, John Rupert. *Winston Churchill and His Inner Circle.* New York: Wyndham Books, 1981.

Eade, Charles, ed. *Churchill by His Contemporaries.* New York: Simon and Schuster, 1954.

Eden, Guy. *Portrait of Churchill.* London: Hutchinson, 1950.

Finlay, Stuart. *What Would Churchill Do? Business Advice from the Man Who Saved the World.* N.p.: Manor Publishing, 2008.

Gilbert, Martin, *Churchill: A Life.* New York: Henry Holt, 1991.

Gilbert, Martin, ed. *The Churchill War Papers.* 3 vols. New York: W. W. Norton, 1993–2000.

Halle, Kay. *Irrepressible Churchill: Stories, Sayings and Impressions of Winston Churchill.* Cleveland: World Publishing, 1966.

Hayward, Steven F. *Churchill on Leadership: Executive Success in the Face of Adversity.* New York: Random House, 1997.

James, Robert Rhodes. *Churchill: A Study in Failure, 1900–1939.* New York: World, 1970.

Jenkins, Roy. *Churchill: A Biography.* New York: Penguin, 2001.

Keegan, John. *Winston Churchill.* New York: Viking, 2002.

Kimball, Warren F. *Forged in War: Roosevelt, Churchill, and the Second World War.* Chicago: Ivan Dee, 1997.

Kimball, Warren F., ed. *Churchill and Roosevelt: The Complete Correspondence.* 3 vols. Princeton, NJ: Princeton University Press, 1984.

Lukacs, John. *Churchill: Visionary, Statesman, Historian.* New Haven, Conn.: Yale University Press, 2002.

Manchester, William. *The Last Lion: Winston Spencer Churchill.* 2 vols. Boston: Little, Brown, 1983–88.

Marchant, James, ed. *Winston Spencer Churchill: Servant of Crown and Commonwealth.* London: Cassell, 1954.

Martin, John. *Downing Street: The War Years.* London: Bloomsbury, 1991.

Moran, Lord. *Churchill, Taken from the Diaries of Lord Moran: The Struggle for Survival, 1940–1965.* Boston: Houghton Mifflin, 1966.

Morgan, Ted. *Churchill: Young Man in a Hurry, 1874–1915.* New York: Simon and Schuster, 1983.

Soames, Mary, ed. *Winston and Clementine: The Personal Letters of the Churchills.* Boston: Houghton Mifflin, 1999.

Stafford, David. *Roosevelt and Churchill: Men of Secrets.* Woodstock, N.Y.: Overlook Press, 2000.

Stansky, Peter. *Churchill: A Profile.* New York: Hill and Wang 1973.

Sutcliffe, J. A., ed. *The Sayings of Winston Churchill.* London: Duckworth, 1992.

Tucker, Spencer C., ed. "Dardanelles Campaign." *The European Powers in the First World War: An Encyclopedia.* New York: Garland, 1996.

# INDEX